NEW YORK STATE
GLOBAL
HISTORY
REGENTS
COACH

BY VIVIENNE HODGES, PH.D.

EDUCATIONAL DESIGN
EDI 806

Acknowledgments

William Rule and Barbara Wuelfing, ninth and tenth grade global history teachers at Wallkill High School, kindly reviewed this manuscript. I wish to thank them for their many helpful comments and suggestions. Hilarie Staton's profound understanding of the reading, writing, and interpretive difficulties that weaker students experience helped to shape my treatment of these topics. I also wish to thank Professor Edward Purcell and Dr. Rachel Vorspan for their thoughtful advice.

This book is dedicated to the memory of Peter Rowe,
a keen student of the world and its history.

ISBN# 0-87694-821-2   EDI 806

Table of Contents

Introduction

At the end of the tenth grade, you will take the **New York State Global History Regents Test**. You will answer questions about what you learned in the ninth and tenth grades— world history from pre-Neolithic times to the present.

You may have forgotten some of the things you studied in previous years. *The NYS Global History Regents Coach* will help you review what you learned. It also gives you practice in reading maps, graphs, tables, and time lines.

Some of you will be taking the **Regents Test** for the first time. To help you face this challenge, *The Coach* will review in depth the reading and writing skills you will need to understand and answer test questions.

The Coach is divided into four units. The first unit reviews your language arts skills and describes the different types of questions you will encounter on the test. The second unit deals with the themes and concepts which New York educators want you to use in your study of global history. Unit Three covers the topics of global history. At the end of each chapter you will find a section review. The last unit is a Practice Test.

The questions in the review sections and on the Practice Test are like the questions you will find on the **Global History Test.** Some are multiple-choice questions, some ask you to analyze documents or graphics, and some ask you to write short or longer answers.

After the Practice Test, you will find a Glossary and a Biography. They will help you understand terms you may not know or learn more about important individuals. *The Coach* ends with two Indexes. The first is an Index of Major Themes and Concepts, and the second is a General Index which you can use to locate particular events, people, or topics.

We hope *The Coach* will help you do well on the test. Good luck!

Part I: Reading and Writing for the Global History Test

To prepare for the **Global History Test**, you must be familiar with many different historical concepts. You will also need to have a good deal of information at your fingertips. But unless you know how to <u>read</u> and <u>understand</u> test questions, and unless you can <u>express</u> your thoughts clearly, you may not get a high score.

In this section of **The Coach**, we will review basic reading and analytic skills. You need these skills to understand and interpret the documents and graphics you will find on the test.

Then you will learn how to answer test questions, in particular, the special kinds of questions found on the **Global History Test**.

Finally, you will learn how to compose an open-ended response—this might be a short answer, or it might be a multi-page essay.

1 Reviewing Your Reading Skills

Questions on the **Global History Test** may ask you to:

1 Find a particular item of information in a text or graphic.

2 Describe the main idea or central purpose of a passage or graphic.

3 Find the details and information that support a particular idea or viewpoint.

4 Identify an author's point of view.

5 Distinguish between facts and opinions.

6 Draw a conclusion based on one or more sources of information.

7 Compare and contrast statements and documents.

8 Make a judgment by combining the information presented to you with your own prior knowledge.

You may also be asked to work out the meaning of a word in a question or document from its context.

These are the skills that you learned in your Language Arts classes. You will need them when you take the **Language Arts Regents Exam**. You need them just as much on the **Global History Test**.

In the pages that follow, you will review these skills one by one along with the strategies that can help you master them. You will practice working with graphics in the next chapter.

Finding Information in a Text

The easiest kind of question to answer is one that asks you to find a particular piece of information. You simply skim through the passage until you find the information you need. It will be *right there* in front of you. Read the following passage about the Ice Age and answer the question.

> In the age of man came the glaciers. They say the glaciers came and went four times. The interval of years between the third and fourth was longer than the years elapsed since the last one. In Greenland, around the polar sea, the ice is still waiting to come back.
>
> —From *A Prairie Grove* by Donald Peattie

1 **The author reports that the glaciers came and went**

   1 an unknown number of times

   2 three times

   3 four times

   4 five times

It is easy to see that Choice 3 is correct. The author writes, "They say the glaciers came and went four times."

Now answer another question based on the same passage. Again, the information is right there in the passage, but it may be harder to choose your answer this time.

Much of Greenland is still covered with ice

2 **The amount of time that has passed since the last glacier disappeared is**

   1 greater than the time that elapsed between the third and fourth glaciers

   2 less than the time that elapsed between the third and fourth glaciers

   3 less in Greenland than in the rest of the world

   4 the same as the length of time man has lived on Earth

The passage tells you that the glaciers came and went four times, so you know the fourth glacier was the last one. It also tells you that more time passed between the third and fourth glaciers than has elapsed since the last glacier. This tells you that Choice 2 is correct. One reason this question is tougher than Question 1 is that the answer choices are harder to understand.

Finding the Main Idea of a Passage

The main idea or central purpose of a passage is what the passage is mostly about. It is what you would come up with if you were asked to summarize the text in a single sentence. The following passage describes an eruption of Mount Vesuvius in 79 C.E.

> In August, 79 C.E., there was a tremendous explosion at the top of Mount Vesuvius. The ancient Roman city of Herculaneum was filled by an avalanche of mud that crept through doors and windows until eventually it rose over the roofs of the buildings. At nearby Pompeii there was no mud. But clouds of sulphurous fumes settled over the city suffocating its inhabitants.

3 What is the central purpose of this passage?

1 to describe where and when the volcano erupted

2 to explain how the remains of two Roman cities were preserved

3 to explain why Mount Vesuvius erupted

4 to explain why the eruption of Vesuvius was so deadly

Choice 4 is correct. The passage describes how the eruption of Mount Vesuvius destroyed Herculaneum and Pompeii and killed their citizens.

When you are asked to decide on the central idea of a passage or the details that support it, you may find it helpful to create a graphic organizer (also known as a semantic map). Graphic organizers allow you to see the connections between different parts of the text in a single glance.

This graphic organizer shows the main idea of the passage in the box on the left. In the boxes that hang off this one you can see two major events and their consequences.

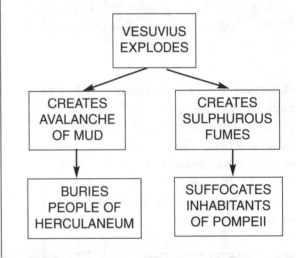

The eruption of Mount Vesuvius in 79 C.E. killed all the inhabitants of the Roman city of Pompeii.

Finding Supporting Details

The following passage describes the Aztec city of Tenochtitlán.

> *There are many temples for their idols in this great city. I have taken these idols—the ones in which the people have the most faith—and thrown them down the great stairways. And the chapels where they were housed I had washed down, for this was where men and women were sacrificed and they were full of blood. In their place, I had images of Our Lady and the other saints put there. This distressed Montezuma and his men very deeply. But I made them understand that they should not put their trust in false idols. For there is only one Lord God, who created heaven and earth and they must worship only him.*
>
> —Excerpt from a letter written by Hernan Cortés to Emperor Charles V in 1520

After you read the passage, complete the graphic organizer on the upper right. Find two supporting details and write them in the empty boxes. The organizer already contains a box describing one action taken by Cortés. In Box 1 describe a second thing he did. In Box 2 write the consequences of his actions.

The Aztec city of Tenochtitlán, the site of many religious rituals.

4

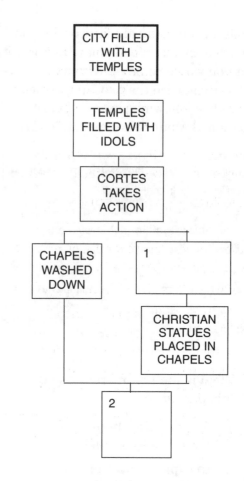

The missing details were (1), Cortés threw the idols down the stairs and (2), Montezuma and his followers were very upset.

Using Context to Work Out Word Meanings

There are several methods for working out what a word means. When you read a word you don't know, see if you can break it down into words you do know. For example, the word *circulation* (the act of moving around) is based on the word *circle*.

Another strategy is to use context clues. Suppose you read the following sentence:

"Archaeologists dig up cultural vestiges."

If you didn't know the meaning of *vestiges*, you might be hard-pressed to understand the sentence. But if you read,

"Archaeologists dig up cultural vestiges. Every year, they unearth more and more pottery fragments. Every year these new finds tell us more about the lives of our early ancestors."

If you read the word *vestiges* in context, you can work out that it means traces or evidence.

Read this excerpt from the diary kept by Meriwether Lewis on his trip through the Louisiana Territory and decide what *extol*

May 5. Last fall Captain Clark gave an Indian man some liniment to rub his knee and thigh for a pain...The fellow soon after recovered and has never ceased to extol the virtues of our medicines and the skill of my friend Captain Clark as a physician...In our present situation I think it is pardonable to continue this deception, for they will not give us any provision without compensation.

—Entry from the Diary of Meriwether Lewis, 1805

is most likely to mean.

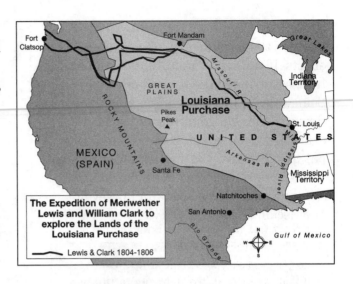

The Expedition of Meriwether Lewis and William Clark to explore the Lands of the Louisiana Purchase
—— Lewis & Clark 1804-1806

5   To extol is to

1   expand

2   itemize

3   praise

4   question

To extol someone's virtues is to praise them. Choice 3 is correct.

Now decide which sentence has the same meaning as some words that Lewis uses.

6   Which of the following has the same meaning as "for they will not give us any provision without compensation"?

1   They refuse to accept our help.

2   They will not provide us with any goods.

3   They will only work for us if we pay them.

4   We have to pay for all our supplies.

Provisions are supplies. Compensation is some kind of payment. The Native Americans refused to provide supplies to the expedition unless they were paid. Choice 4 is correct.

Identifying an Author's Point of View

Writers and speakers use many techniques to make their points and achieve their effects. If you read carefully, you can usually discover the author's point of view. Sometimes it will be clearly stated. At other times, the language the author uses, the examples given, and the way a passage is put together give you a good idea of where its author stands. Read the following speech by President Franklin Roosevelt and decide on his point of view.

Many U.S. battleships were damaged or destroyed during the attack on Pearl Harbor

> December 7, 1941—A date which will live in infamy—the United States of America was suddenly and deliberately attacked by naval and air forces of the Empire of Japan. The United States was at peace with that nation and…looking towards the maintenance of peace in the Pacific. Indeed, one hour after the Japanese air squadrons had commenced bombing in Oahu, the Japanese Ambassador …delivered a formal reply to a recent American message. While this reply stated that it seemed useless to continue the existing diplomatic negotiations, it contained no threat or hint of war or armed attack.
>
> —President Roosevelt's Speech to Congress, December 8, 1941

The angry language that President Roosevelt uses tells us that he is outraged by the attack on Pearl Harbor. Choice 4 is correct.

7 **What is President Roosevelt's response to Japan's attack on U.S. forces?**

   1 He is relieved that war has come at last.

   2 He hopes it will distract his enemies in Congress from domestic political problems.

   3 He fears the U.S. will soon be conquered by Japan.

   4 He is outraged by the sudden, unprovoked attack.

Distinguishing Fact from Opinion

When you analyze a text, it is important to distinguish between facts and opinions.

Facts can be checked. If a meteorologist claims: "Five inches of rain fell on New York City yesterday," you can verify this statement. An opinion is based on the writer's feelings. It can't be proven the way a fact can. Words like *think, feel,* and *believe* indicate that what you are reading is an opinion.

Read the excerpt from Roosevelt's speech again and decide which portion is an opinion.

President Roosevelt signs the declaration of war against Japan.

> December 7, 1941—A date which will live in infamy—the United States of America was suddenly and deliberately attacked by naval and air forces of the Empire of Japan. The United States was at peace with that nation and...looking towards the maintenance of peace in the Pacific. Indeed, one hour after the Japanese air squadrons had commenced bombing in Oahu, the Japanese Ambassador ...delivered a formal reply to a recent American message. While this reply stated that it seemed useless to continue the existing diplomatic negotiations, it contained no threat or hint of war or armed attack.
>
> —President Roosevelt's Speech to Congress, December 8, 1941

8   Which of President Roosevelt's statements is an opinion?

1   December 7, 1941, a date which will live in infamy

2   The United States was at peace with Japan.

3   An hour after bombing began, the Japanese Ambassador delivered a reply to a U.S. message.

4   The Japanese replied that negotiations seemed useless.

9   What tells you that the statement you have selected is an opinion?

_____

_____

_____

Choice 1 is the correct answer to Question 8. The other choices are factual information, but Choice 1 is clearly the President's opinion.

You know that the President is stating an opinion because he is making a claim that cannot be verified (Question 9).

Comparing Statements and Documents

You will learn more about interpreting documents in Chapter Four. At this point, you will review the *reading skill* that allows you to compare two different texts.

During the day one of the boys brought in a Virginia paper in which it was stated that "one Southerner could lick five Northern mudsills" [building blocks]. It was not so very comfortable to feel that we were to be killed off in blocks of five... Some time during the night an alarm was sounded by the beating of the "long roll" and we were ordered into line to drive the terrible foe, who was thought, even then, to be in our midst. Immediately everything was excitement and confusion... When it was discovered, as it shortly was, that all this excitement was caused by a pig who strolled into camp and was mistaken by the officer of the guard for the rebel army, many of us were imbued [filled] with a courage we hardly felt before.

—From the Diary of Charles E. Davis,
August 1, 1861

"Well, Stephen, I've just read the darnedest thing in this Virginia newspaper—I'm sure surprised anyone in this ignorant rebel state can read or write. Anyway, this scribbler boasts that any one of their reb soldiers can whip the hide off five of us Yankees."

Stephen's friend burst out laughing. "You remember how those boys acted ten days ago when we had them surrounded at Bull Run? Hey, they were as scared as a bunch of skunks!"

Just then a warning shot was fired and the troops fell silent. They remembered their drill. Each man fell into his proper place, rifle in hand. As they waited for the order to advance, the men prepared themselves for battle. This time, they would whip those boys in gray like they'd never been whipped before.

Of the two passages on this page, the one on the left is a primary source. It is part of a diary written by a young soldier in the Civil War. On the right is a piece of fiction. In this passage a soldier describes how he and his comrades behaved during an emergency. This fictional story is based on the account given in the soldier's diary. But it has a different point of view: its soldiers act very differently from the soldiers in the diary.

This suggests one of the features to look for when you compare texts: their authors' points of view. Another important clue is style. Style may reflect the date at which a passage was written, or it may reflect the educational or socioeconomic status of the author. The diary was written nearly 140 years ago, whereas the other passage is a contemporary piece; their literary styles reflect this difference.

10 Compare and contrast these two authors' attitudes towards the behavior of men in battle.

_____

_____

_____

_____

_____

_____

_____

_____

Some Union soldiers playing dominoes

A good answer to this question might stress this important difference between the two accounts: Whereas Charles Davis, the diarist, describes the confusion and chaos that occurred when a pig entered the army camp, the other author describes well-drilled soldiers who kept their heads.

11 Pick a phrase or sentence from each passage that reveals its author's point of view regarding the behavior of men at war.

_____

_____

_____

_____

A Venn diagram can help you to see both how people or things differ, and also how they are similar. Venn diagrams consist of two overlapping circles. The parts of the circles that don't overlap contain the differences between the things being compared. The overlapping area contains what they share in common.

Read the following passage about two Mexican revolutionaries and then observe how the information in the passage is entered into a Venn diagram.

Emiliano Zapata and Pancho Villa led the Mexican Revolution which began in 1910.

Zapata was a poor man from a village in southern Mexico. He wanted to redistribute the land held by great landowners among the poor. His army was successful for a while. They fought in many parts of southern Mexico. But in 1919 he was murdered.

Villa fought in the north. Like Zapata, he was also very successful in the first part of the war. Sometimes he too fought for people, sometimes he robbed them. In 1916, angered by American support for one of his rivals, he invaded the United States and killed 16 Americans. U.S. troops chased him back into Mexico but failed to catch him. After the revolution, Villa settled on a ranch given him by the new government. After a few years, he too was murdered.

The characteristics and events that are true only of Zapata or true only of Villa are listed under their names. The things they share are listed in the center where the circles overlap. Find another characteristic they share to complete the diagram.

12

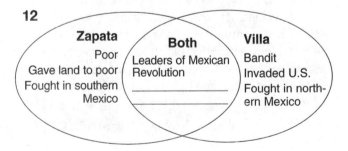

Drawing Conclusions

We are often asked to make inferences or to draw conclusions from the information we are given. If we see people jumping into the ocean waves, we are likely to judge that the seawater is warm enough to swim. If we see a lightning flash and the lifeguard whistles for everyone to come out of the swimming pool, we conclude (if we don't already know it) that storms are particularly dangerous if you are in the water. Our assumptions may not always be correct, but they are the best guesses we can make from the information we have.

Read the speech that Elizabeth I of England made to her troops. As you read, decide what conclusions you can draw about the queen's character.

Queen Elizabeth I as a young woman. She was 55 when she spoke to her troops at Tilbury.

My loving people,

We have been persuaded by some that are careful of our safety, to take heed how we commit ourselves to armed multitudes for fear of treachery; but I assure you, I do not desire to live to distrust my faithful and loving people. Let tyrants fear. I have always so behaved my self, that under God, I have placed my chiefest strength and safeguard in the loyal hearts and goodwill of all my subjects, and therefore I am come amongst you, as you see, at this time, not for my recreation and disport, but being resolved in the midst and heat of the battle, to live or die amongst you all, to lay down for my God, and for my kingdom, and for my people, my honour and my blood, even in the dust. I know I have the body but of a weak and feeble woman, but I have the heart and stomach of a king, and of a King of England too, and think foul scorn that Parma or Spain, or any Prince of Europe should dare to invade the borders of my realm; to which, rather than any dishonour shall grow by me, I myself will take up arms, I myself will be your general, judge, and rewarder of every one of your virtues in the field. I know already for your forwardness, you have deserved rewards and crowns; and do we assure you, in the word of a Prince, they shall be duly paid to you.

—Queen Elizabeth I, Speech to Her Troops, Tilbury, August 8, 1588

13 **Based on this speech, which statement about Queen Elizabeth is most likely to be correct?**

   1 **She always tried to get others to take responsibility for any decisions she made.**

   2 **She inspired love and respect among her people.**

   3 **She was an educated woman and preferred reading and theater going to sports and outdoors activities.**

   4 **She was terrified of war and avoided it wherever possible.**

This is a stirring speech and it stirred the hearts of the people who heard it back in 1588. Choice 2 is correct.

Making a Judgment by Combining Information from Documents with Your Own Knowledge of History

Most questions on the **Global History Test** will ask you to use your prior knowledge, as well as any information you can obtain from the documents you are given to read.

Reread Queen Elizabeth's speech and then use the information it contains, along with your own knowledge of history, to answer the question. Even if you don't recall the events of this period, the text may still allow you to guess at the answer.

> My loving people,
>
> We have been persuaded by some that are careful of our safety, to take heed how we commit ourselves to armed multitudes for fear of treachery; but I assure you, I do not desire to live to distrust my faithful and loving people. Let tyrants fear. I have always so behaved my self, that under God, I have placed my chiefest strength and safeguard in the loyal hearts and goodwill of all my subjects, and therefore I am come amongst you, as you see, at this time, not for my recreation and disport, but being resolved in the midst and heat of the battle, to live or die amongst you all, to lay down for my God, and for my kingdom, and for my people, my honour and my blood, even in the dust. I know I have the body but of a weak and feeble woman, but I have the heart and stomach of a king, and of a King of England too, and think foul scorn that Parma or Spain, or any Prince of Europe should dare to invade the borders of my realm; to which, rather than any dishonour shall grow by me, I myself will take up arms, I myself will be your general, judge, and rewarder of every one of your virtues in the field. I know already for your forwardness, you have deserved rewards and crowns; and do we assure you, in the word of a Prince, they shall be duly paid to you.
>
> —Queen Elizabeth I, Speech to Her Troops, Tilbury, August 8, 1588

14 **Why were Elizabeth's troops gathered together at Tilbury?**

1 to invade Ireland

2 to launch an attack on the French city of Calais

3 to oppose the troops carried by the Spanish Armada

4 to set sail for the New World

15 **What information in the speech helped you select your answer?**

_____

_____

_____

_____

The speech provides a major clue as to the occasion upon which it was spoken. The queen says, "and think foul scorn that Parma or Spain, or any Prince of Europe should dare to invade the borders of my realm." King Philip of Spain was planning to invade England. He sent a mighty fleet (the Spanish Armada) to ferry troops (led by the Duke of Parma) across the English Channel from the Netherlands. For students who are good at dates, the date of the speech is a give-away.

More Practice

Now you can practice some of these reading skills. Read each passage and answer the questions that follow it.

> By driving him [the African] off his ancestral lands, the Europeans have robbed him of the material foundations of his culture, and reduced him to a state of serfdom incompatible with human happiness...It is not in his nature to accept serfdom forever. He realizes that he must fight unceasingly for his own complete emancipation; for without this he is doomed to remain the prey of rival imperialisms.
>
> —Jomo Kenyatta, *Facing Mount Kenya*, 1938

16 Which sentence is the best summary of Kenyatta's words?

  1 Europeans believe that their culture is vastly to superior to African culture.

  2 Europeans have seized lands that belonged to Africans for generations.

  3 The African must fight for his freedom in order to end European exploitation.

  4 The imperial nations are more interested in fighting each other than in carving out colonies in Africa.

17 Describe one way in which the life of an African under colonial rule resembled that of a serf in medieval Europe.

_____

_____

_____

_____

> I have only tried to persuade you all, young and old, not to put body or property first, but to care chiefly about improving the soul. For virtue does not come from money; money comes from virtue, as does every other human good, public or private. This is what I teach, and if it corrupts the youth, then I _am_ a trouble-maker. Men of Athens, acquit me or convict me; but whichever you do, know that I shall never change my ways, even if I must die many times.
>
> —Adapted from Plato's *The Apology of Socrates*

18 On what occasion do you think Socrates made this speech?

  1 at a debate in the market-place of Athens

  2 before a battle

  3 during a philosophy lecture

  4 when he was on trial for his life

19 What argument does Socrates use to defend himself?

  1 If you trust in God, you will behave like a good citizen.

  2 Life is less important than dishonor.

  3 Nothing matters as much as having a virtuous soul.

  4 Young Athenians have learned from him how to make an honest living.

2 Analyzing and Interpreting Pictures, Maps, and Graphs

When you look at a map, notice its title, scale, compass, and key.

The map opposite is entitled, "South America and the Amazon Basin." This tells you that the map will show which part of the South American continent the Amazon Basin occupies. The map also shows which South American countries include parts of the Amazon Basin and which do not. Other maps of South America might show you its physical features, or its climate regions, or its major roads and railways. A map's title tells you what kind of information the map contains.

1   **Which of these nations contains a part of the Amazon Basin?**

    1   **Argentina**

    2   **Chile**

    3   **Uruguay**

    4   **Venezuela**

Find this symbol on the map of South America. It is a compass and has four points:

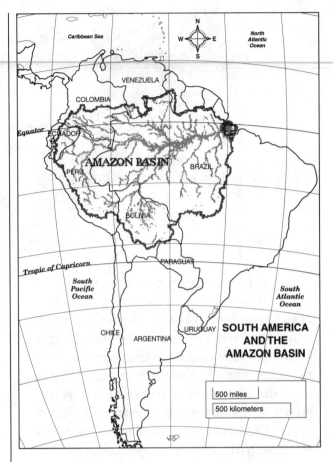

N (north)

E (east)

W (west)

S (south)

A compass tells you about direction. Its northern point (N) points to the North Pole and its southern point (S) to the South Pole.

2   **In which direction would you travel to get to from Chile to Uruguay?**

    1   **East**

    2   **North**

    3   **South**

    4   **West**

Suppose you want to know how far one place is from another. The map's scale tells you this. The scale on this map shows distances in miles and kilometers. Half an inch represents about 500 miles. Use this information to answer the next question.

3   **About how many miles would you cover if you traveled from the northernmost tip of Colombia to Bolivia's southern border?**

    1   **1,000 miles**

    2   **1,500 miles**

    3   **2,250 miles**

    4   **3,000 miles**

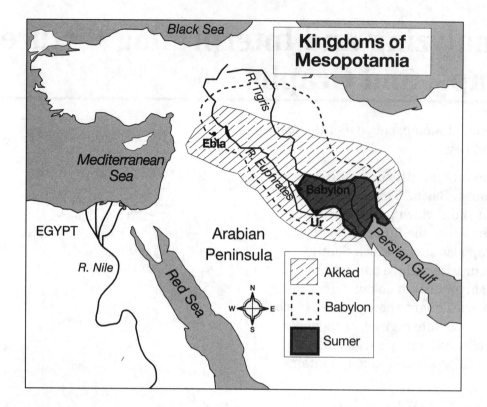

Map keys often contain symbols. On a road map, these symbols typically represent interstate highways and state highways, and cities and state capitals. On an agricultural map, the symbols may represent the crops grown or the animals that graze in different areas. The keys of historical maps may show empires, battles, or the routes taken by traders or conquerors.

The map above shows the location of three early Middle Eastern civilizations, Akkad, Babylon, and Sumer. Each one was dominant at a different time. The key helps you identify the overlapping boundaries of these three empires.

4 **The boundary of which civilization lay closest to the Black Sea?**

1 Akkad

2 Babylon

3 Egypt

4 Sumer

5 **Which statement describes one difference between the geography of Egypt and that of the other three empires?**

1 Egypt does not lie in a river valley.

2 Egypt is somewhat further to the north.

3 Egypt lies between the Red Sea and the Persian Gulf.

4 Egypt lies outside the Tigris-Euphrates Valley.

6 **The civilizations of Mesopotamia and Ancient Egypt relied on water to irrigate their crops. Where did these civilizations get their water?**

_____

_____

_____

Graphs are a means of organizing and presenting numeric data. The most commonly used graphs are the bar graph, the line graph, and the pie chart.

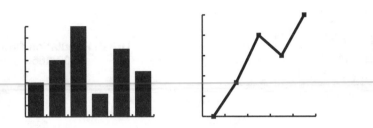 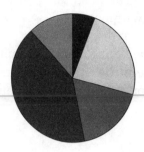

You studied a map of the Amazon Basin on page 21. The pie chart opposite shows how much of the Basin lies within six South American nations. Use the size of the different pie slices and the information about the Basin's total acreage to answer the question.

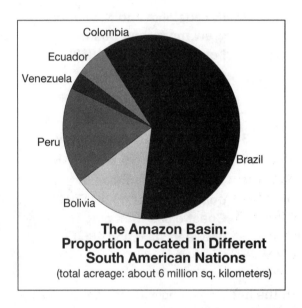

**The Amazon Basin:
Proportion Located in Different
South American Nations**
(total acreage: about 6 million sq. kilometers)

7 **About how much of the Amazon Basin's total acreage is in Brazil?**

    1   3.5 square kilometers

    2   25,000 square kilometers

    3   300,000 square kilometers

    4   3,200,000 square kilometers

8 **About how much Amazon Basin acreage lies in the other five South American nations?**

    Bolivia: _____

    Colombia: _____

    Ecuador: _____

    Peru: _____

    Venezuela: _____

In line graphs and bar graphs, time is usually shown along the horizontal axis. In both the graphs on this page, the vertical axis shows quantities.

It is important to note the unit in which these quantities are shown. In the bar graph opposite the unit is thousands. The graph shows city populations in thousands of persons.

9 **What information is provided by the bar graph?**

1 **Philadelphia and New York grew more than Boston between 1800 and 1860.**

2 **The cities shown in the graph saw a tenfold increase in population after 1860.**

3 **More than 80% of all immigrants settled in New York.**

4 **The largest increase in the populations of major East Coast cities took place between 1800 and 1860.**

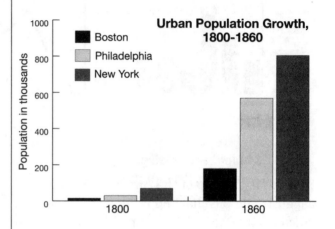

In the line graph opposite, the figures are percentages. The graph shows what percentage of children were working at a given point in time.

10 **According to the line graph, what percentage of children were employed in 1880?**

1 **7 percent**

2 **12 percent**

3 **17 percent**

4 **22 percent**

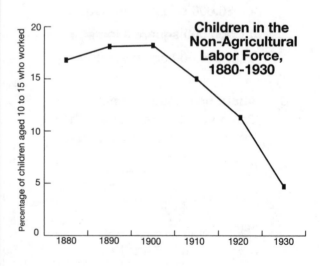

Many of the documents you will be asked to interpret on the **Global History Test** are pictures and cartoons. You may have heard the saying, "A picture is worth a thousand words." Pictures can contain a tremendous amount of information.

Look carefully at this photograph of a trench where soldiers fought during World War I.

11 **Soldiers crouched in trenches to shield themselves from enemy fire. This picture of a trench shows one difficulty presented by this form of warfare. What was it?**

_____

_____

_____

_____

Picture captions can provide useful information about the people, places, or time period that is depicted. Use the caption of this picture and the information contained in the map below to answer the next question.

British soldiers in Flanders in 1917

12A Which battle is depicted in this picture?

_____

12B What tells you this?

_____

_____

_____

_____

GREAT BRITAIN NETH. GERMANY • Tannenberg 1914 RUSSIA _Eastern Front →_ FLANDERS Ypres 1915 •• Passchendaele 1917 Somme 1916 • Lemberg 1915 _Western Front →_ Marne 1914 • • Verdun 1916 AUSTRIA-HUNGARY FRANCE ITALY ROMANIA SERBIA BULGARIA _Black Sea_ _Adriatic_ TURKEY Gallipoli 1915

World War I in Europe 1914-1918

• Major Battles

Cartoons express the artist's view of events in the news. To understand cartoons, you usually need to have some background knowledge of the events they depict. As with paintings or photographs, captions or bubbles with dialog contain important information, so don't ignore them.

The cartoon shown on the right reflects many Americans' attitudes towards the United Nations. Decide which answer choice reflects the attitudes shown.

13 **The characters shown in this cartoon view the United Nations as**

    1 **a body that has become too powerful and should be abolished**

    2 **a costly but valuable instrument for dealing with global issues**

    3 **an expensive institution where debates are endless and little is achieved**

    4 **an opportunity for nations to talk together to resolve their disputes peacefully**

14 **Create another bubble dialog with the same point of view as the ones shown in the cartoon.**

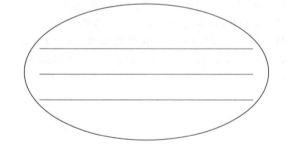

3. Understanding and Analyzing Test Questions

QUESTIONS ON THE GLOBAL HISTORY REGENTS TEST			
TYPE OF QUESTION	NUMBER OF QUESTIONS	TIME ANTICIPATED	PERCENTAGE OF SCORE
Multiple-choice	50	60 minutes	55%
DBQ or Document-based		70 minutes	
Short Written Answers	about 6–8		15%
Document-based Essay	1		15%
Thematic Essay	1	50 minutes	15%
TOTAL		**about 3 hours**	**100%**

The **Global History Regents Test** asks you three kinds of questions: Multiple-choice, Document-based, and Thematic Essay. The table shown above tells you, for each type of question, how many questions you will be asked, how much time you will probably need, and what percentage of your total mark comes from answering them.

For two years (2000 and 2001), the passing mark will be 55%. Then in 2002, the passing mark will be raised to 65%.

Notice that there are no time limits for taking this test. The times shown in the table above are <u>estimates</u> of how long most students take to answer the questions. But because this test is so important, you can take as much time as you need to finish.

It is important to prepare yourself <u>in advance</u> for answering each type of question. You should be able to tackle <u>all</u> kinds of questions. The rest of this chapter will show you what these questions look like and give you a chance to practice answering them.

On this page we will discuss some general strategies which can be used to answer several different kinds of questions.

Always begin by reading the question very carefully. Underline key words. These might be instructions that tell you what to do, or concepts, or names of people and places, issues, time periods, or other important information.

For example, if you were asked:

Compare life in ancient Sparta and ancient Athens.

You might underline like this:

<u>Compare</u> <u>life</u> in <u>ancient Sparta</u> and <u>ancient Athens</u>

<u>Compare</u>	What you must do with the knowledge you have
<u>life</u> in	What you must compare
<u>ancient Sparta</u> and <u>Athens</u>.	The places which you must compare

You may know from the question or from a document you are asked to study what themes, places, and time periods you are dealing with. Before you begin to study a document in depth, write down what you know about this theme, and the places and eras involved. You will be working with documents when you answer *some* multiple-choice questions and *all* document-based questions. When you are ready to look at a document, check first to see if you are told who wrote it, when, and where.

The date of the document below provides a big clue. 1914 was the year World War I began in Europe. A quick glance at the document tells you that it deals with Serbia.

The main motive which guided me in my deed was the avenging of the Serbian people…I am a nationalist. I aimed to free the Yugoslavs. For I am a Yugoslav…As far as Serbia is concerned, it is her duty to free us.

— Gavrilo Princip, 1914

Had there been no date, you might think it referred to a more recent Serbian conflict.

JOIN, or DIE.

Published by Benjamin Franklin, 1754

You might have difficulty making sense of the cartoon: *Join or Die*. But if you notice that it was published by Ben Franklin in 1754, you know that it refers to events in the British colonies. Now you may be able to guess the kind of message Franklin was trying to get across. Use whatever you know about an author's background or point of view when you interpret documents. Maybe you know that 1754 was the year the French and Indian War began. The French were threatening the British colonies which were divided among themselves. This tells you why Franklin wanted the colonies (the different parts of the snake) to join together.

Even if you don't know an author's name, you may still be able to guess his or her point of view from the caption or other non-text information. The passage below was used in a question about imperialism.

[Progressive nations] can establish schools and newspapers for the colonies [and] give these people the benefit of other blessings of civilization which they have not the means of creating themselves."

— O.P. Austin, "Does Colonization Pay?," *The Forum*, 1900

O.P. Austin sounds English rather than African or Asian. 1900 was the heyday of imperialism, and many Europeans ardently supported it. You might guess, even without looking at the text, that Austin believed that colonization does pay.

When you are ready to analyze the body of the document, use the same technique of underlining key words that you used to analyze questions.

Suppose you had to read the following document:

> Lycurgus allowed no one to travel abroad, lest they contracted foreign manners and saw lives with little discipline and different forms of government. He forbade foreigners to come to Sparta unless they had good reason lest they taught his people some evil.

You might underline sections as follows:

> <u>Lycurgus</u> <u>allowed</u> no one to <u>travel abroad</u>, lest they <u>contracted foreign manners</u> and <u>saw lives with little discipline</u> and <u>different forms of government</u>. He <u>forbade foreigners</u> to come to <u>Sparta</u> unless they had good reason lest they <u>taught his people some evil</u>.

These underlined sections allow you to focus on key points of the document. Lycurgus was clearly a ruler of Sparta. He wanted to protect its citizens against bad foreign influences. He wanted to keep them well disciplined and he wanted to keep Sparta's form of government intact. This information, which is all right there in the document, allows you to draw several conclusions. For example, it allows you to infer what Spartans meant by good citizenship.

1   **Describe how Spartans expected a good citizen to behave.**

_____

_____

_____

_____

Usually you must combine your prior knowledge with the information contained in a document. If you jot down what you can recall of the period that a document covers, even before you study it in depth, it will help you place the text in a historical context. It will help you to connect what you already know with the information in the document.

You may also need to compare and contrast different documents. Underlining words and tapping your prior knowledge will help you here as well. So will the reading skills you reviewed in Chapter 2.

Suppose you were asked to compare the two songs below. A good place to begin is to look for the theme or main idea of each one. Then you can compare them. How are the themes of these songs similar? How are they different?

> It is we who dug the ditches
> Built the cities where they trade
> Blasted mines and built the workshops,
> Endless miles of railroad laid
> Now we stand outcast and starving
> 'Mid the wonders we have made,
> But the union makes us strong…

> Too old to work, too old to work
> When you're too old to work and too young to die
> Who will take care of you, how'll you get by
> When you're too old to work and too young to die?

2   **What common theme can you find in these two worker songs?**

_____

_____

_____

_____

Multiple-Choice Questions

Here is a multiple-choice question that was used in an earlier version of the **NYS Global History Test**. Most of the multiple-choice questions you will see on the actual test will look pretty much like this.

---

1 A physical geographer would most likely study

   1 landforms and ocean currents

   2 systems of government

   3 the customs and traditions of a country

   4 the religious practices of a culture

When you answer a question requiring a multiple-choice answer, read the passage and then read the question carefully. Examine the four choices and choose the answer you think is best. If you're not sure of the answer, reread the passage until you find the information you need.

There are always four answer choices. Even if you're not sure of the answer, always check off one of the choices. There is no penalty for guessing.

To answer most multiple-choice questions, including the one shown above, you must use your prior knowledge. (Later in this chapter you will learn some ways to help you tap this knowledge.) Sometimes you will be shown a graphic and then asked a question. Usually you will need to combine the information in the graphic with your own knowledge to answer it. Even if you lack this knowledge, you might be able to work out the answer from the graphic alone. Look at the map and the question on the right.

---

2 Which statement best explains why water rights are a vital issue in the Middle East?

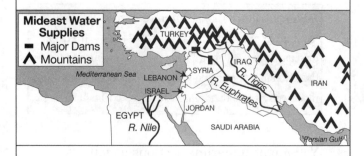

1 Most of the region's water lies underground.

2 Only one country in this region has a river.

3 The source of water for one country often lies in another country.

4 Turkey uses most of the region's water for irrigation of its crops.

You must decide which statement explains why water rights are a vital Middle East issue. A good strategy is to eliminate the answer choices that are clearly incorrect. The map shows three rivers and four other bodies of water (three large seas and the Persian Gulf), so it is unlikely that Choice A is correct. The Euphrates River runs through three countries, so Choice B must be incorrect. You may be unsure about Choice D—Turkey may or may not use most of the region's waters. But the map does show that the Euphrates and Tigris Rivers rise in Turkey and flow through Syria and Iraq where they drain into the Persian Gulf. And Choice C says: "the source of water for one country often lies in another country." By a process of elimination and good sense, you can guess that Choice C is correct.

Document-Based Questions

There are two parts to document-based questions (DBQs). In *Part A* you study between six and eight documents. Most documents will be in text format, but at least two will be graphics (maps, charts, cartoons, etc.). Each document is followed by a question to which you will provide a short written answer.

In *Part B*, you will answer an essay question on the same topic as the documents. An essay that gets a good score will easily fit into two or three hand-written pages.

On this page and the page that follows you will read a sample DBQ. It consists of directions, three documents with questions, and an essay question. The topic of the documents is imperialism, one of the key themes in New York's global history curriculum.

Please note: You do not have to write out answers to the questions posed in this section at this time. Simply read through the material carefully and think of what kind of answers you would come up with.

SAMPLE DOCUMENT-BASED QUESTION

This task is based on the accompanying documents. Some of these documents have been edited for the purpose of the task. The essay is designed to test your ability to work with historical documents. As you analyze the documents, take into account both the source of the documents and the author's point of view.

Directions:

- Write a well-organized essay that includes an introduction with a thesis statement, several paragraphs explaining the thesis, and a conclusion.
- Analyze the documents.
- Use evidence from the documents to support your position.
- Do not simply repeat the content of the documents.
- Include specific related outside information.

Historical Context:

Imperialism has been interpreted from a variety of viewpoints. The comments below express various viewpoints about the positive and negative effects of European imperialism.

Task A:

Evaluate both the positive and negative effects of imperialism.

Part A

Short Answer

The documents below relate to the positive and negative effects of imperialism. Examine each document carefully and then answer the question which follows it.

Document 1

"Colonialism's greatest misdeed was to have tried to strip us of our responsibility in conducting our own affairs and convince us that our civilization was nothing less than savagery, thus giving us complexes which led to our being branded as irresponsible and lacking in self-confidence..."

—Sekou Toure, West African nationalist, 1962

1. In 1962, what was the response of this West African nationalist to years of colonialism?

_____

_____

_____

Document 2

"Learning civilized ways is hard work."

2. What did colonization mean for the native people?

_____

_____

_____

_____

Document 3

"Modern progressive nations lying in the temperate zone seek to control 'garden spots' in the tropics [mainly in Africa, Latin America, and Asia]. Under [the progressive nations'] direction, these places can yield tropical produce. In return, the progressive nations bring to the people of those garden spots the foodstuffs and manufactures they need. [Progressive nations] develop the territory by building roads, canals, railways, and telegraphs. They can establish schools and newspapers for the colonies [and] give these people the benefit of other blessings of civilization which they have not the means of creating themselves."

—O.P. Austin, "Does Colonization Pay," *The Forum, 1900*

3. According to the author, what benefits did the colonies receive from the "modern progressive nations"?

_____

_____

_____

_____

Part B

Essay Response

Evaluate both the positive and negative effects of imperialism.

We will review these three documents and see how you might answer questions based on them.

Document 1

"Colonialism's greatest misdeed was to have tried to strip us of our responsibility in conducting our own affairs and convince us that our civilization was nothing less than savagery, thus giving us complexes which led to our being branded as irresponsible and lacking in self-confidence..."

—Sekou Toure, West African nationalist, 1962

1. In 1962, what was the response of this West African nationalist to years of colonialism?

You learn that the author of this document is a West African nationalist, and his words make his anti-imperial position quite clear.

The question asks you how Sekou Toure responded to years of colonialism. Your answer should take into account what he said and the angry and bitter tone in which he said it. You might answer as follows:

<u>Toure was bitterly angry with the colonial powers for depriving native peoples of the right to govern themselves and for trying to persuade them that they were uncivilized savages.</u>

Document 2

"Learning civilized ways is hard work."

2. What did colonization mean for the native people?

Your first task with this document is to work out what the cartoon means. Remember that cartoons usually have two aspects: the picture and the caption. Both are important. The picture shows an Asian and an African pulling a rickshaw containing a colonial ruler. He sits back comfortably while they sweat. The caption says, "Learning civilized ways is hard work." You have to probe below the surface to find the meaning of the cartoon. Cartoons are usually symbolic; their images mean something else. Pulling a rickshaw represents oppression. The white ruler oppresses the native peoples. The caption talks about "civilized ways," but this is *ironic*. There is nothing civilized about oppression and forced labor.

So you might answer as follows:

2. What did colonization mean for the native people?

From the native people's viewpoint, colonial rule was oppressive. The people were forced to work hard to satisfy the needs of the colonial powers and received very little benefit in return.

Document 3

"Modern progressive nations lying in the temperate zone seek to control 'garden spots' in the tropics [mainly in Africa, Latin America, and Asia]. Under [the progressive nations'] direction, these places can yield tropical produce. In return, the progressive nations bring to the people of those garden spots the foodstuffs and manufactures they need. [Progressive nations] develop the territory by building roads, canals, railways, and telegraphs. They can establish schools and newspapers for the colonies [and] give these people the benefit of other blessings of civilization which they have not the means of creating themselves."

—O.P. Austin, "Does Colonization Pay," *The Forum, 1900*

3. According to the author, what benefits did the colonies receive from the "modern progressive nations"?

You are asked what benefits the author believes the colonies received from the "modern progressive nations." To answer this question, you must be clear about three things:

- <u>meaning</u>: The colonies described in the question are what the author calls *garden spots.*

- <u>comparison</u>: You need to distinguish between what the colonies provided (tropical produce) and what they received from the "progressive nations."

- <u>author's point of view</u>: The author believed that everything the "progressive nations" brought to the colonies was a benefit.

Once you are clear about this, you will find the answer right there in the document.

3. According to the author, what benefits did the colonies receive from the "modern progressive nations"?

<u>Austin claimed that the "progressive nations" brought food and manufactured goods to the colonies. They brought technological improvements like roads and railways. They also provided such benefits of their civilization as schools and newspapers.</u>

When you have finished analyzing the documents and answering questions about them, you will be ready to write an essay about imperialism.

Here are the instructions you will be given:

Part B

Essay Response

Evaluate both the positive and negative effects of imperialism.

Your essay should be well organized with an introductory paragraph that states your position. Develop your position in the next paragraphs and then write a conclusion. In your essay, include specific historical details and refer to the specific documents you analyzed in Part A. You may include additional information from your knowledge of global history.

Keep these strategies in mind as you prepare to write your document-based essay:

- Analyze each document carefully.

- Use evidence from the documents to support your position.

- Interpret the theme or concepts that underlie each document.

- Do not simply repeat the content of the documents. Restate the supporting ideas that the documents provide using your own words.

- If you are asked to use only some of the documents in your answer, choose the documents you understand best and the documents that prompted you to recall your prior knowledge.

- You will need to use over half the documents on your essay to get a high score.

In the next chapter you will learn how to prepare and write a document-based essay or a thematic essay.

4. Writing Your Answers

Planning Your Essay

Before you begin to plan your answer to an essay question, you need to:

- read all parts of the question carefully

- underline key words in the question

- activate your prior knowledge about the concepts, names, and topics mentioned in the question

- obtain all the information you can from the documents given you to study

A key word in the question is the verb that tells you what to do. Here are some verbs that are often used in essay questions together with their meanings:

Compare
Show similarities and differences

Contrast
Compare by showing differences

Define
Explain the meaning of

Describe
Give an account of

Discuss
Give facts to support both sides

Evaluate
Make a judgment taking into account information from both sides

Explain
Make clear so that the reader knows you understand

Trace
Follow the development

Be sure you arrange your essay so that you do what the verb tells you.

Now you are ready to plan your answer. Most essay questions focus on a historical theme—it might be nationalism, or industrialization, or imperialism, or some other general topic that spans places and times. You will be asked to take a position on this theme. For example, you might be asked:

Define the term "nationalism." Select one country you have studied and give specific examples of nationalism within that country. Describe a situation where nationalism was either a positive or a negative force in that country's history.

OR

Belief systems and religions have an impact on the culture, history, and daily lives of the people of a region. Write a five-paragraph essay that supports and develops the above statement using at least three religions.

OR

The encounter between Europeans and Native Americans in the 16th and 17th centuries has been described as "the discovery of a new world which resulted in great changes in both worlds" or "an invasion of a highly civilized people which benefitted the Europeans more than the Americans." Choose one of the descriptions and write a well-organized essay supporting your choice.

OR

Evaluate both the negative and the positive effects of imperialism.

You can use the same strategies for planning a DBQ essay and a thematic essay. The essay topic, like the topics you have just read, will revolve around a major theme. This theme and your response to it will be the main idea of your essay.

Let's take the first topic, nationalism. You are asked to define nationalism. It's a good idea to begin an essay by defining the major concepts you plan to discuss. You could begin your answer to the other essay questions by defining "belief systems," and "The Encounter," and "imperialism."

Most essay questions ask you to take a position on a topic. The essay questions on the previous page ask you:

- to describe a positive or negative consequence of nationalism

- to trace the impact of at least three religions on cultures and history

- to decide whether or not "The Encounter" was about the exploitation of one people by another

- to evaluate the positive and negative aspects of imperialism

But you can't form an opinion on a topic without having information to base it on. This is where you must use your prior knowledge and, if it's a DBQ, the information contained in the documents.

You may want to create a graphic organizer to sort out your ideas and information. The organizer on the right deals with the topic of imperialism. Much of its information and ideas comes from the documents you read in the last chapter. It's perfectly fine to use these sources provided you remember that their authors may be biased. One piece of information in the organizer was not contained in the documents: imperialism caused conflict among the colonial powers. You would need to tap your prior knowledge for this.

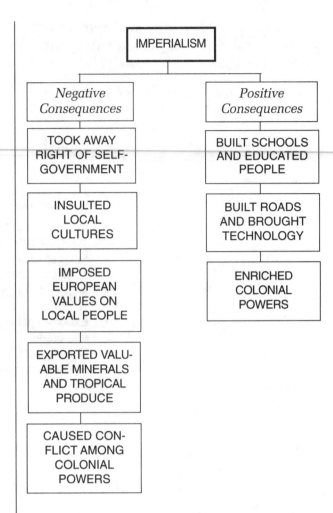

The imperialism question asked you to <u>evaluate</u> its <u>negative</u> and <u>positive</u> aspects. This means you must separate the data that makes imperialism look good from the data that makes it look bad. That's why the information in the diagram has been arranged in two columns. The column on the left shows the negative aspects of imperialism; the column of the right shows its positive aspects. When you decide whether information is positive or negative you have to make judgments. You might think, for example, that the fact that imperialism enriched the colonial powers was a negative rather than a positive effect. On the other hand, European imperialists thought they were doing something beneficial in imposing their values upon colonial peoples.

You may find a different kind of graphic organizer helpful when you are sorting out your information.

You might want to use a Venn diagram like this:

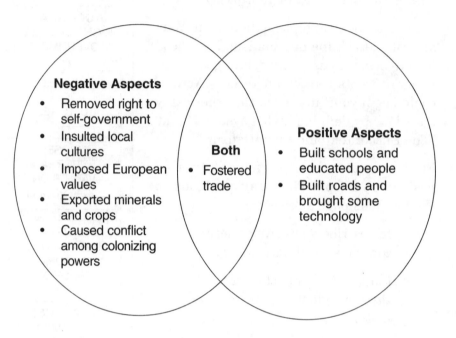

Or it might be important to arrange data about imperialism in chronological sequence or according to cause and effect like the graphic on the right:

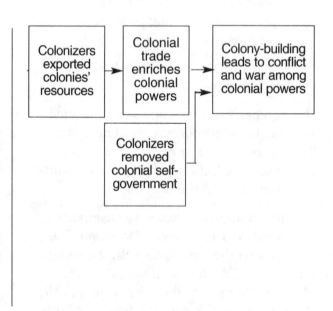

Once you have grouped your data, you must decide what position you want to take. If the topic has no special significance for you, you will probably be guided by your data when you make this decision. But many topics are "hot potatoes." You may already have strong feelings about imperialism. In this case, your emotions may guide you to a particular position. This is perfectly okay provided you find details and information to support it.

NOTICE: Photocopying any part of this book is prohibited by law.

Writing Your Essay

You have already:

- Understood what the question asked you to do
- Taken notes and jotted down ideas (including information contained in the documents if you're answering a DBQ)
- Arranged your information and ideas into a meaningful order
- Used your information to help you take a position

Now you are ready to begin writing. You should begin your essay with a strong introduction in which you restate the question and take a position on it. If you were evaluating imperialism, you might begin:

> Imperialism has caused deep misery for millions of people. For this reason, my evaluation of its negative and positive aspects will stress the negative consequences of imperialism.

You could continue this introduction by noting the issues and topics you will discuss in the body of your essay to support your position. Suppose, for example, that the question asked you to evaluate imperialism using two different examples. You would choose the areas you know best and mention them in your introduction:

> This essay will show how European economic exploitation of China and British rule in Ireland brought civil war and economic backwardness to those areas.

In the body of your essay, you will use a separate paragraph to discuss each topic, issue, or argument. You may want to begin a paragraph with an issue statement, and then use specific examples to illustrate it. Remember that you should always provide details to support your generalizations. Be sure that the facts you use are facts, not opinions or propaganda.

If the question asks you to evaluate (or compare or contrast), you will need to consider the pros and the cons of the issue. Don't ignore information that doesn't seem to support your position. Outline *non*-supporting details. Then you can adopt one of three strategies. You may feel you can argue that these details *do* support your position. For example, you might suggest that while the colonial powers benefitted economically from imperialism, they did so by stealing the assets of the people they ruled. Or you can acknowledge information that doesn't support your position—for example, that the colonizers built roads and railways in Africa and China—but argue that they did so to help their own traders, not to benefit the local people. Or finally, you can concede that some facts contradict your position but suggest that they are outweighed by the details that *do* support your argument.

If you quote from documents in your essay, don't use long quotations. Summarize their content and use only a sentence or phrase from the document, always remembering to surround it with quotation marks.

Throughout the essay, bear in mind the question you are answering and the position you are supporting. Don't stray from the topic. Stay on target; don't include irrelevant information. Don't repeat yourself.

End your essay with a conclusion where you restate your position and summarize your main arguments.

It is important to review your essay before you put your pen down. You will not be penalized for mistakes in grammar, capitalization, or spelling **UNLESS** these mistakes prevent the reader from understanding what you are trying to say.

Editing Your Essay

Before you begin to review your essay, ask yourself these questions:

- Did you answer the question that was asked and cover all parts of it?
- Did you write a strong introduction stating your position and summarizing how you will support it?
- Did you provide accurate facts to support your position?
- Did you check to see that there is no information in the body of the essay that doesn't belong there?
- Does your conclusion restate and summarize your position?
- Did you write legibly?

If the answer to any of these questions is "no," make any necessary changes. Then check to make sure your essay is clear and accurate.

Now you will have an opportunity to edit an essay that a student has written. First, read the essay question (below) and the student essay (opposite). Then rewrite the essay so that it follows the rules for good essay writing given at the top of the page. (You may need to add some words of your own to follow these rules.) Leave out information you don't think belongs in the essay but otherwise keep the student's information and ideas.

Question

Define the term "nationalism." Select one country you have studied and give specific examples of nationalism within that country. Describe a situation where nationalism was either a positive or a negative force in that country's history.

The history of Yugoslavia illustrates that nationalism is devotion to one's country. Yugoslavia was created after World War I. Its people had belonged to different nations before the war.

It split into many different nations in the 1990's, Croatia, Serbia, Bosnia, and so on. Each of these new nations had different religious beliefs, ethnic backgrounds, and cultures. They fought each other for their independence and many atrocities were committed. In the end the United Nations sent troops including Americans to bring peace.

In conclusion I would like to say that nationalism has been harmful in the nation of Yugoslavia for the reasons I have shown.

_____

_____

_____

_____

_____

_____

_____

_____

_____

_____

_____

_____

_____

Part II: Concepts, Themes, and Skills in the Social Sciences

When New York State educators considered how students would handle the vast topic of global history, they recognized that this posed a problem. It is simply not possible, even at a superficial level, to get a grasp on what has happened since time began throughout the world. So the people who set the curriculum devised a way to make global history manageable. Where possible, it would be organized into *concepts* and *themes*. These would provide the hooks that would allow students to connect events and movements in different parts of the world at different times.

The Coach will examine these concepts and themes and see how they can help make global history manageable. It will also take a look at the different disciplines that make up the social sciences: history, geography, economics, and political science. Each discipline has its own concepts and themes and its own subject matter. ***The Coach*** will take a look at the subject matter covered by each of the different social sciences and see what special skills an understanding of this subject matter may require.

5. History

Historical Concepts and Themes

In this chapter we will look at the concepts and themes that help you classify and group information as you study history.

Concepts allow you to understand and relate to people and events. Themes help you see patterns in how individuals, groups, and nations have behaved towards each other across place and time.

The terms "concept" and "theme" will come up again and again throughout *The Coach.* You will be asked to write an essay about either a concept or a theme on the **Global History Test**. Remember that themes and concepts cover all the ages of history and all parts of the world.

Read this passage by the Arab traveler Ibn Battuta who visited the African kingdom of Mali in 1352. Then answer the question.

> The women are treated with more respect than the men, an amazing state of affairs. A man's heirs are his sister's sons, not his own sons. I have never seen such a custom anywhere else in the world except among the Indians of Malabar. But the Indians are heathens, while the people of Walata are Moslems, most careful about making their prayers, studying books of law, and memorizing the Koran. Yet their women show no shyness before men and do not veil themselves, though they go to prayers faithfully.
>
> —Ibn Battuta

Concepts

Belief Systems   The structures that groups or individuals create in order to fulfill their religious faith or beliefs

Change   The basic alteration in things, events, and ideas

Choice   The right or power to select from a range of alternatives

Culture   Patterns in human behavior (ideas, beliefs, values, artifacts, and ways of making a living) that a society transmits to succeeding generations to meet its basic needs

Diversity   Differences in language, gender, socioeconomic class, religion, and other human characteristics and traits

Empathy   The ability to understand the behavior of others because one can identify similar responses in oneself

Identity   Awareness of one's own values, attitudes, and capabilities as an individual and as a member of different groups

---

1   Which concepts does Battuta touch on in this passage?

_____

_____

_____

2   Choose two of the concepts you listed and explain how they are illustrated by Battuta's account.

Concept 1:

_____

_____

_____

Concept 2:

_____

_____

_____

Themes

Interdependence

Observing how people rely on other people in interactions and exchanges that benefit all those involved

Imperialism

Analyzing the domination by one country of the political and/or economic life of another country or region

Movement of People and Goods

Knowing that there has been a constant exchange of people, ideas, products, technologies, and institutions from one region or civilization to another throughout history

Nationalism

Identifying the feeling of devotion and pride in one's country, or the desire of a people to control their own government, free from foreign interference or rule

Urbanization

Observing the movement of people from rural to urban areas

3   **Now read the passages that follow. Beneath each passage, identify the theme (or themes) that it illustrates.**

When they had finished, I told Montezuma [the Emperor of Mexico] that you needed gold. And he ordered his people to go to the provincial chiefs and bring back jewelry, and gold ingots, and gold and silver sheets. When the gold ingots and sheets were melted down, Your Majesty's share came to 32,400 gold pesos. The gold and silver jewelry I had already set aside for Your Holy Majesty.

—Excerpt from letter written by Hernan Cortés, October 30, 1520, to Emperor Charles V

Theme: _____

It was a town of red brick, or of brick that would have been red if the smoke and ashes had allowed it…It was a town of machinery and tall chimneys, out of which interminable serpents of smoke trailed themselves for ever and ever, and never got uncoiled. It has a black canal in it, and a river that ran purple with ill-smelling dye…It contained several large streets all very like one another, and many small streets still more like one another, inhabited by people equally like one another, who all went in and out at the same hours.

—Charles Dickens, *Hard Times*, 1854

Theme: _____

The volume of world trade has tripled, providing new material security for human life—and resulting in a rapid increase in the world's population. People hitherto isolated have been brought into worldwide circulation, with new opportunities for personal development.

—Perry, Chase, et al. 1989

Theme: _____

As never before, thousands and hundreds of thousands felt what they should have felt in peace time, that they belonged together. A city of two million, a country of nearly 50 million, in that hour felt that they were participating in world history, in a moment that would never recur…All differences of class, rank, and language were flooded over at that moment by the rush of fraternity. Strangers spoke to one another in the streets, people who had avoided each other for years shook hands.

—Stefan Zweig recalling the news of the outbreak of war in Vienna in 1914

Theme: _____

Interpreting History from Multiple Perspectives

You have learned to distinguish between primary and secondary historical sources. As fingerprints are to the detective, so primary sources are to the historian. Diaries, letters, government documents, business accounts—these are the materials that historian use to build a picture of the past. (Archeologists use different kinds of evidence—pottery fragments, bones, jewelry, ruins.)

The records left by the past do not speak for themselves. Historians must interpret this evidence to make sense of it. But historians are human beings. They reflect the class and culture within which they have been raised. They have absorbed beliefs and attitudes from parents, friends, religion, and schools. It is not hard to see, then, that they interpret evidence differently.

Interpretations of the past offered by today's American (or Russian, or Indian, or Arab) historians vary from individual to individual. Interpretations of history also vary from one era to another. British historians used to believe that their history was a gradual and inevitable journey towards freedom and democracy. Marxist historians insist that history consists of class struggle. Twentieth century historians stress the importance of geography, demography (population studies), and culture in helping us make sense of the past.

The Ancient Greeks fought a prolonged and bitter war that destroyed their economies. Before it began, both sides, the Athenians and the Spartans, were convinced that they would win. Accounts of their different viewpoints have survived. As you read them, observe how very differently two intelligent observers, both of them Greek, could view the same situation at the same point in time.

Perspective A:

> We have many reasons to expect success, first, superiority in numbers and military experience, and second, our general and unvarying obedience in the execution of orders. The naval strength which [the Athenians] possess shall be raised by us from...the monies at Olympia and Delphi. A loan from these enables us to seduce their foreign sailors by the offer of higher pay... A single defeat at sea is in all likelihood their ruin.
>
> —Thucydides, account given by one of Sparta's allies, 432 B.C.E.

4   Why do the Spartans expect to defeat the Athenians?

_____

_____

_____

Perspective B:

> Personally engaged in the cultivation of their land, without funds either private or public, the [Spartans]...are also without experience in long wars across the sea...Our naval skill is of more use to us for service on land, than their military skill for service at sea. Even if they were to...try to seduce our foreign sailors by the temptation of higher pay...none of our foreign sailors would consent to become an outlaw from his own country, and to take service with them.
>
> —Pericles of Athens, 432 B.C.E.

5   Why do the Athenians believe that the Spartans will fail?

_____

_____

_____

Chronology and Periodization

The First Americans

25,000 B.C.E.	10,000 B.C.E.	9000 B.C.E.	8000 B.C.E.	7000 B.C.E.	6000 B.C.E.	5000 B.C.E.
25,000 B.C.E. - before 10,000 B.C.E. Hunters cross Bering Straits to North America	Large grass-eating animals die out. Native Americans make new weapons to hunt faster animals like deer	End of glacial period		Hotter weather turns western grasslands into deserts		Native Americans begin first attempts at agriculture
People spread rapidly throughout North and South America						

Time lines show events in **chronological order**. This time line shows you when people first reached the continents of North and South America and what happened to them over the next 5,000 years or so.

Always check the title of a time line to understand what it contains. Also, remember that most time lines deal with events that occurred during the Common or Christian Era (C.E.). Events that occurred before the year 1 C.E. are labeled B.C.E. (Before the Common Era). Some older textbooks use B.C. instead of B.C.E. and A.D. instead of C.E.

Time lines generally show you what happened in one part of the world. But events occur throughout the world all the time. While hotter weather was turning grasslands into desert in Central America, some communities in Western Asia were building the world's first villages.

Compare the time line below with the one at the top of the page.

6 **Compare the development of farming in the Americas and in the Middle East.**

_____

_____

_____

_____

_____

_____

_____

_____

_____

Early People and the Neolithic Revolution

50,000 B.C.E.	20,000 B.C.E.	10,000 B.C.E.	9000 B.C.E.	8000 B.C.E.	7000 B.C.E.	6000 B.C.E.	5000 B.C.E.
Homo Sapiens in Africa	Cro-Magnon Man (European name for homo sapiens) in Europe	End of last Ice Age		First crops grown in Middle East	Settlement at Jericho on West Bank of Jordan River	Settlement at Catal Hüyük in Turkey	Invention of plow and use of fertilizers in agriculture	Invention of wheel; used for transport
Humans begin using language	Cave paintings in Europe	Domestication of goats					
		Invention of pottery and bone tools	Domestication of cattle, pigs, sheep, chickens			Looms used to weave clothes	

Periodization refers to the grouping of events over a specific time period. For example, the history of Europe from the fall of the Roman Empire until the fifteenth century is usually called the Middle Ages. The history of Asia and Africa between 1880 and 1914 is often labeled the *Age of Imperialism*. These labels have a tremendous influence on how we view the past. For instance, we view Africa in 1900 in the context of how Europeans were dividing up the region.

Periodization is both useful and harmful. It allows us to characterize a region at a particular place and time. But it can also distort our understanding of history. After all, no age has a clear beginning and end. Some parts of Europe had left the Middle Ages behind as early as 1350; in others, aspects of medievalism lingered until the French Revolution.

Whenever you read about the *Age of…*, remember that a historian created this label. Ask yourself what the label means. What were the characteristics of this place in time? What else was happening at this place in time that might justify the use of a different label? What reason is there for beginning the *Age* at a certain date and ending it at a certain date?

On the right you can see a passage about the rule of the Ming dynasty in China. As you read the passage, ask yourself what would be an appropriate way to characterize this period of Chinese history. Then answer the questions.

The first Ming ruler, Hong Wu, came to power in 1368. He and his successors rebuilt the Great Wall along the northern frontier. This helped to keep out the nomadic tribes. With peace came economic prosperity.

The early Ming emperors were interested in exploring the world outside China. Between 1408 and 1433, Chinese fleets under their captain Zheng He sailed to India, Arabia, and Southeast Asia. Their mission was to impose the emperor's authority and collect tribute. These voyages also began trading relationships, and Chinese merchants settled in southern and southeastern Asia.

Later Ming rulers chose to cut off contact with the outside world. Their officials considered the navy too costly, and Confucian philosophy despised trade and traders. After this, the building of ships was forbidden. These rulers preferred court pleasures to attending to official business. The expense of the luxurious court reduced the money available for defense. Once again, invaders crossed the frontier and established their own dynasty in 1644.

7   Which is the best way to label the rule of the Ming dynasty?

   1   An Age of Expansion

   2   An Age of Consolidation

   3   Chinese Imperialism

   4   The Chinese Renaissance

8A   If none of these choices seems accurate, choose your own label to describe Ming rule in China.

   _____

8B   Defend your choice of label for the Ming dynasty.

   _____

   _____

   _____

   _____

   _____

NOTICE: Photocopying any part of this book is prohibited by law.

6. Geography

Six Elements of Geography

Geography is the study of the earth. It is concerned with the earth as a physical environment and also with the people and animals who live there.

Geographers have divided their subject into the following six elements:

The World in Spatial Terms

Mapping the relationships among people, places, and environments into a spatial context

Places and Regions

Studying the identities and lives of individuals and people in terms of the places and regions in which they live

Physical Systems

Studying the physical processes that have shaped the Earth's surface; observing how plant and animal life interacts with this physical environment to create, sustain, and modify ecosystems

Human Systems

Studying how people have created settlements and structures on the Earth's surface and how they compete for control of the Earth

Environment and Society

Studying how the Earth (through its physical features and processes) impacts human activities and how human activities (largely through their use of natural resources) modify the Earth

The Uses of Geography

Knowing how the relationships between people, places, and settlements have changed over time.

These elements may be summarized as maps, regions, the physical world, human societies, and the relationship between the Earth and its people. It is important to understand how much human life has been shaped by the geography of the *place* where a person lives. This is still true today; in the past, it was overwhelmingly important.

Geographers often specialize in different aspects of their discipline. Cartographers are map-makers. Physical geographers study the earth's physical processes such as climate and landforms. Human geographers study human societies and their relationship to their physical environment.

1   **After the death of Mohammed in 732, C.E., there was a massive migration of Arabs from the Arabian Peninsula into North Africa and the Middle East. Which of the six elements of geography would help you understand how and why this migration occurred?**

_____

_____

_____

_____

_____

_____

Regions of the World

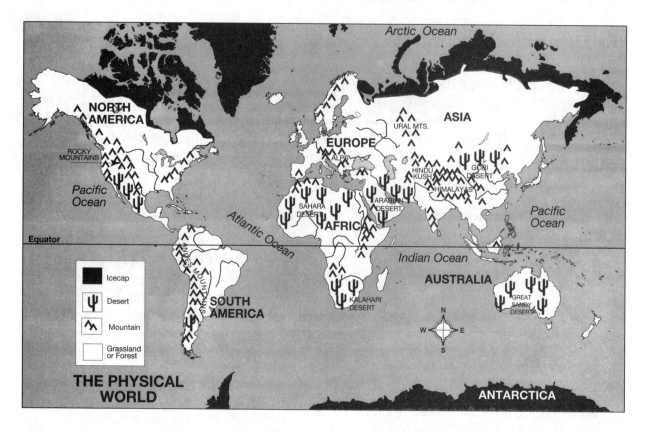

The study of regions and the people who live there is one of the six elements of geography. The term *region* is used to identify an area with certain characteristics that distinguish it from another area. These characteristics could be climate, elevation (height above sea level), natural vegetation, agricultural use, landforms, political boundaries, and many others.

The map shown above illustrates the world's physical regions: its mountains, deserts, and major rivers. These landforms have had a tremendous impact on human history. High mountain ranges and wide rivers reduce contact between peoples; vast plains encourage movement. Regions filled with icecaps or deserts rarely support much human activity and are largely uninhabited.

You may want to refer to this map as you learn how geography has affected the lives of people in different parts of the world

2   **Based on the information shown in the map, which of the following statements about the world's physical features is correct?**

1   **Australia contains several high mountain ranges.**

2   **Both North America and Asia contain deserts, grasslands, mountains, and icecaps.**

3   **Most of the land that lies on the equator is desert.**

4   **The continent with the largest area of icecap is Europe.**

7. Economics

Major Economic Concepts

You read in Chapter 5 about the themes and concepts that concern historians. In this chapter you will learn about the concepts that economists study. These concepts, which are listed on the right, deal mainly with how humans satisfy their survival needs and how governments help them to achieve these (and their own) goals.

Historians use economic concepts in their study of the past. Whether their subject is the beginning of farming, or the Industrial Revolution, or feudalism, or China's Great Leap Forward, they need to know:

- what goods and services were produced within a region
- who made this decision
- for whom were these items produced

1   An agricultural nation exports the sugar that it grows. Now its government wants to build factories to process sugar before it is exported. Which economic concepts will be involved in making this change or will be affected by it?

_____

_____

_____

_____

_____

_____

_____

Needs and Wants

Knowing that needs are essential goods and services (food, clothing, and shelter) and wants are the goods and services that people would like to have to improve their quality of life such as education, security, health care, and entertainment

Scarcity (and supply and demand)

Identifying the conflict between a limited **supply** of natural and human resources and unlimited **demand** in the form of needs and wants

Opportunity Costs

Understanding that because of scarcity, we must make choices; the items we do without are the opportunity costs of the items we choose to have. (Say you have $3.00 to spend. Big Macs and shakes both cost $3.00. If you buy the Big Mac, and pass up the shake, then the shake is your opportunity cost.)

Economic Systems

Understanding how economic systems (traditional, command, market, and mixed systems) determine what goods and services will be produced

Resources (the Factors of Production)

Identifying the resources, human (labor), natural (land), and capital, that are combined to produce goods and services (food, for example)

Science and Technology

Identifying the tools and methods people use to get what they need and want

Global Interdependence

Understanding that the economies of nations around the world are highly intermingled and depend on each other to supply those goods that they do not provide for themselves

8. The Concepts of Political Science

The concepts and themes of political science can be grouped as follows:

- Purposes of Government
- Political Systems
- Rights and Responsibilities of Citizens

Government

Definition:

The groups of people who make up the institutions and processes through which a society makes and enforces its laws

Functions:

Protect basic human rights (economic, political, and social) such as the right to life, liberty, and security, and the right to an adequate standard of living

Provide justice—the fair and equal treatment of individuals by government and society

Methods:

To achieve these aims it uses its power to influence others or to compel their obedience. Legitimate power is called authority.

Political Systems

Definition:

Political systems determine the powers that governments (monarchies, dictatorships, democracies, etc.) have and how they function.

Where they exist:

In nation-states which unite people in a geographic area under one government

---

Rights and Responsibilities of Citizens

Definition of Citizenship:

Belonging to a community (world, nation, state, town, school, or neighborhood) and accepting the rights and responsibilities of membership in this community

Civic Values:

These include justice, honesty, self-discipline, due process, majority rule with respect for minority rights, and respect for people and property.

Decision Making:

Citizens must often make decisions for the well being of the community. This process means working with others to reach agreement and manage conflict by building coalitions, seeking consensus, and negotiating compromises.

---

1   How would citizenship in a totalitarian dictatorship differ from citizenship as described above?

_____

_____

_____

_____

_____

_____

_____

_____

Part III: Global History

9. The Ancient World: First Civilizations and Belief Systems

In 10,000 B.C.E. humans lived and hunted together in small groups and worshiped nature spirits. By the year 500 C.E., most people lived in farming communities where they grew their own food. Some individuals lived in cities working as artisans, traders, and officials. Most of the people of southern Europe, the Middle East, India, and China now participated in belief systems that required good conduct from their followers. In this chapter we will examine how these huge changes came to pass.

These are the questions we will ask and seek to answer:

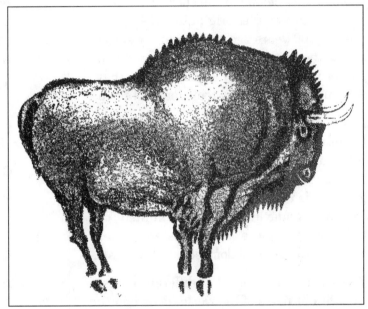

This cave painting of a bison was created about 14,000 years ago during an Ice Age. It was found in a Spanish cave.

What role did technology play in the development of human civilization?

What contributions did early and classical civilizations make to the history of mankind?

How did these early civilizations develop trading links with each other and how did cultural change pass along these links from one people to another?

What similarities and differences can we find in the major religions that developed during this period? How do these belief systems affect our lives today?

Early Peoples, 10,000–3500 B.C.E.

Early People and the Neolithic Revolution

50,000 B.C.E.	20,000 B.C.E.	10,000 B.C.E.	9000 B.C.E.	8000 B.C.E.	7000 B.C.E.	6000 B.C.E.	5000 B.C.E.
Homo Sapiens in Africa	Cro-Magnon Man (European name for homo sapiens) in Europe	End of last Ice Age	First crops grown in Middle East	Settlement at Jericho on West Bank of Jordan River	Settlement at Catal Hüyük in Turkey	Invention of plow and use of fertilizers in agriculture	Invention of wheel; used for transport
Humans begin using language	Cave paintings in Europe	Domestication of goats					
		Invention of pottery and bone tools	Domestication of cattle, pigs, sheep, chickens			Looms used to weave clothes	

People today belong to the species *homo sapiens*. This species originated in Africa over 50,000 years ago and gradually spread across the world. These people hunted and gathered their food. By 10,000 B.C.E., they were using pottery and tools made of bone

It was around this date that the **Neolithic Revolution** began. The glaciers that had covered the earth during the last Ice Age melted, and this allowed new forests and grasslands to emerge. People began to shift from a nomadic life where they hunted their food to a more settled existence where they grew crops and domesticated animals.

These changes occurred at different times in different parts of the world. People in the Middle East planted wheat and barley as long ago as 8000 B.C.E., but rice was not grown in China until 3,000 years later.

The beginning of agriculture had two major results: it provided a steady supply of food, and it allowed people to settle in one place—hunters had lived a nomadic life.

1   Several developments made it possible for early people to live settled lives as farmers. Which was one of these developments?

A   the ability to make warm clothes

B   the domestication of animals

C   the invention of pottery

D   the use of the wheel

2   Which of the following occurred first?

A   the building of village communities

B   the manufacture of woven fabrics

C   the use of horse-drawn carts

D   the use of speech

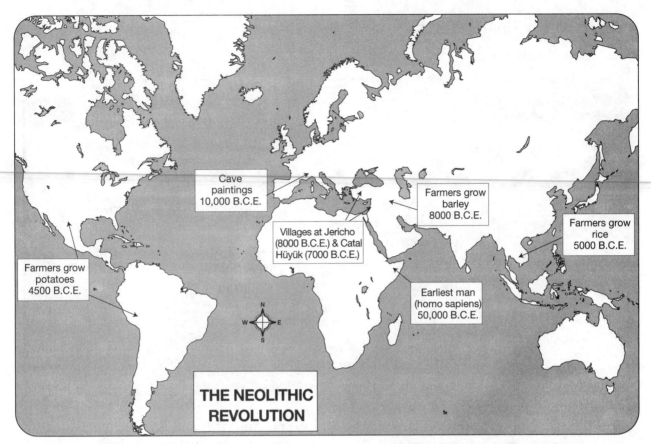

THE NEOLITHIC REVOLUTION

New sources of food allowed the world's population to grow from about two million in 15,000 B.C.E. to 90 million by 4000 B.C.E. Farming families built villages in areas where there was fertile soil and plentiful water. The time line and the map show some of these early villages.

New inventions made farming easier. Oxen were trained to pull plows; fields were fertilized with manure to make them yield more crops. Farmers needed to know when they should plant their crops. They developed calendars to help them measure the seasons. Farmers claimed that the land they farmed was theirs. Disputes over land ownership led to conflict and war.

Inventions also changed cultural life. People who had worn nothing but animal skins could now weave clothes from their sheep's wool. They could travel in carts once the wheel was invented. They could build their houses from bricks once they learned how to bake clay.

3A **List three ways that new technologies changed farming?**

_____

_____

_____

3B **Choose one of these technologies. Describe how farmers coped before it was available.**

_____

_____

_____

3C **Give reasons to support your answer to the above question.**

_____

_____

_____

River Valley Civilizations

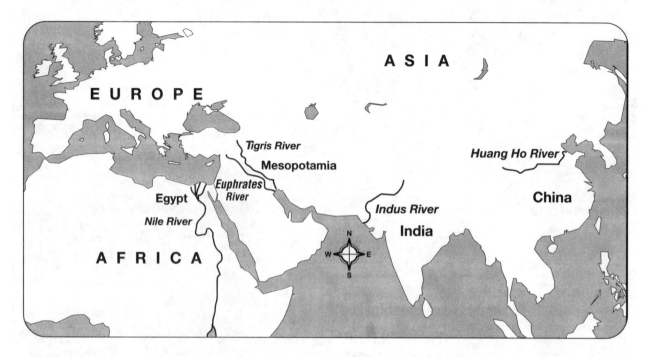

Over thousands of years, some of these farming communities grew into great cities. Life in these cities was much more complex than in the agricultural villages. Urban citizens specialized in different occupations: they were traders, craftsmen, priests, and government officials, as well as farmers. New technologies and an organized system of government allowed them to build irrigation systems and other group projects. Citizens shared a system of values and beliefs. Richer individuals could read and write. These cities are known as **civilizations**.

The major ancient civilizations grew up around the great rivers shown in the map. The earliest ones developed around 3500 B.C.E. in the valleys of the Tigris and Euphrates Rivers in present-day Iraq. Soon thereafter the Ancient Egyptians built cities in the fertile Nile Valley, and by about 2500 B.C.E. settlements began to appear around the Indus River. One thousand years after that the first Chinese civilization flourished along the banks of the Huang Ho (Yellow River). By 750 B.C.E. there were cities in

Europe, America, and East Africa. Even so, most people continued to live in smaller farming communities.

4A In which four regions were the River Valley civilizations located?

_____ _____

_____ _____

4B Cities were possible only after farmers increased their output. Why?

_____

_____

4C Describe what is meant by the term "civilization."

_____

_____

_____

Egypt, 3000–945 B.C.E.

Between about 3000 B.C.E. and 945 B.C.E., Egypt was ruled by **pharaohs** believed to be gods as well as kings. The pharaohs held **absolute** power and created a **bureaucracy** to help them govern. These officials oversaw trade, collected taxes, and supervised irrigation projects that spread the Nile's waters and its fertile silt (known as **loess**) over nearby farmland.

Egyptians believed that the souls of the pharaohs continued to rule, even after death, so they preserved their rulers' bodies and placed these **mummies**, along with the pharaohs' possessions, in the magnificent tombs we know as **pyramids**.

Ancient Egypt is often divided into three eras: the Old Kingdom (2686–2181 B.C.E.), the Middle Kingdom (2040–1786 B.C.E.), and the New Kingdom (1570–1005 B.C.E.). The Old Kingdom saw the unification of the country under one ruler and the building of the pyramids. During the Middle Kingdom, the pharaohs extended their empire south to include the Sudan. They also built a canal linking the Nile with the Red Sea that allowed traders to travel to Arabia and East Africa. The pharaohs of the New Kingdom expanded their empire north to include Syria. Egypt's power waned after 945; it came under Kushite control in the south and Libyan rule in the west.

Egyptian society was highly stratified: the royal family, nobles, and priests were at the top. Craftsmen and merchants were in the middle. Most Egyptians were at the bottom of the ladder. They were poor farmers who rented their land from the king in return for a part of their crops. Occasionally they worked on state building projects.

Religion was central to Egyptian life. The people were **polytheistic,** worshiping many gods whom they held responsible for the climate, their health, and their fortunes in general. By 1500 B.C.E., the poor believed that they, as well as the rich, would enjoy an afterlife.

Egyptians developed a picture writing system called **hiero-glyphics**—a simple form of it was used in everyday business. Many of the **artifacts** created by Egyptian scribes, craftsmen, and builders—writing, pyramids, and temples—have survived. We learn from them that the Egyptians were skilled in astronomy and medicine. Their calendar enabled them to predict when the Nile would flood, and their doctors were able to treat fractures, wounds, and diseases.

5   **Arrange the following events in chronological order to create a time line. Place the letter next to each event in the correct box.**

A   The New Kingdom began.

B   The pharaohs conquered the Sudan.

C   The pyramids were built.

D   Western Egypt was conquered by the Libyans.

Mesopotamia, 3500–1600 B.C.E.

Mesopotamian civilizations were built around the Tigris and Euphrates Rivers. Unlike the Nile, the Tigris and Euphrates did not provide a regular supply of water—when there was no rain, they dried up. At times, floods swept away whole villages. The Sumerians built dams and canals to control river waters and this allowed local farmers to grow grains and other crops. Even so, the rivers could bring disaster. This affected people's attitudes: they felt that they had no control over their lives and regarded their gods (the people were polytheistic like the Egyptians) as selfish creatures who brought floods and famines.

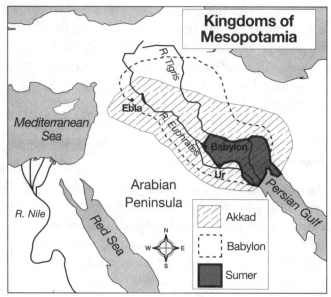

The Sumerians built the first Mesopotamian civilization. Their city-states were built around massive **ziggurats** that contained tombs like Egypt's pyramids but also served as temples for the priests. Located on a wide open plain, the Sumerians were much more exposed than the Egyptians to the threat of invasion. Accordingly, their self-governing city-states chose military leaders who then became hereditary kings. Like the pharaohs, the kings also served as the high priests of the local gods.

Sumerians developed **cuneiform** writing as early as 3100 B.C.E. and engraved its symbols on clay tablets. Scribes wrote business records and literary epics like the poem *Gilgamesh* on these tablets. The Sumerians were an inventive people and developed a metal plow, the wagon wheel, the potter's wheel, the making of bronze from copper and tin, and a calendar with 12 months based on the cycles of the moon.

In about 2300 B.C.E., the Sumerians were conquered by the Akkadians who had migrated north from Arabia. Sargon, the Akkadian king, was mainly interested in military conquests, but his people adopted many aspects of Sumerian culture. By about 1900 B.C.E., Mesopotamia was ruled by the Babylonians. **Hammurabi**, their greatest ruler, created a law code for the region. Some of its laws seem harsh to us, but it did make crime a community concern and it provided legal protection for weaker citizens. In about 1600 B.C.E., the Hittites, who were the first in the region to use iron weapons, put an end to the kingdom of Babylon.

6 **What does the following excerpt from the epic poem *Gilgamesh* suggest about the Mesopotamians' view of life?**

"Where is the man who can clamber to heaven? Only the gods live forever...but as for us men, our days are numbered, our occupations are a breath of wind."

—*The Epic of Gilgamesh*

_____

_____

_____

_____

Indus Valley and Yellow River Civilizations, 2500–1000 B.C.E.

Like the Tigris and Euphrates, the Indus and Ganges Rivers of northern India are unpredictable. Summer **monsoon** rains cause them to flood, enriching the soil. But the heaviest rains destroy homes and villages, while light or late rains can lead to starvation.

The cities of Harappa and Mohenjodaro were built on the flood plain of the Indus in about 2500 B.C.E. and survived for about 800 years. The food surplus created by local farmers enabled town citizens to work as potters, metal toolmakers, and merchants. The merchants traded with the Mesopotamians from whom they may have borrowed their written language. But until we decode this language, the Indus Valley civilization will remain a mystery to us.

The Huang Ho carries large amounts of loess downstream. When melting snow and monsoon rains cause the river to flood, this loess is spread over the North China Plain, making it one of the richest agricultural areas in the world. It was in this region

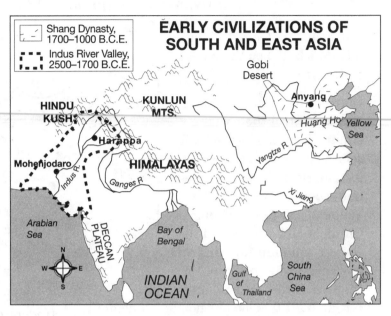

that the first Chinese civilization emerged around the year 2500 B.C.E.

The Shang was the first dynasty for which records have survived; they ruled this area between about 1700 and 1100 B.C.E. Like other early kings, the Shang were priests as well as rulers. The people worshiped nature gods. The priests developed a complex language which was written on bones. Chinese craftsmen made bronze weapons and jade and ivory statues. They wove garments from silk and made pots from a fine white clay.

Summary Question. Pick any two of the River Valley civilizations: Egypt, Mesopotamia, India, or China.

7A For each choice, explain how geography affected its development.

1 _____

2 _____

7B Compare the political systems of the two civilizations you have selected.

_____

_____

_____

Classical Civilizations and Empires

Zhou, Qin, and Han Dynasties in China, 1028 B.C.E.–220 C.E.

The history of China is divided into eras based on the names of its **dynasties**.

China's rulers had to find a way to control their vast empire. The Zhou gave their relatives areas to govern, but in time these kinsfolk seized power for themselves. The Qin emperor (after whom China is named) divided the country into military districts and took away the power of the local lords. He built the **Great Wall** to keep out nomadic invaders from the north. The Han also centralized control of government and extended their rule west to the borders of India and south to Indochina.

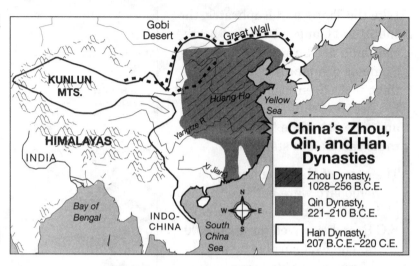

China's Zhou, Qin, and Han Dynasties

Zhou Dynasty, 1028–256 B.C.E.

Qin Dynasty, 221–210 B.C.E.

Han Dynasty, 207 B.C.E.–220 C.E.

During the chaos of the Zhou era, Chinese philosophers developed ideas for bringing peace and order. **Confucius** taught that ethics should guide personal conduct. He believed that better-educated, ethical officials could restore social harmony and good government. **Wudi**, the greatest Han ruler, wanted to put these ideas into practice. To raise the quality of his officials, he required them to take long, written exams to obtain their posts. This system created a new class of scholar civil servants called **mandarins**.

Other important philosophical ideas came from the **Taoists** and **Buddhists**. Taoists believed people should be guided by nature, not by rules of conduct. Buddhism, which entered China from India by way of Central Asia in the first century C.E., stressed escape from suffering through meditation.

Social life in China was influenced by these ideas. The family was at the center of daily life; its members had well-defined roles and duties. Society was divided into three tiers.

At the bottom were the merchants and traders, despised for their pursuit of wealth. Next came the peasants (perhaps 90% of the population) who rented their land from their lords and lived in rural villages. At the top were the aristocrats whose homes and lives were filled with art and literature.

Chinese inventors created silk, paper, and gunpowder. Traders carried this silk to the Middle East along the route known as the Silk Road. There they exchanged it for glasswares and wool and linen cloth. Chinese engineers built suspension bridges and mines. Their doctors recognized the importance of nutrition and developed the technique of **acupuncture**.

8   The map suggests that the Great Wall of China

  A   kept invaders from the North out of Han empire

  B   prevented Indian culture from spreading into China

  C   helped the Zhou emperors to centralize their kingdom

  D   was in the valley of the Huang Ho

Kingdoms and Trade in the Middle East, 1500–400 B.C.E.

After Hammurabi's Mesopotamian empire was destroyed by the Hittites, the region was controlled by a series of warlike people. The Hittites were followed by the Assyrians who were conquered in turn by the Chaldeans. These warriors frequently deported whole populations and resettled them in other parts of their empires. They were excellent soldiers, and the Assyrians, at least, were fine administrators, but they were more interested in conquest than culture. The Hittites and Assyrians borrowed the legal system, the gods, the script, and the art forms of the Mesopotamians. The short-lived Chaldean Empire reached its peak under King **Nebuchadnezzar**, a talented general and statesman. He rebuilt the city of Babylon and created the famous Hanging Gardens in his splendid new palace.

The peoples conquered by these warrior states included the Phoenicians and the Israelites. The Phoenicians were great traders. They sailed around the Mediterranean and beyond to West Africa from their ports of Tyre, Sidon, and Byblos. They carried cedar wood, dyed textiles, glass, and jewelry. To help them keep track of their accounts, the Phoenicians developed an alphabet which became the basis of the alphabets used in Western languages.

The Israelites lived in the small kingdoms of Israel and Judah. Israel was conquered by the Assyrians; the people of Judah were deported by the Chaldeans to Babylon in 586 B.C.E. and their temple at Jerusalem was destroyed. But their legacy of **monotheism** (belief in one God) and a commitment to ethics survived this and subsequent **diasporas**.

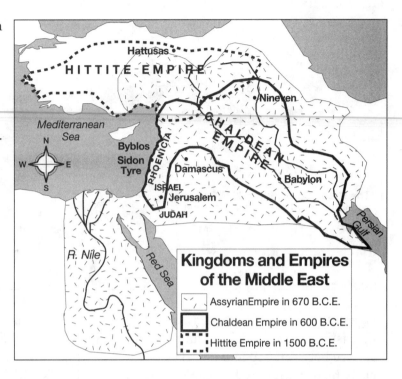

Kingdoms and Empires of the Middle East

- AssyrianEmpire in 670 B.C.E.
- Chaldean Empire in 600 B.C.E.
- Hittite Empire in 1500 B.C.E.

9 Identify the people described by the sentences below.

A "At its height, their empire stretched from the Persian Gulf to Egypt."

B "These daring explorers established towns along the west coast of Africa, on the islands of the western Mediterranean, and in Spain."

C "In the 1300's B.C.E. their empire reached its peak and included much of Asia Minor and northern Syria."

D "Their exile is known as the Babylonian Captivity."

A _____

B _____

C _____

D _____

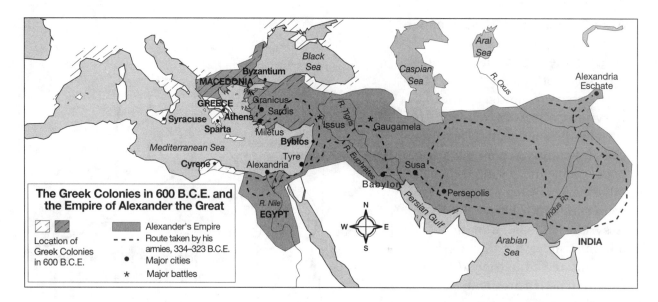

The Greek Colonies in 600 B.C.E. and the Empire of Alexander the Great

Location of Greek Colonies in 600 B.C.E.

Alexander's Empire

- - - - Route taken by his armies, 334–323 B.C.E.

● Major cities

★ Major battles

One of the world's greatest civilizations flourished on the mainland and islands of Greece between 750 and 336 B.C.E. Its early history and myths were celebrated by the blind poet **Homer** in two epic poems, the *Iliad* and the *Odyssey*. In the centuries that followed, the Greeks adopted the Phoenician alphabet and wrote plays, poems, histories, and books on philosophy and science that are still performed and studied.

The coastline of Greece is filled with fine harbors; the interior, apart from a coastal plain, is mountainous. Not surprisingly, the Greeks became sailors, traders, and fishermen. Rugged geography separated one part of Greece from another and so it was never united under one government. It consisted instead of independent city states—cities and the farmland and villages that surrounded them. When a city could no longer feed itself, it created colonies along the Mediterranean and Black Sea coasts. The colonies supplied the parent city with food and stimulated the growth of trade.

Originally, Greek communities were ruled by kings. By 750 B.C.E., power had passed to noble landowners. By 500 B.C.E. most city states were either **oligarchies** like Sparta or democracies like Athens. In the latter, all free Athenian-born males (about 20% of the total population) were citizens. As such they were equal before the law and could serve on juries and participate in the Assembly. The Assembly made the laws, served as a supreme court, and appointed army generals. Everyday government decisions were made by a Council of 500 whose members were chosen by lottery each year.

Pericles, a great Athenian general and democrat

Sparta also had a law-making assembly, but its political life was controlled by a handful of citizens. The army dominated Spartan life. Although they were allowed to marry at age 30, Spartan males spent most of their active lives drilling and fighting. The Spartans' iron discipline allowed them to control their large **helot** (slave) population. But it made them resist change, trade, and culture. Sickly babies who would make poor soldiers were left to die. Surprisingly, women were encouraged to be active and healthy and given more freedom and power than women in other cities. Athenian women were not even trusted to do the shopping!

The Greeks believed in striving for excellence and calmly accepting one's fate. They put man at the center of their philosophy and culture. Their dramas focused on the interplay between man and destiny. Their architecture, painting, and sculpture stressed beauty, balance, and simplicity. Philosophers like Socrates, Plato, and Aristotle wrestled with the meaning of truth and the nature of government. Historians tried to separate truth from legend in their study of the past. Scientists based their theories on experiments and on observations of the world around them.

A famous sculpture of a discus thrower

The Greeks humanized their gods, too, and made them into a family that lived on Mount Olympus. Each god controlled his or her own sphere: Zeus, the chief god, ruled the sky; his brother, Poseidon, was lord of the sea; and his daughter, Aphrodite, was the goddess of love. The Greeks believed that their quarrelsome, selfish gods created physical events like storms and sunshine and brought to mankind both good fortune and disaster.

Before the Golden Age of Athens (490–431 B.C.E.) could begin, the Greeks had to join together to keep out the Persians. In 546 B.C.E., the Greek colonies in Asia Minor had become part of the mighty Persian Empire. Fifty-six years later, the Persian king, **Darius**, decided to conquer mainland Greece. He was stopped by two Greek victories: a land battle at Marathon and a sea battle at Salamis. But cooperation among the city states was short lived. Between 431 and 404, city leagues headed by Athens and Sparta fought each other in the Peloponnesian War. The war destroyed the spirit and weakened the economies of the Greeks and made it easy for Philip of Macedonia to conquer them in 338 B.C.E. His son, **Alexander the Great**, became ruler of Greece and Macedonia. His career was spent as a conqueror, leading his men as far east as India. Alexander tried to blend Greek and Persian cultures and to spread Greek language and **Hellenistic** culture throughout his vast empire.

10A List the achievements of the Greek people that were passed on to later ages.

_____

_____

_____

_____

_____

10B Choose the achievement that you consider most important for the history of humankind and explain your choice.

_____

_____

_____

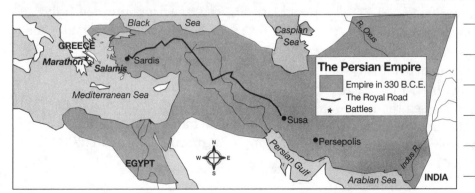

_____

_____

_____

_____

Rome: Republic and Empire, 509 B.C.E.–476 C.E.

By 146 B.C.E., the Greek city states and most of the remains of Alexander the Great's empire had been swallowed up by Rome. In the process, the Romans absorbed much of Greek culture and scientific achievement.

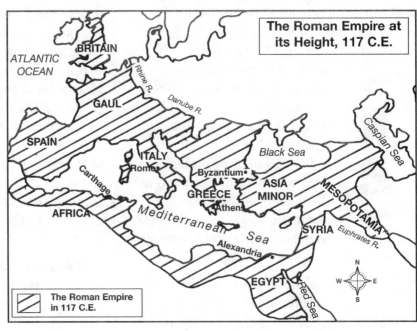

The Roman Empire at its Height, 117 C.E.

The Roman Empire in 117 C.E.

Rome had begun as a small city on the Italian peninsula. In 509 B.C.E., Rome's citizens expelled their Etruscan ruler. By 264, they controlled the whole of Italy. Roman expansion was halted briefly in 216 by General **Hannibal** of Carthage. Hannibal with his army and his elephants invaded Italy and threatened to destroy Rome. But Roman troops finally defeated Hannibal. In 146 they burned Carthage and this gave them control of the western Mediterranean. The conquest of Greece and Macedonia had secured the eastern Mediterranean. The lands around this sea were the core of Rome's empire, though later generals would extend its boundaries north and east.

Rome began as a **republic**. There were two classes of citizens: the aristocratic **patricians** and the majority of citizens, the **plebeians**. Both groups had some civic rights, but only patricians could be elected to office. Rome's government was divided into executive and legislative branches. Two **Consuls** headed the executive branch. The Senate dominated the legislature. Its 300 patrician members, who were elected for life, advised the Consuls and debated foreign policy and legislation. In 494 B.C.E., a revolt by the plebeians increased their political power and established the principle that all free citizens were protected by the laws.

Rome's military success was based on its well-organized and highly disciplined army. At first, when most Romans were small farmers, all male citizens served as soldiers. But military conquests changed that. Thousands of conquered people were brought as slaves to Rome and replaced the paid workers. At the same time, many small farmers lost their lands to great landowners who also used slave labor. Rome's swelling population of the poor and unemployed now provided army recruits.

These new soldiers were loyal to the generals who paid them, not to the state. Powerful generals used their soldiers to gain political control. The most important was **Julius Caesar**. After conquering Gaul and Britain, Caesar's army invaded Italy. In 45 B.C.E. he began to rule as dictator for life. Caesar carried out many social reforms, but some senators viewed him as a tyrant and murdered him in 44 B.C.E. Caesar's nephew, Octavian, defeated his rivals and made himself Rome's first emperor as **Augustus Caesar** in 27 B.C.E.

Statues of Emperor Augustus showed him in a heroic pose

Emperor Augustus and the "good emperors" who ruled from 96 to 180 C.E. reformed the administration of the empire. They appointed capable governors to rule the provinces; fine new roads allowed them to communicate with Rome.

Imposing public buildings were constructed and **aqueducts** were built to carry water to the cities. Roman law applied to rich and poor alike and was used across the empire.

The provinces sent luxury items from the East and raw materials to Rome. Italian craftsmen made pottery, cloth, glass, and jewelry for the provinces. The profits of trade and agriculture allowed wealthy Romans to lead comfortable and cultured lives. Most citizens were poor but they were consoled by free grain and public spectacles such as chariot races and gladiator fights.

The period of peace and prosperity between 27 B.C.E. and 180 C.E. is known as the **Pax Romana**—the peace brought by Rome. Literature, art, and science flourished. Latin poets like Virgil and Horace and historians like Livy celebrated Rome's greatness. Doctors and astronomers developed theories based on the observations made earlier by Greeks and Egyptians.

But by 200, the Roman empire was threatened from inside and out. Christianity was spreading, especially among poor city folk. Christians refused to fight in the army or to honor Roman gods (including the emperor who was viewed as a god). They were widely persecuted and even though their numbers were small, their influence was considerable. By 392, Christianity was so widespread that it became the official religion of the empire.

After 192, emperors were appointed by the army. Most of them ruled only briefly. Army factions fought each other constantly. This internal fighting disrupted trade and industry and destroyed harvests and farms.

To make matters worse, Germanic groups whom the Romans called **barbarians** began to threaten the empire. Rome's army was too divided, and its borders too long to be defensible. Emperor **Diocletian** recognized that it was impossible for one man to rule such a vast area and appointed separate rulers for the eastern and western provinces (the empire was formally divided into two halves in 395). In 330, Emperor **Constantine** moved the capital to the Greek city of Byzantium which was easier to defend than Rome. The city of Rome was finally conquered in 476, but the eastern half of the empire survived for another 1,000 years.

11A Which forces caused the Roman Empire to expand?

_____

_____

_____

_____

_____

_____

11B Which forces caused its decline?

_____

_____

_____

_____

_____

The Emergence and Spread of Belief Systems

FIVE GREAT RELIGIONS					
	Buddhism	**Christianity**	**Hinduism**	**Islam**	**Judaism**
FOUNDERS	Siddhartha Gautama, known as Buddha	Jesus Christ	Unknown	Mohammed	Abraham and Moses
PLACE AND DATE OF ORIGIN	Northern India about 500 B.C.E.	Palestine about 30 C.E.	India before 1500 B.C.E.	Arabia 622 C.E.	Palestine about 2000 B.C.E.
HOLY BOOKS		Holy Bible (Old & New Testaments)	The Vedas	Koran	Torah
SYMBOLS	Wheel of life	Cross		Crescent	Star of David
BASIC BELIEFS	Right thinking, speech, and action lead to *enlightenment*	*Salvation* of the souls of those who have faith in Christ	*Reincarnation*; good or bad fortune (*karma*) comes from good or bad behavior	One God, Mohammed his prophet; five obligations for the Faithful	One God, who gave the law to his people

The development of belief systems is a major theme in human history. Belief systems are the structures that groups or individuals create in order to fulfill their religious faith. The table shows five of the world's principal belief systems. As the map indicates, they all originated in southwest or southern Asia. These five religions evolved over a relatively short space of time—between 2000 B.C.E. and 622 C.E. *The Coach* uses two chapters to cover this historical period, but these religions are treated together here so that they may be compared.

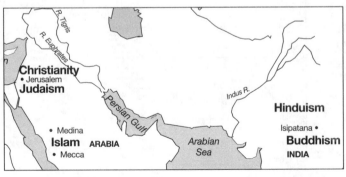

12 Which three major religions originated in the Middle East?

A Buddhism, Hinduism, and Islam

B Christianity, Hinduism, and Islam

C Christianity, Hinduism, and Judaism

D Christianity, Islam, and Judaism

13 Unlike the other major religions, Hinduism

A has no holy books

B stresses belief in one God

C was founded after the end of the Neolithic period

D was not developed by anyone that we can identify

66

Hinduism and Buddhism

Unlike other belief systems, Hinduism does not have a founder. It originated in the beliefs and practices of the people who lived in India before 400 B.C.E. From them, Hinduism adopted the belief in several gods (the most important were Brahma, Shiva, and Vishnu), and in the idea of **reincarnation**. This teaches that when a being dies, his/her/its soul is reborn in another body. This is painful for the soul which yearns to end the reincarnation process by achieving unity with the universal spirit. The kind of body that a soul is reborn into depends on **karma**. This means that the soul of an individual who lives an evil life may be reborn as a lowly creature, but the soul of someone whose life is filled with good deeds will be reborn into a higher social class and move closer to universal oneness. Good deeds consist of a life filled with prayer, self-denial, and the rejection of worldly goods.

The founder of Buddhism was an Indian prince called **Siddhartha Gautama**. When Gautama learned that suffering and poverty exist, he wanted to understand how suffering could be ended. After years of meditation and fasting, he reached a new understanding of the human condition. In the **Four Noble Truths**, he taught his followers:

- all beings suffer—it is part of being human

- people are driven by worldly desires which cause the soul to be reincarnated

- by eliminating desire, people can eliminate suffering

- desire can be eliminated by truthfulness, resisting and freeing the mind of

Siddhartha Gautama, the Buddha

evil, not harming others and working for their well being, respecting life, controlling one's thoughts, and meditation.

Many Buddhist teachings (Buddha means "Enlightened One") are derived from Hindu beliefs. But the Buddha did not believe in the Hindu gods who brought warfare and good fortune, nor in the Hindu **varna** system which teaches that a person's destiny depends on the **caste** into which he or she is born. Hinduism is deeply rooted in Indian cultural practices and did not spread much beyond India. But Buddhist monks carried their master's ideas to China, Japan, Indochina, and Korea.

14A Which of the Hindu beliefs did Buddhists share?

_____

14B Did the Buddhist version of this belief differ from the Hindu version? If so, how?

_____

_____

_____

14C Which Hindu beliefs did Buddhists NOT share?

_____

_____

_____

_____

Judaism and Christianity

Judaism is the faith of the Jewish people. It is based upon a compact between God and the ancient Israelites that is described in the Bible. In return for worshiping Him only and obeying His laws, God promised special honor to the Jewish people and a homeland in Canaan (Palestine).

The first five books of the Bible are known as the **Torah**. They describe the early history of the Israelites and the religious and ethical laws received by the prophet **Moses** at Mount Sinai. The Torah teaches that man is made in God's image and is therefore uniquely precious. It stresses that people have a commitment to obey the law and to work with God for the betterment of mankind. Other books of the Bible describe the teachings of prophets who, acting as God's spokesmen, urged the Israelites to remain faithful to Him or be punished.

The Jews were driven from Palestine first by the Assyrians and Chaldeans, and then, following an unsuccessful rebellion in 132 C.E., by the Romans. After this latter exile, communities of Jews were scattered around the Mediterranean and the Middle East. But they continued to study the Torah in home and in special schools called **yeshivas**. Between 200 and 500, learned **rabbis** wrote commentaries on the Torah. The **Talmud** is a collection of these writings.

Jesus was a Jew who was raised in Palestine. He preached that God was for-giving and compassionate when people repented of their sins, and that people should behave with loving kindness towards each other. Jesus claimed that he was the son of God, and the followers of Jesus believed he was the **messiah**, the savior of the Jews. This troubled Roman rulers who feared he might cause political unrest. Accordingly, he was crucified in 33 C.E.; but Christians believe that he rose from the dead after three days.

While Jesus lived, his followers were Jews who remained within Judaism. After his death, the apostle **Paul** spread his message among **gentiles**. He preached that God sent Jesus to bring **salvation** to mankind. Paul preached to small Christian communities (after his death, Jesus was known as Christ) in the Mediterranean world; the apostle **Peter** allegedly set up a church in Rome. Many Christians including Paul and Peter were **martyred** (killed for their beliefs). But the faith became legal in the Empire in 322 and spread throughout Europe. European missionaries later spread the teachings of Christianity through Asia, America, and other parts of the world.

15A Identify one belief shared by Judaism and Christianity.

_____

_____

15B What did the Apostle Paul tell people about Jesus?

_____

_____

_____

_____

A typical Christian painting of Jesus teaching his followers

Islam

Milestones in the History of Islam

600	650	700	750	800	1250

622 Hijrah to Yathrib

624 Medina Compact

630 Mecca becomes Islam's spiritual center

635 Koran compiled

632 Mohammed dies; Abu Bakr first calif

631 Islam spreads across Arabia

661 Calif Ali killed; Umayyad dynasty begins

680 Ali's son, Hussein, murdered; split between Sunni and Shiite Moslems

716 Moslems conquer Spain

732 Moslem defeat at Battle of Tours halts spread of Islam into France

747 Umayyads defeated; Abbasid califate at Baghdad

786–809 Calif Harun al-Rashid makes non-Arabs equal with Arabs

1258 Mongols destroy Baghdad; end of Abbasid califate

In 613, an Arab named **Mohammed** began preaching in the city of Mecca. He taught that there was one God whom everyone should worship and obey, that those who believed in God were equal, that the rich should share their wealth with the poor, and that God judged people according to their deeds. Most Meccans opposed these ideas, so Mohammed and his followers went to Yathrib which became the center of Islam under its new name, Medina. In the Medina Compact, Mohammed decreed that the community would be ruled by the law and scriptures he had received from God (they were later recorded in the **Koran**). As judge and commander, he would settle all disputes.

Islam spread first to Mecca, then across Arabia, and then throughout the Middle East and beyond. The murder of the fourth calif and his son (Mohammed's descendant) by the troops of the Umayyad calif caused a deep division within the faith. A majority of Moslems (**Sunni**) believed that any devout Moslem could serve as calif. The **Shiites** stressed the spiritual aspects of leadership and insisted that only Mohammed's descendants could be califs. The division continues today; the Shiites, who live mainly in Iran and Iraq, stress suffering and martyrdom as the hallmarks of Islam.

The Koran teaches similar moral values to Judaism and Christianity: kindness to others and condemnation of cruel and criminal behavior. It decrees that the word of Mohammed is law in private and public life and it lists the Five Pillars of Islam, the five duties all Moslems must follow:

- Faith in one God, the God of Christians, Jews, and Moslems, whose prophets include Moses and Jesus, and the last and greatest of them, Mohammed
- Prayer offered five times a day in the direction of Mecca
- Alms-giving to the poor
- Fasting during the month of Ramadan
- Annual pilgrimage to Mecca (the **hajj**)

The Koran also includes laws relating to diet, family life, and property ownership.

16 **Which event was the most important for Shiite Moslems?**

A **Mohammed's journey to Medina**

B **the murder of Ali and his son**

C **the spread of Islam beyond the Middle East**

D **the victory of the Abbasids**

Section Review: The Ancient World

Part A

The documents below indicate how the people of ancient and classical civilizations viewed life and the society in which they lived. Examine each document and answer the question that follows it.

Document 1

> What is good in a man's sight is evil for a god,
> What is evil to a man's mind is good for his god.
> Who can comprehend the counsel of the gods in heaven?
> The plan of a god is deep waters, who can fathom it?
> Where has befuddled mankind ever learned what is a god's conduct?
>
> "The Epic of Gilgamesh," composed between 3000 and 2000 B.C.E.

1. What view of life is being expressed here?

_____

_____

Document 2

And Moses went up unto God, and the Lord called unto him out of the mountain saying: "Thus shalt thou say to the house of Jacob and tell the children of Israel:…if ye will hearken unto My voice indeed, and keep My covenant, then ye shall be Mine own treasure from all peoples; for all the earth is Mine; and ye shall be unto Me a kingdom of priests and a holy nation."

> *The Book of Exodus*, chapter 19, verses 3-6, composed in about 1250 B.C.E.

2. What beliefs would you expect that the ancient Israelites had from this passage?

_____

_____

Document 3

We are called a democracy, for the administration is in the hands of the many and not of the few. But while the law secures equal justice to all alike in their private disputes, the claim of excellence is also recognized; and when a citizen is in any way distinguished, he is [selected for] public service…as the reward of merit. Neither is poverty a bar, but a man may benefit his country whatever may be the obscurity of his condition…A spirit of reverence pervades our public acts; we are prevented from doing wrong by respect for authority and for the laws…

> A funeral oration delivered by Pericles during the Peloponnesian War (431-404 B.C.E.)

3. What values does Pericles hold most highly?

_____

_____

Document 4

Hour by hour resolve firmly, like a Roman and a man, to do what comes to hand with correct and natural dignity, and with humanity, independence, and justice. Allow your mind freedom from all other considerations. This you can do, if you will approach each action as though it were your last…See how little a man needs to master, for his last days to flow on in quietness and piety.

> —Marcus Aurelius, *Meditations,* about 170 C.E.

4. How would you expect Marcus Aurelius to respond if his troops were defeated in battle?

_____

Part B

Summarize how attitudes towards life and society changed between 2500 B.C.E. and 200 C.E. Include specific historical details and refer to the documents you analyzed in Part A.

_____

_____

_____

_____

_____

_____

_____

_____

_____

_____

_____

_____

_____

_____

_____

_____

_____

_____

_____

_____

_____

_____

_____

_____

_____

_____

_____

_____

_____

_____

10. Expanding Zones of Exchange and Encounter, 500–1200 C.E.: Setting the Stage for the Future

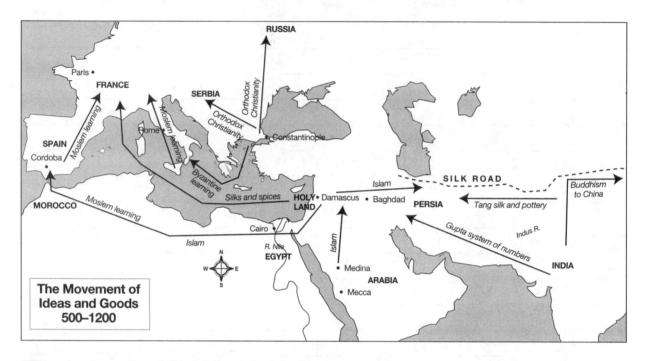

The Movement of Ideas and Goods 500–1200

In the years that followed the fall of the Roman Empire, new centers of economic prosperity and learning evolved. They included the Gupta Empire in India, China under the Tang Dynasty, the Byzantine Empire, and the Umayyad and Abbasid califates based in Damascus and Baghdad.

As the map shows, the spiritual and intellectual achievements of these centers fanned out east and west along the trade routes of Europe, Asia, North Africa, and the Middle East. Byzantine monks brought Orthodox Christianity to the Eastern Slav peoples of Russia, Bulgaria, and Serbia. Buddhism spread east from India to China. Islam moved west along the southern coast of the Mediterranean and east towards India. The classical learning of Greece and Rome was kept alive by Byzantine, Arab, and Jewish scholars and carried from them to the culturally backward areas of Western and Northern Europe.

At the same time, an active trade developed among the peoples of this vast region. The Crusades gave Western Europeans a taste for the luxuries of the East.

These various exchanges would set the stage for still more global interactions in the centuries that followed and for the resurgence of Europe.

NOTICE: Photocopying any part of this book is prohibited by law.

The Gupta Empire in India

Until 321 B.C.E., large sections of India were ruled by foreign invaders. The Aryans poured into the Indus-Ganges Plain from Central Asia in about 1500 B.C.E. They were followed 1,000 years later by Darius of Persia and then by Alexander the Great. Chandragupta Maurya was the first Indian to unite and rule large areas of India. His grandson, **Asoka**, extended the Mauryan empire until it covered most of the Indian subcontinent. The bloodthirstiness of battle persuaded Asoka to become a Buddhist. From military conquest, he turned to projects that would benefit his people: free hospitals, fine roads, and compassionate laws. After 184 B.C.E., the Mauryan Empire disintegrated into smaller, warring kingdoms.

In about 310 C.E., another Indian ruler named Chandragupta I built an empire that was smaller than the Mauryan Empire but covered some of the same area. As the map shows, the Gupta Empire stretched from east to west across central India. This empire lasted for 200 years. It was based on a strong central government, a powerful army, and the use of terror to intimidate opponents if necessary.

Unlike Asoka, the Guptas were Hindus and encouraged the spread of Hinduism across their empire. They believed in the importance of learning; their court included poets, dramatists, philosophers, and scientists. Much of their work was devoted to religious themes, but their astronomers

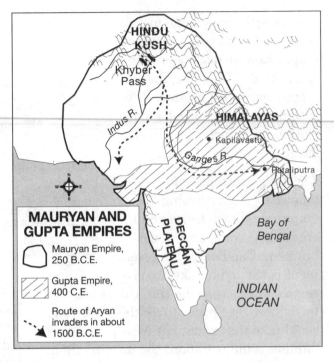

MAURYAN AND GUPTA EMPIRES

▢ Mauryan Empire, 250 B.C.E.

▨ Gupta Empire, 400 C.E.

⋯▶ Route of Aryan invaders in about 1500 B.C.E.

understood that the world is round and their mathematicians invented the zero and devised the numbers 1 through 9. Because Gupta traders traveled the land and sea routes to Arabia, Central Asia, China, and the Mediterranean, Gupta learning was able to spread to these areas. Their number system was adopted by Arab traders (hence they are called Arabic numerals) and provided an important tool for scientists around the world.

> Gupta doctors were the first to use inoculation to stop the spread of disease. They injected their patients with small amounts of cowpox to stop the spread of the deadly smallpox germ. Their surgeons could set broken bones and use plastic surgery to repair injured ears and noses. They also understood how important it was to sterilize their surgical instruments.

1 List three major contributions to learning that the Gupta made.

_____

_____

_____

_____

_____

China's Tang Dynasty

The Tang dynasty came to power in China soon after the Gupta Empire disappeared from India. Under Tang rule, the empire expanded northwest to include parts of Mongolia, and southwest to include parts of Tibet.

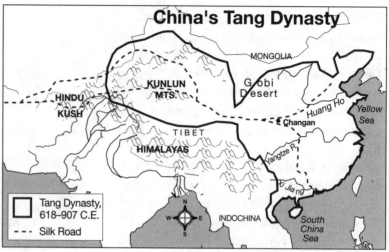

The Tang controlled their vast empire by strengthening the empire's military forces and by creating a strong central government. Candidates for government posts had to take the civil service exams that the Han rulers had introduced (see page 60). In theory, anyone could take the exams, but most peasant families could not afford the tutoring their sons would need.

Land reforms helped the Tang keep the support of their people. Land was given to farmers, and in the Yangtze region, farmers learned to grow strains of rice with higher yields. Now that crops could be planted and harvested in peace, farm output expanded and the population was able to grow.

Trade grew in importance during this period. The Tang built new trade routes throughout their empire. Caravans of merchants traveled these roads and the Silk Road which the Han had built to Central Asia. Water routes took them to Japan, India, and the Middle East. The traders carried silk and pottery and brought back foreign goods and ideas. Boosted by the growth in trade, the Tang capital of Changan became the world's largest city with over two million people.

Chinese potters, painters, and poets flourished under the Tang. Buddhism, which had already entered China through Central Asia, gained many converts during the Tang period. Scholars wrote dictionaries and encyclopedias and histories of the empire. The earliest form of printing was developed by monks who carved letters onto wood blocks, inked the blocks, and then pressed them onto paper.

The prosperity, security, and cultural achievements of China under the Tang make it a Golden Age in Chinese history.

2   **What entered China from India during the rule of the Tang?**

   A   Buddhism

   B   Christianity

   C   printing techniques

   D   silk

3   **Which of the following was inherited by the Tang from the Han dynasty?**

   A   control over parts of Indochina

   B   Moslem communities

   C   printing techniques

   D   the use of civil service exams

The Byzantine Empire

When the Roman Empire was divided, its eastern half continued the traditions of Rome. Its emperor spoke Latin and many ruling families were from Rome. But Greek language and culture became increasingly dominant, especially after the fall of Rome. After all, Byzantium was a Greek city, and the old Greek city states lay at the core of its empire. The city's position at the crossroads of the trade routes between Asia and Europe brought a multicultural flavor (and prosperity) to the empire.

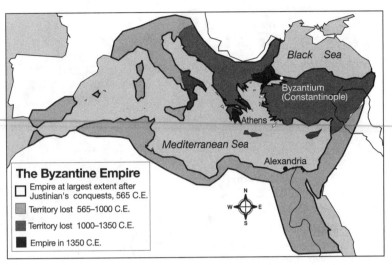

The Byzantine Empire
☐ Empire at largest extent after Justinian's conquests, 565 C.E.
Territory lost 565–1000 C.E.
Territory lost 1000–1350 C.E.
Empire in 1350 C.E.

Despite serious threats from the Persians on its eastern borders, the Emperor **Justinian** set about reconquering the western empire. His success was short-lived. Germanic tribes soon regained control of Italy and Spain. Syria, Palestine, and North Africa were lost to the Arabs. Constantinople itself—Byzantium was renamed to honor Emperor Constantine—was seized and ruled by Western Christians from 1204 to 1261. Constantinople finally fell to the Ottoman Turks in 1453.

During its 1,000 year existence, the Byzantine Empire played a vital role in preserving ancient learning. Scholars copied the writings of the ancient Romans and Greeks. Justinian codified Roman law, and the **Justinian Code** would become the basis for many European legal systems.

The Orthodox Church was central to daily life. **Icons, mosaics**, illuminated manuscripts, and literature depicted religious themes. The Byzantines, and this included the emperor, the clergy, and the ordinary people, were deeply involved in religious topics. Issues such as the relationship between God and Jesus, and the use of icons could lead to violence. Many men and women chose to live in monasteries and convents. They helped the needy and sent missionaries among the Slavs of Eastern Europe to spread the Christian faith. The monk **Cyril** created a Slavic alphabet and script that is still used today. The Eastern and Western branches of the Church became increasingly divided over issues of doctrine, politics, and power: the Pope at Rome claimed to be head of the Church, a claim that the **Patriarch** at Constantinople opposed. Finally, in 1054, there was a **schism** from which two churches emerged: the Eastern Orthodox and the Roman Catholic.

> And the Empress Theodora said:...Now is a poor time for flight...One who has been an emperor cannot endure to be a fugitive. There is the sea, there are the boats. But take care that after you are safe, you do not find that you would gladly exchange that safety for death.

4   **The historian Procopius described a riot that erupted in Constantinople in 532. Why did the Empress Theodora urge her husband Justinian not to flee?**

_____

_____

The Arab World: Arab Origins and the Spread of Islam

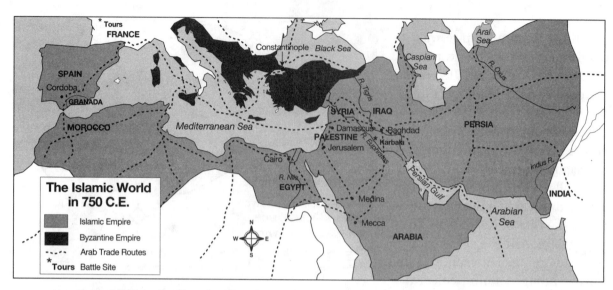

The Islamic World in 750 C.E.

Before 500 C.E., the Arabs were nomadic animal herders. Warfare was their way of life: Arab tribes raided each other's cattle and battled over water holes. By 550, many tribes had become traders or settled as farmers in fertile areas. But the land could not support the growing population. And although they shared a common language, the Arabs had no central government to unite them against the Byzantines and Persians who threatened their lands.

Islam was introduced into this world by Mohammed in 622. By 631 it had spread across the Arabian Peninsula. After Mohammed died, the armies of the first four califs carried Islam across the Byzantine and Persian Empires, conquering Syria, Iraq, Persia, Egypt, and Palestine. Their success was fueled by the belief that they had a **jihad**, or religious duty, to bring Islam to other lands and by the desire to obtain farmland to feed their people.

When Calif Ali was murdered in 661, the political center of Islam shifted to Syria, home of the Umayyad califs. The Umayyads made Arabic the official language and improved the treatment of non-Moslem Jews and Christians in the empire. Umayyad warriors and traders carried Islam to India and China, across North Africa, and into Spain.

In 747, the Umayyads were defeated by the Abbasid califs and Baghdad became the political center of Islam, though Mecca remained its spiritual capital. Under the great calif **Haroun al-Rashid**, Persians ran the government, Turks commanded the army, and Arabs controlled religious and legal life. (Indeed, Turkey and Persia became the only parts of the Middle East and North Africa where a majority of the people were not Arab.) Haroun tried to create equality among Moslems, Arabs and non-Arabs. After 810, Abbasid power declined as groups in Persia, Central Asia, and North Africa broke away and set up independent Islamic states. In 1258, the Mongols destroyed Baghdad and killed the last calif.

5 Create a time line by placing the letter next to each event in the correct box.

A the Mongol invasions

B the death of Mohammed

C the rule of Haroun al-Rashid

D the spread of Islam to Spain

76

Life and Culture in the Arab World

The Koran laid down the rules for family and business life. Husbands could have as many as four wives. A woman was her husband's responsibility. Her life centered on the home and family, though she could control her own property. Men worked as farmers, merchants, administrators, and soldiers, and much of their leisure time was spent at public baths and meeting places.

Until 1400, Moslem merchants controlled trade across Central Asia, the Middle East, much of the Mediterranean area, and North Africa. The Arab world produced carpets, spices, and textiles which it exchanged for Chinese silks, Asian spices, African gold and ivory, and African and European slaves. Cargoes were shipped across the seas and carried overland by caravan to the great **bazaars** of Baghdad, Damascus, and Cairo.

Because the Koran was written in Arabic, Moslems everywhere began to speak the same language. This allowed scholars, poets, rulers, and philosophers to communicate with each other. Between 800 and 1300, the Islamic world was the center of learning and culture—by contrast, much of Western Europe remained in the Dark Ages. Moslem colleges and cities were filled with Arab, Jewish, Greek, and Persian scholars who shared their ideas and translated them into other languages. Arabs used their knowledge of trigonometry and geometry to build mosques, survey land, and design pumps and fountains. Their astronomers' observations allowed them to predict eclipses and tidal movements. They invented the **astrolabe** that helped them to navigate and to measure the size of the earth. The chemist **al-Razi** and the physician **Ibn Sina** identified many diseases and described how the body functions.

Islamic philosophers tried to make the Koran compatible with Greek philosophy

> **On a Blind Girl**
> **by Bahä Ad-Dïn Zuhayr**
>
> They called my love a poor blind maid:
> I love her more for that, I said;
> I love her, for she cannot see
> These gray hairs which disfigure me.
> We wonder not that wounds are made
> By an unsheathed and naked blade;
> The marvel is that swords should slay,
> While yet within their sheaths they stay,
> She is a garden fair, where I
> Need fear no guardian's prying eye;
> Where, though in beauty blooms the rose,
> Narcissuses their eyelids close.

by using logic to analyze its teachings. Similarly, **Moses Maimonides**, a Jewish scholar who lived in Cairo and wrote mainly in Arabic, used Aristotle's philosophy to explain the mysteries of the Torah.

The Koran banned the representation of living creatures and so art was based on **calligraphy,** plants, and complex patterns. Architects designed mosques and homes that were works of art. Arabs were famous for love poetry (see the example above) and for fantastic tales such as *The Arabian Nights*. The works of Persian poets like Omar Khayyám were also widely read by rich Moslems who took pride in their culture.

6 "Islam's greatest cultural achievement was the part it played in preserving classical learning." Do you agree with this statement? Give your reasons.

_____

_____

_____

_____

_____

Medieval Europe

Feudalism

A period known as the "Dark Ages" descended on most of Europe after the fall of the Roman Empire. Cities and roads deteriorated, trade declined, as did law and order, and **barter** replaced money. There was some revival of order and learning during the reign of **Charlemagne**, a **Frankish** king whom the pope crowned the first **Holy Roman Emperor** in 800. But invaders from all directions soon created chaos again. Arabs attacked southern Italy, Magyars stormed through Central Europe until they settled in Hungary, and Vikings from over-populated Scandinavia conquered and ravaged many parts of Europe.

These raids severely weakened royal power, and communities were often isolated and left to fend for themselves. A political system known as **feudalism** evolved to deal with this situation. It was based on a grant of land in return for military service. Kings gave land **fiefs** to their **vassals** (nobles). In return, vassals pledged to provide knights (horse soldiers) to fight for the king. To protect their families, **retainers**, and villagers against attack in these lawless times, nobles built castles where they lived and held court.

Manorialism had evolved during the last years of the Roman Empire when peasants were unable to defend their farms against attack. Huge estates had sprung up where hundreds of peasants worked for lords who provided food, shelter, and protection in exchange. The economy of medieval Europe was based on the same system. A manor consisted of the lord's house, his home farm, grazing areas, woods, and the fields and housing that the peasants used. Manors were largely self-sufficient: they produced tools and clothing as well as food. In return for land to farm, peasants gave their lords some of their crops and some days of labor. Most peasants were **serfs**, unable to leave

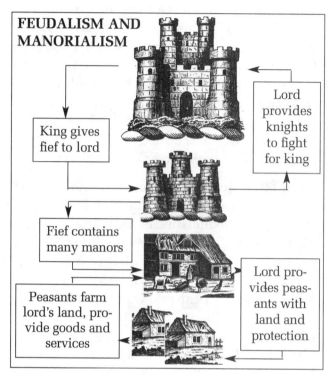

FEUDALISM AND MANORIALISM

King gives fief to lord

Lord provides knights to fight for king

Fief contains many manors

Lord provides peasants with land and protection

Peasants farm lord's land, provide goods and services

the manor without the lord's permission. Their lives were harsh, but predictable.

> God himself has willed that among men, some must be lords and some serfs, in such a fashion that the lords venerate and love God, and that the serfs love and venerate their lord following the word of the Apostle. Serfs, obey your temporal lords with fear and trembling. Lords, treat your serfs according to justice and equity.

7 **Use this passage by a medieval clergyman to describe how the church viewed feudalism**

_____

_____

_____

_____

_____

The Church and the Crusades

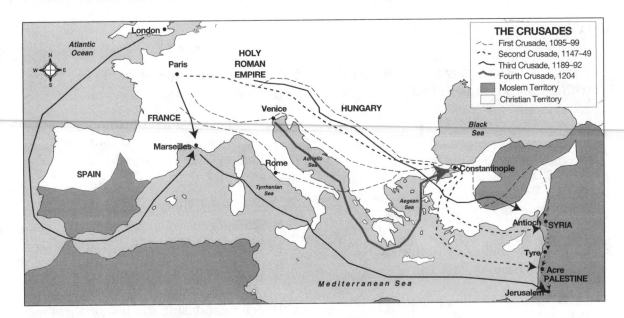

The Catholic Church helped to fill the political vacuum created by the fall of Rome. As successors to the Apostle Peter, the Popes at Rome claimed leadership over all Christians. Anyone, peasant, lord, or king, who disobeyed church law could be punished. The Popes sent missionaries to convert the English and Germans and led the fight against **heresy** (refusal to accept church doctrine). The **Inquisition** Court was created to try and punish heretics.

The Church was organized as a hierarchy. At the top was the Pope who was elected by a body of **cardinals**. Below him, the bishops governed **dioceses**, usually larger cities and surrounding areas. At first, councils of bishops settled disputes over doctrine, but over time the Popes gained this power. Dioceses were divided into **parishes** that were led by priests. Priests were the connection between the Church and the people. They celebrated the **sacraments**, which included marriage, baptism, and burial (as well as others), and conducted church services, including the **mass**. After **St. Benedict** founded the first monastery in the West in 529, monasteries and convents were built throughout Europe for men and women who wished to leave society and live in poverty, chastity, and obedience.

When the Moslem Seljuk Turks conquered the Holy Land and threatened Constantinople, the Byzantine emperor begged the Pope for help. Pope Urban II urged Christians to win back the Holy Land. So began the First Crusade. This Crusade and those that followed—the eighth and last was in 1270—failed to achieve this goal, but their impact was powerful. They heightened religious hatred, particularly anti-Semitism. Many nobles died fighting; this weakened feudal ties and increased the power of the king. By introducing the Crusaders to silk, spices, sugar, and other goods, the Crusades created a demand for luxury goods which stimulated trade.

8 **Which of the Crusades shown on the map was supported by England?**

A the First Crusade

B the Second Crusade

C the Third Crusade

D the Fourth Crusade

Section Review: Expansion, 500–1200 C.E.

Part A

1 Which of the following terms connected with European feudalism refers to a parcel of land?

   1 fief

   2 retainer

   3 serf

   4 vassal

2 Which of the following Arabic words means pilgrimage to Mecca?

   1 bazaar

   2 hajj

   3 hegira

   4 jihad

3 Which of the following is a Christian sacrament?

   1 diocese

   2 heresy

   3 mass

   4 parish

4 One way in which India under Mauryan rule and China under Tang rule were similar was that in both

   1 Buddhism became a major religion

   2 contact with the outside world was discouraged

   3 there was constant civil war

   4 local cultures were heavily influenced by Europeans

5 Which event occurred first in Byzantine history?

   1 A schism divided Christianity into the Eastern Orthodox Church and the Roman Catholic Church.

   2 Crusaders occupied and ruled Constantinople.

   3 Emperor Justinian issued a law code.

   4 The Seljuk Turks conquered the Holy Land.

6 Which relationship did manorialism regulate?

   1 the relationship between a knight and his squires

   2 the relationship between a lord and his peasants

   3 the relationship between a noble and his knights

   4 the relationship between the king and his nobles

7 The split between Shiite and Sunni Moslems began with

   1 the death of Mohammed in 622

   2 the destruction of Baghdad by the Mongols in 1258

   3 the murder of Calif Ali in 661

   4 the victory of the Abbasid califs over the Umayyad califs in 747

Part B

CHINA'S DYNASTIC CYCLE

New dynasty creates peace and prosperity. It has the <u>Mandate of Heaven</u>

Dynasty declines and loses its power; widespread corruption and high taxes

Rebellion and violence; old dynasty overthrown by new dynasty that claims Mandate of Heaven

Natural disasters like floods and famines and political problems like peasant rebellions and foreign invasions

Clearly old dynasty has lost the Mandate of Heaven; rebellion is justified

Select from your knowledge of the Tang and earlier Chinese dynasties two examples to illustrate the working of the Dynastic Cycle. Identify each dynasty and then describe how and why it achieved power, prospered, and then declined.

Dynasty 1: _____

_____

_____

_____

_____

_____

_____

_____

Dynasty 2: _____

_____

_____

_____

_____

_____

_____

_____

NOTICE: Photocopying any part of this book is prohibited by law.

81

11. Global Interactions, 1200–1650: Retreat and Advance in Eurasia

In 1200, the Arab world was still ruled by the calif at Baghdad, and Islamic invaders had conquered northern India. China was governed by the Song dynasty. The Byzantine Empire continued to shrink, and Europe continued to recover from its economic and intellectual Dark Age.

Mongol Warriors advance fiercely on their way to invade a nearby country.

By 1650, the Ottoman Turks had conquered the Byzantine Empire and replaced the Arabs as the leading Moslem power. Compact and unified nation states had emerged in Western Europe, and Europe's cities had become centers of commerce and culture.

In between these two points in time, there were large-scale movements of peoples. Mongol and Turkish invaders advanced across Asia and Eastern Europe, conquering as they went. The Black Death, too, spread from Mongolia to Russia and then across Europe, killing millions of people and profoundly impacting regional economies.

We can see expansion and contraction within different regions. China's Grand Fleet traveled as far west as Arabia, seeking to expand Chinese power and commerce. But then China withdrew into isolation. Japan, too, kept out foreign invaders and foreign influences as it developed its unique culture and governmental structure.

The economies and societies of Europe also contracted after the Black Death. But the Renaissance and commercial growth created a new confidence in human progress.

Feudalism in Japan

Milestones in the Early History of Japan

400	500	600	700	800	1000	1100	1200	1300	1600	1850

400 Head of Yamato clan becomes emperor

552 Buddhism introduced into Japan

593 Shotoku imports Chinese learning

710 Nara becomes first capital

646 Taika reforms (Great Change) proclaim all land belongs to emperor

794 Kyoto becomes capital

752 Buddhism reaches peak popularity with building of temple at Nara

1010 Lady Murasaki writes *Tale of Genji*

1274 and **1281** Kubla Khan unable to invade Japan

1543 Portuguese missionaries in Japan

1598–1603 Japan unified by shogun Tokugawa

1636 Act of Seclusion isolates Japan

1853 Perry visits Japan

1638 Christian community at Nagasaki destroyed

Japan lies on an **archipelago** (a group of islands) off the coast of China. For most of its history, it has been isolated by its geography and by choice from the rest of the world. Before 400 C.E., it was populated by clans who worshiped ancestral spirits. This practice is called **Shintoism**. In about 400, a warrior from the Yamato clan became emperor. After 550, the emperor's role became purely ceremonial. Japan patterned its government on China's strongly centralized rule and Kyoto became the seat of government. The strength of the clans was reduced by the decree that all land belonged to the emperor. For centuries, power lay in the hands of various noble families. In 1185, the emperor formalized this tradition by making a leading noble the **shogun** and giving him political and military power. Later shoguns repelled the attempts by the Mongol **Kublai Khan** to invade Japan (in 1274 and 1281).

After 1300, shogun power declined and a form of feudalism developed. **Samurai** warriors pledged loyalty to a **daimyo**, a powerful landowning noble. The Samurai, who included women, followed a strict code of honor known as **bushido**. Farmers paid taxes to the daimyos who in return protected them from attack. By 1598, the power of the daimyo had been tamed. The **Tokugawa** family seized control. Under them the land of the daimyos was redistributed. New laws froze social classes, preventing peasants and merchants from becoming warriors.

Buddhism had reached Japan from Korea. By 1200, it was the religion of the common people as well as the nobility, though it never replaced Shinto. The samurai practiced **Zen Buddhism**, which stressed living in harmony with nature and reaching enlightenment by meditation and bodily discipline. Christianity came to Japan after 1543; the Catholic missionary **Francis Xavier** won many converts before Christianity was outlawed in 1587. This move reflected a growing fear that contact with the outside world was dangerous. Between 1636 and 1853, Japan was effectively sealed off from the rest of the world.

1   What characteristic did Japanese and European feudalism share?

_____

_____

_____

_____

The Mongol Empire

Between 1000 and 1400, clans of nomadic horsemen from Central and East Asia invaded areas to the west and south. The most successful were the Mongols whose leader was **Genghis Khan**. Genghis codified Mongol law and transformed his horsemen into disciplined cavalry units.

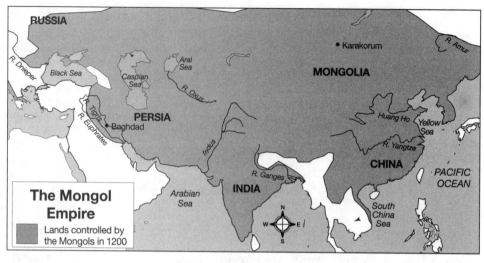

The Mongol Empire

⬛ Lands controlled by the Mongols in 1200

By 1215 he had conquered much of northern China. Between 1218 and 1224 his armies swept west over most of Central Asia and up to the borders of Persia and Eastern Europe.

Genghis' successors conquered the rest of China and established a Mongol dynasty, the Yuan. Gunpowder rockets which the Chinese had invented helped the Mongols in their conquests. Genghis' grandson, Kublai Khan, ruled China until 1294. He insisted that official documents be written in Mongol as well as Chinese and made Mongols his chief officials. In 1368 the Yuan dynasty was overthrown and the Mongols were expelled from China.

Other groups of Mongols continued to move westward. One Mongol army conquered Russia. Another moved southwest into the Middle East. In 1258, they overwhelmed the Abbasid Califate, conquering Baghdad and enslaving its people.

The Mongols used terror to subdue their enemies. They slaughtered thousands and burned countless cities and villages. But once in control, the Mongols brought peace and prosperity to the lands they ruled. They built roads and encouraged trade with Europe—it was during Kublai Khan's reign that the Italian trader **Marco Polo** visited China.

If they respected the culture of the people they conquered (the Chinese, for example) they copied it. Mongol settlers in Persia and Central Asia intermarried and converted to Islam. The Mongols in Russia, however, governed at a distance, from the khanates they created north of the Caspian Sea. They imposed a heavy tax and required Russians to serve in the Mongol army, although they did not impose their culture on them. Mongol rule isolated Russians and other eastern Slavs from the changes that were sweeping Western Europe. At first, Mongol rulers were loyal to the khan in Mongolia, but by 1300 they had become independent.

2   **What were the consequences of the Mongol conquests?**

_____

_____

_____

_____

_____

_____

The Revival of Commerce

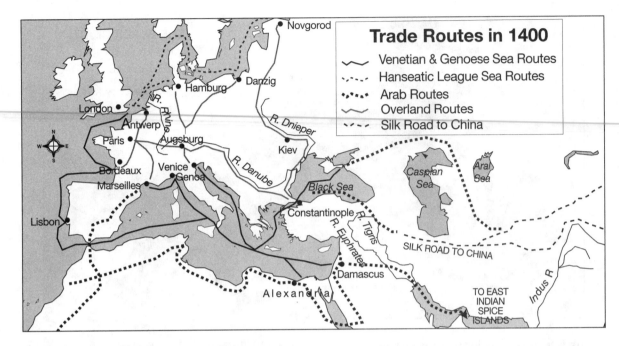

During the early Middle Ages, Islamic and Byzantine merchants kept trade alive. After 1000, the European economy slowly recovered and local and long-distance trade revived. Italian cities like Venice and Genoa grew prosperous from the lucrative Mediterranean trade. At first they acted as middle men between Arab and Byzantine traders and those of Western Europe. Later their ships sailed to India and China for luxury items like spices and silks. For a brief time after 1400, Chinese merchants such as **Zheng He** sailed their precious cargoes as far west as Arabia.

The merchants of northern Europe formed a trade association called the **Hanseatic League.** The League had a profitable trade in Flanders cloth, English wool, Russian firs, and German iron and timber. Huge fairs like those held in northeastern France were occasions when merchants could sell goods from around the world.

Towns were built where trade could flourish: along rivers, on seacoasts, at crossroads and market sites, and also outside of castles and monasteries. Most towns were small and surrounded by walls built to protect them from robbers.

3A Describe one route by which silk could reach London and identify which merchants transported it there.

_____

_____

_____

_____

3B Describe how Russian furs could be carried Antwerp.

_____

_____

_____

_____

Medieval Towns and the Plague

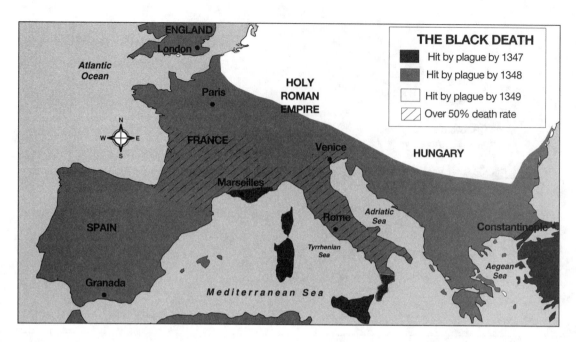

THE BLACK DEATH
- Hit by plague by 1347
- Hit by plague by 1348
- Hit by plague by 1349
- Over 50% death rate

Towns had a revolutionary impact on medieval society. By providing new economic opportunities for men and women, they contributed to the decline of feudalism and manorialism. A new class arose that did not depend on land for its livelihood. This could only happen because of the increase in agricultural output. More food meant that the countryside could support city populations of craftspeople, merchants, and professionals. These artisans—masons, weavers, and so on—organized themselves into **guilds** to protect themselves against competition.

Medieval cities were not healthy places. Sewage and garbage were thrown into the streets. People lived so crowded together that disease spread rapidly. The prosperity and abundant harvests of earlier centuries ended in the fourteenth century. The climate turned colder and food shortages were widespread. Into this situation came the **Black Death**, an epidemic of bubonic plague spread by fleas that lived on black rats. It originated in Mongolia and spread from there to Russia and the Black Sea. Rats that lived aboard cargo boats carried the plague along trade routes. Plague-

infested fleas swiftly infected an undernourished population. The mortality rate was highest in the crowded cities. Perhaps 20 million people, one third of Europe's population, died.

More than ever, nobles needed the labor of the serfs who survived and tried to tie them still more closely to their manors. In much of Europe they were successful. But in parts of Western Europe, peasants were able to win more freedom now that their labor was more valuable.

4 **List two developments that furthered the decline of feudalism.**

1 _____

2 _____

5 **What were the consequences of the Plague?**

_____

_____

_____

European Recovery

The Commercial Revolution

The **commercial revolution** is the term used to describe the economic changes that occurred in Europe between 1200 and 1600. These changes included the creation of a money economy, new ways of raising money, and new ways of organizing businesses. Historians have identified this revolution as the beginning of **capitalism** (a system of private enterprise where economic decisions are made by individuals) and associate it with the rise of the middle classes.

During the medieval era, traders began to use money instead of barter. Merchants came from many nations, so many currencies were in use. Money exchangers converted one currency into another. The first of these middlemen were Arab traders. European middlemen evolved into bankers: they transferred funds from one place to another and made business loans. By the 1600's they were also issuing checks.

War and the plague also contributed to the growth of a money economy. Earlier, kings and barons had relied on their feudal relationships to provide them with soldiers. Now they found that they needed to pay their armies and borrowed money from bankers. They imposed taxes to repay these loans. Serfs were used to paying their rent with labor and crops. Now, those who could benefit from the labor shortage (see opposite) bought their freedom with cash.

Overseas trading ventures were costly. So merchants began to raise money by pooling their resources. They created **joint-stock companies** (with the monarch's permission) and invited other investors to share the risks and profits of an ocean voyage.

Profit-making and money-lending became respectable—at least in the commercial centers of Italy, England, and the Netherlands. Individuals and companies that made money were able to expand their businesses by plowing back their profits. These **entrepreneurs** were to be found in agriculture and industry as well as trade.

In the feudal era, social rank was based on land ownership. With the development of trade and a money economy, fortunes could be based on non-landed sources. Rich merchants and artisans, professional men like lawyers and doctors, and government officials created a new "middle" class. Their wealth and power might even surpass that of great nobles. Great merchant families governed the Italian city states of Venice and Florence. Most merchants lived in the cities, but in England and France the most successful bought landed estates.

> To sell dearer or to buy cheaper than a thing is worth is itself unjust and unlawful.
>
> St. Thomas Aquinas, *Summa Theologicae*

6 **Thomas Aquinas defines the medieval idea of the <u>just price</u>. In what way did the commercial revolution reject this idea?**

_____

_____

_____

_____

_____

_____

Renaissance and Humanism

Economic changes were paralleled by changes in cultural and spiritual attitudes at the end of the Middle Ages. The Church had been the center of learning—clerics were the only people who could read and write. A belief in church teachings and in salvation through Christ had been at the core of intellectual life. After 1400, people began to focus their minds on humanity, society, and the world around them.

This period saw a **Renaissance**, or rebirth, of learning that began in Italy. Ancient Greek and Latin texts had only recently become known to scholars in the West via Arab translators and from the manuscripts carried west when Constantinople fell. These texts revealed a set of beliefs and values very different from those the church taught. Classical writers had stressed ideas like individual worth and a belief that people can improve themselves through their own efforts. **Humanists** who studied these ideas, like **Erasmus** of Rotterdam in the Netherlands, were impressed. They opened schools based on the Greek model and taught Greek, Latin, history, and philosophy.

Writers explored human feelings and ambitions. **Machiavelli** wrote *The Prince* in which he analyzed contemporary rulers to see what personal qualities were the most effective. He concluded that the best rulers were those most willing to use force and most able to deceive their opponents. His ideas are often summarized as "the end justifies the means."

The visual arts gave the most powerful expression to Renaissance ideas. Painters and sculptors continued to use religious themes, but they used new techniques to make their work more lifelike. Their study of the human body allowed them to depict muscles and flesh realistically in the Greek style (as, for example, in this drawing by

Michelangelo). **Leonardo da Vinci**, the artist who painted the Mona Lisa, was also interested in anatomy, medicine, and engineering. Buildings, too, reflected classical styles: architects put Roman columns and arches into the buildings they designed.

After 1400, the Renaissance spread north to Germany, France, the Netherlands, and England. The tales written by **Rabelais** in France suggested that people should enjoy life and forget the afterlife. In his plays, **Shakespeare**, England's greatest writer, examined the human character and the power of emotions like ambition and love.

7   **Use this map to show how the Renaissance spread from Italy. Write the names of its artists and writers in the correct location.**

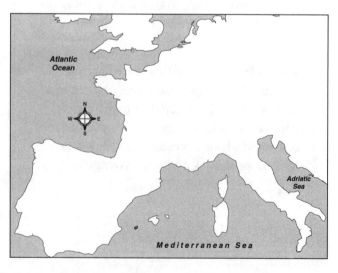

Reformation and Counter Reformation

During the later Middle Ages, the reputation of the Church declined. Many of its leaders were worldly or corrupt, and many parish priests were as uneducated as their parishioners.

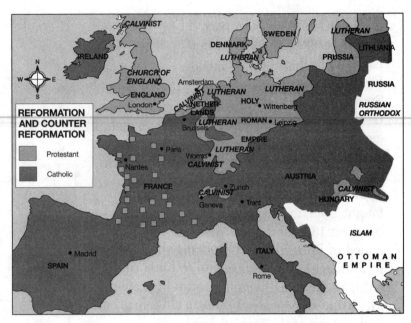

The Protestant Reformation began in 1517 when a monk named **Martin Luther** nailed **95 theses** to a church door in the German city of Wittenberg. Luther opposed the sale of **indulgences**—documents that supposedly allowed people to avoid punishment for their sins—and other church practices. Luther was swiftly condemned by the Pope, but the people cheered his stand, and his prince, Frederick of Saxony, protected him from punishment. Luther's ideas spread through northern Europe. He down-graded the importance of the church, the clergy, and ritual. Instead, he emphasized that salvation was based on faith alone and that everyone could find religious truth in the Bible. Since Luther had translated the Bible into German, it was now available to all who could read. Luther also preached passionately against the Jews. He had hoped to convert them to Christianity with his teachings but had failed.

John Calvin, another Protestant reformer, argued that God decides the fate of each one of us, a doctrine known as **predestination**. Calvin tried to make the Swiss city of Geneva a model religious community; all aspects of its citizens' lives were controlled by a church council of elders. Calvinism took deep root in the Netherlands and Scotland. It would also influence the Reformation that **Henry VIII** began in England. Henry wanted a divorce; the Pope refused to grant him one. So Henry removed England from the Catholic Church.

The Catholic Church fought back. At the **Council of Trent** in 1563, the church ended many abuses including the sale of indulgences. The Inquisition was given new power to stamp out heresy. **Ignatius of Loyola** founded the Jesuit order. Its missionaries, along with Catholic soldiers, won back large areas of southern and eastern Europe for Catholicism. The map shows those areas that remained Protestant after this **Counter Reformation**.

> 6. The Pope has no power to pardon any guilt.
> 37. Every Christian...has a share of all the benefits of Christ and of the Church, given by God.
>
> —Martin Luther, The Ninety Five Theses

8 **Use this quotation to help you explain why Luther's attack was so serious for the Roman Catholic Church.**

_____

_____

_____

The Emergence of Nation States

During the fifteenth century, the monarchs of Spain, France, and England united their kingdoms. **Ferdinand and Isabella** of Spain drove the last Moors from Granada in 1492. To create religious unity, they offered Moors and Jews the choice of converting to Christianity or leaving Spain. England and France fought the Hundred Years War between 1338 and 1453. When it ended in French victory, the king of France finally controlled most of his realm. For England's kings, defeat was a victory of sorts. Many of the English nobles survived the fighting in France only to be killed in a bloody civil war. This allowed England's monarchs to reassert their authority and to unify the nation.

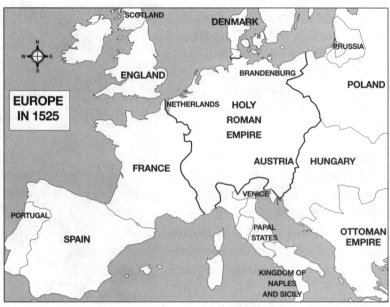

Wise rulers like Ferdinand, Henry Tudor in England, and Louis XI in France reformed their bureaucracies, reined in the power of the nobles, used middle class officials, encouraged trade, and restored order to their nations' finances.

In these kingdoms, the monarch was powerful enough to select the people's religion. Protestantism was never an issue in Spain. In France it provoked bloodshed and strife until 1590 when the Protestant **Henry IV** won the throne by promising to became a Catholic. England swung back and forth between Protestantism and Catholicism at the whim of its ruler. Finally in 1559, **Elizabeth I** and her **Parliament** created a compromise, the Church of England.

By contrast, the **Hapsburg** rulers of the Holy Roman Empire, could not impose religious unity on their people nor control their semi-independent princes. The power of the land-owning class also prevented the kings of Poland from creating a strong nation state. Italy also remained divided into independent city states and small kingdoms.

9 **Describe two factors that enabled rulers to create powerful nation states. Give an example to illustrate each factor.**

_____

_____

_____

_____

_____

_____

_____

_____

_____

_____

_____

Section Review: Early Global Interactions

Part A

1 Which sentence best describes Renaissance humanism?

   1 Scholars attacked church abuses.

   2 Thinkers gave their ideas a scientific basis.

   3 Writers stressed piety and reflection.

   4 Writers suggested that individuals might enjoy life without offending God.

2 Which development was the cause of the other three?

   1 the rise of nation states

   2 the decline of feudalism

   3 the growth of commerce

   4 the development of a money economy

3 Which of the following developments originated in India?

   1 the creation of a system of numbers

   2 the development of the Cyrillic alphabet

   3 the invention of gunpowder

   4 the invention of the astrolabe

4 Which of the following were Moslem?

   1 Genghis Khan

   2 the Seljuk Turks

   3 the Gupta emperors

   4 the Tokugawa shogun

5 What was the Hanseatic League?

   1 a group of German princes who rebelled against the Holy Roman Emperor

   2 an association of North European trading cities

   3 an association of Protestants

   4 the cities which were allowed to hold international fairs

6 Why were the Mongols so successful in promoting trade?

   1 They maintained friendly relations with neighboring states.

   2 They protected the trade routes they controlled.

   3 They encouraged the development of independent city-states.

   4 They were a sea-faring people.

7 A map showing the path of the Black Death in Europe would indicate that

   1 it traveled overland along the same routes as the Mongol invaders

   2 outbreaks of the disease were haphazard and random

   3 the first and hardest hit areas lay near Mediterranean ports

   4 the worst affected areas were in Northern Europe

Part B

The documents below relate to European family life in the Middle Ages. Examine each document and answer the question that follows it.

Document 1

When your little brother, whose name I still do not know, has been baptized in Christ, do not fail to instruct him, to educate him, to love him...for he is your flesh and your brother...above all to your lord and father Bernard [husband of Dhuoda], in his presence as in his absence, you owe fear, love, and loyalty...Obey him in every important matter, listen to his advice.

Dhuoda, Manual for My Son, 841–843

1. What was the main duty of the Lady Dhuoda's son?

Document 2

The family was the basic labor unit, its tasks subdivided into a men's and women's share. Men did the "outside" work—plowing, hoeing, reaping, haying, winnowing, threshing—as they had always done. Women performed their traditional "inside" jobs...cooking, milking, making butter and cheese, spinning and weaving, feeding the poultry, cultivating the vegetable path, foraging in the woods and fields for berries, nuts, and greens.

—Frances and Joseph Gies, Marriage and the Family in the Middle Ages

2. What class of society are the authors describing?

Document 3

Right worshipful husband, I recommend me to you, beseeching you that you be not displeased with me, though my simpleness caused you for to be displeased...and if I have [displeased you] I am sorry thereof and will amend it. Wherefore I beseech you to forgive me, and that you bear no heaviness in your heart against me, for your displeasure should be too heavy for me to endure with."

Margaret Paston, The Paston Letters, 1422–1509

3. Generalize from this passage how women believed they should conduct themselves towards their husbands.

Document 4

If there is anything which combines handsomely with nobility or is a worthy adornment in human life or gives grace, authority, and reputation to a family, certainly it is the cultivation of letters...A father should make sure that his sons devote themselves seriously to their studies. He should teach his children to read and write correctly...They must learn the abacus...geometry...the poets, orators, philosophers...good morals may be gained as well as a knowledge of literature.

Leon Battista Alberti, Books of the Family, 1437-1441

4. What about the text tells you that this passage was written during the Renaissance?

Document 5

The young women of Avignon...give themselves in marriage without the endorsement or consent of their fathers and mothers and other kinsfolk, which is a thing most wonderfully scandalous and injurious to the public well being.

—Complaint to the City Council of Avignon, 1546

5. Why is this document particularly surprising when compared with Document 3?

Part C

Describe how family life, particularly the role of women, changed over the course of the Middle Ages. Include specific historical details and refer to the documents you analyzed in Part B.

_____

_____

_____

_____

_____

_____

_____

_____

_____

_____

_____

_____

_____

_____

_____

_____

_____

_____

_____

_____

_____

_____

_____

_____

_____

_____

_____

_____

12. The First Global Age, 1450–1770: The Empire Builders

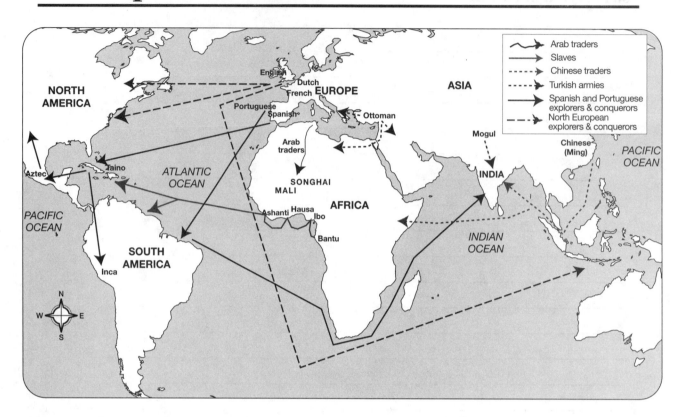

This period is dominated by the encounters between the peoples of Europe, Africa, Asia, and North and South America. In 1490, there were prosperous empires within each of these continents: the Ottoman Turks in Europe and Western Asia, the Ming dynasty in China, the Aztecs and Inca in the Americas, Mali and Songhai in West Africa, and within 60 years, the Mogul empire of Akbar the Great in India. Conquest and commerce linked many of the peoples of Africa and Eurasia.

But in 1492 we see an Encounter with a capital E. When Christopher Columbus crossed the Atlantic Ocean, he initiated a whole new set of relationships. For the first time, the people of Europe and Africa met with the native people of the Americas. The meeting would change the lives, the geography, and the culture of all the peoples and places involved. The encounters between Europeans and the peoples of South, Southeast, and East Asia would also have momentous consequences in the centuries to come.

Within the empires of Asia and the kingdoms of Europe, rulers were consolidating their power and centralizing their governments. An age of absolutism was beginning. By contrast, we can also see a return of the classical practice of divided authority: the English parliament was evolving into a body summoned frequently by and sharing power with the monarch.

Mesoamerica and South America

The first American civilization appeared in about 1500 B.C.E. Within a few hundred years the Chavin of Peru and the Olmecs of Mexico were building large religious centers. The Olmecs developed a form of writing. They were active traders and brought their culture to the Maya of Guatemala and southern Mexico.

Religion was a central part of Maya life. Human sacrifice played an important role in religious ceremonies designed to soothe their gods. The political power of Maya priests was based on an understanding of astronomy and of their complicated calendar. The Maya were farmers and traders. They used irrigation and **slash-and-burn** methods to fertilize the fields where they grew squash, pumpkins, and tomatoes. The Maya of Guatemala declined after about 800 C.E., but the Yucatan Maya thrived for another 200 years. They built towering pyramids for their priestly rulers. Maya states continued to play a role in Mexico right up to the time of the Spanish conquest.

In about 1325, the warlike Aztecs settled at Tenochtitlán in Mexico. There, where Mexico City now stands, they built a beautiful city of gardens, canals, and temples. Since farmland was scarce, they built rafts filled with soil from the bottoms of lakes. Farmers grew beans and corns on their floating farms as they poled them around the lakes. Influenced by the Maya, the Aztecs slaughtered thousands of prisoners to satisfy their gods and to assure abundant harvests. By 1500, they had built an empire that covered much of Mexico.

In the Andes Mountains of South America, the Inca built a civilization that included present-day Peru and parts of Ecuador, Chile, and Bolivia. Good roads and skilled administrators enabled the Inca to control their vast empire. Flat farmland was scarce,

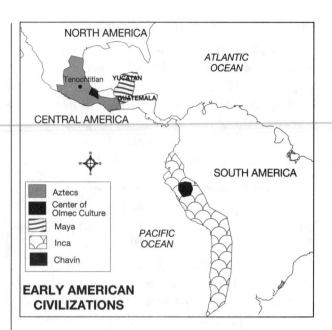

EARLY AMERICAN CIVILIZATIONS

so crops were grown on terraces cut into the hillside. Inca artists created fine metal sculptures and ornaments from the gold and silver found in local mines.

1   Use the map to decide which statement about early American civilizations is correct.

   A   The Aztec Empire included areas previously ruled by the Olmecs.

   B   The Aztecs dominated North America.

   C   The Inca ruled much of Central America.

   D   Olmec culture replaced that of the Incas.

2   Which part of the Maya civilization would you guess still exists?

   A   human sacrifices

   B   their large empire

   C   their form of government

   D   their language and pyramids

The Kingdoms of West Africa

The power of the West African kingdoms of Ghana, Mali, and Songhai was based on the gold they mined and the taxes they imposed on the Moslem trade caravans that crossed the Sahara. Despite frequent local wars and the threat of invasion by peoples to the north, the greatest rulers brought power and prosperity to their lands.

King Sundiata of Mali encouraged the planting of peanuts, rice, beans, and other crops which were fertilized by burnt grass. **Mansa Musa** (reigned 1312–1337) expanded the lands and wealth of Mali by opening up trade routes and exchanging gold for much-needed salt. He brought Islam and Islamic culture to his court and made the city of Timbuktu a major center of Moslem learning and art. Musa went on a famous hajj to Mecca. It was during the reign of his successor that the Arab traveler **Ibn Battuta** visited Mali.

Songhai broke away from Mali and by 1493, it had replaced it as the most powerful kingdom in West Africa. Its greatest ruler was **Askia Mohammed**. Askia divided his lands into provinces with their own governors. He used his cavalry to maintain internal peace and to repel foreign invaders. Like the kings of Mali, Askia was a zealous Moslem. He introduced a legal system based on the Koran and appointed Islamic judges.

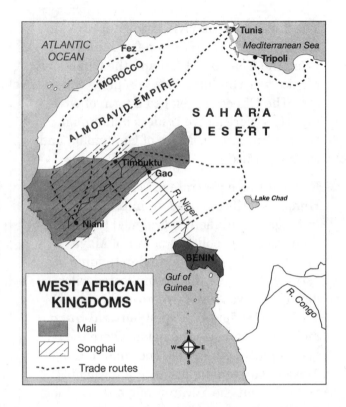

WEST AFRICAN KINGDOMS

- Mali
- Songhai
- ----- Trade routes

The Songhai empire disappeared after Moroccan troops defeated its army in 1589.

3   Explain the rise and fall of the kingdoms of Mali and Songhai?

_____

_____

_____

_____

_____

_____

_____

_____

_____

_____

_____

_____

West African Empires				
300	900	1200	1500	
Ghana builds trade empire Islam reaches Ghana via trade routes	North African Almoravids destroy Ghana's empire	**1235** Conquests of Sundiata, king of Mali	**1324** Mansa Musa, King of Mali, makes pilgrimage to Mecca Sunni Ali of Songhai captures Timbuktu	Collapse of Mali **1493–1528** Askia rules Songhai **1589** Moroccans defeat Songhai

The Ming Dynasty in China

After ruling China for 89 years, the Mongol Yuan dynasty was overthrown by Hong Wu in 1368. Hong Wu established the Ming dynasty which ruled China until 1644.

One of Hong Wu's first tasks was to replace Mongol bureaucrats with men of Chinese ancestry. Once again, Confucianism became the state religion. Hong imposed a more efficient tax collection system and reformed local government. New, harsher laws imposed corporal punishment on anyone (even nobles) who displeased the emperor.

Hong Wu and his successors rebuilt the Great Wall along the northern frontier. This helped to keep the nomadic tribes outside and Chinese culture inside the empire. Once again, with peace came economic prosperity. Farmers were encouraged to move to northern China by the offer of free land and seed. The now thriving population of this area provided soldiers when needed. In 1421, Emperor Yong Le moved the capital to Beijing which was closer to the northern border. This totally rebuilt city contained the splendid palaces of the Forbidden City where the imperial family lived.

Inside China, an increase in food production led to an expansion of trade. Farmers sold their surplus food to artisans who made silk textiles and pottery— the Ming dynasty is famous for its porcelain. Trade brought wealth to merchants and craftsmen, and growth to cities like Shanghai.

The early Ming emperors were interested in exploring the world outside China. Between 1408 and 1433,

A Ming vase

Chinese fleets under their captain Zheng He sailed to India, Arabia, and Southeast Asia. Their mission was to impose the emperor's authority and collect tribute. At the same time, these voyages began a trading relationship and Chinese merchants settled in southern and southeastern Asia.

China's foreign policy has often swung like a pendulum between expansionism on the one hand and a sense of cultural uniqueness and geographic isolation on the other. The idea that China lies alone at the center of the earth led the Chinese to call their land **Zhong Guo** (Middle Kingdom). These feelings of **ethnocentrism** helped bring about a decline in the Ming dynasty. Later rulers chose to cut off outside contacts. They discontinued adventures like Zheng's. Their officials considered the navy too costly and Confucian philosophy despised trade and traders. The building of ships was forbidden. These rulers preferred court pleasures to attending to official business. The expense of the luxurious court reduced the money available for defense. Once again, invaders, this time the Manchu from Manchuria, crossed the frontier and established their own dynasty in 1644.

4   Why did the Ming emperors change their attitude towards economic and commercial expansion after 1433?

_____

_____

_____

_____

_____

_____

_____

The Ottoman Empire

The Seljuk Turks who conquered the Holy Land had migrated west from Central Asia. They were followed in about 1200 by another Turkish people, the Ottomans. Settling in Asia Minor, they attacked the power of Byzantium. Once Constantinople fell in 1453, they made the city their capital. The Ottomans had converted to Islam, and as their empire expanded, so did their religion. Most peoples along the southern Mediterranean coast had been Moslem for centuries. After overcoming Serbian resistance at Kosovo in 1389, the Ottomans were the first Moslems to bring Islam to the people of the Balkans. That is why most Bosnians today are Moslem.

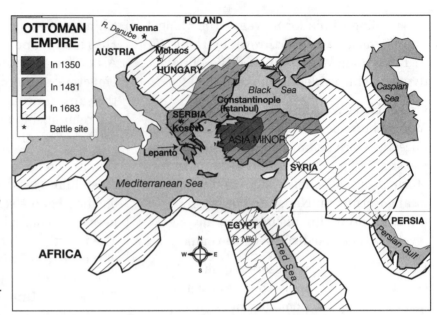

Europeans viewed the Ottomans as a major threat. At the battle of Mohacs in 1526, the Turks defeated the King of Hungary and absorbed his kingdom. Spain was alarmed by the fact that the Ottomans controlled the Mediterranean trade routes. It raised a fleet which defeated the Ottoman navy at Lepanto in 1571. But Turkish sea power was not broken. In 1683, the Ottoman empire reached its greatest extent when its troops besieged Vienna. Their defeat by the Polish king began a long period of decline.

Suleiman I, the "Magnificent," was **sultan** of Turkey from 1520 to 1566. His power was absolute: he was political leader, and, as calif, the religious head of his people. One of the world's greatest commanders and administrators, Suleiman reorganized the bureaucracy under a **grand vizir**. Religious advisors known as the **Ulema** decided questions of Islamic law. The Ottoman army was officered by men from across the empire. One such group, the **janissaries,** were taken as children from their Balkan Christian families, converted to Islam, and trained as soldiers.

The Turks granted religious toleration and the right to run their own communities to their non-Moslem people, Jew, Catholic, and Orthodox. Their culture was enriched by elements borrowed from those they conquered: Arab, Persian, and Byzantine. In particular, they are remembered for their magnificent mosques, mosaics, and illuminated manuscripts.

5 **Use the text and map to create a time line showing the expansion of the Ottoman empire. Put the letter next to each conquered area in the correct box.**

A **Constantinople**

B **Serbia**

C **Syria**

D **western Asia Minor**

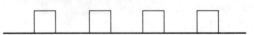

European Expansion

Advances in Technology

New Inventions and Ocean Travel

1200	1300	1400	1500

1190 Magnetic compass (invented in China) first used in Europe

About 1200 Rudders make it easier to steer ships

About 1300 Cannon (guns) first used on ships

1400's Arab triangular sail used on European ships

1400's Caravels built with multiple sails and masts

1454 First printing press; knowledge can spread faster

1400's Ptolemy's maps showing latitude & longitude reintroduced

About 1480 Improved astrolabe measures distances accurately

Spices like nutmeg and pepper were highly prized in medieval Europe. They were used to preserve meat, and also as medicines and perfumes. They were grown in the East Indian Spice Islands and shipped overland to Europe by Arabs who controlled the trade routes. European merchants wanted to sail across the oceans to the East. But their ships needed to be strong enough to handle an ocean voyage, their sailors needed maps to tell them which way to sail, and they needed navigational instruments to get them there. Until these were available, ships had to hug the coastline.

The time line shows the inventions and new knowledge that made ocean-going voyages possible. Many of these inventions had been developed by Chinese and Arab sailors many centuries before they were used on European ships. During the 1400's, Portuguese shipbuilders created a new ship, the **caravel**, that included many of these new features. The use of rudders eliminated the need for oarsmen as steerers; triangular sails allowed them to sail into the wind; multiple sails and masts enabled ships to take full advantage of wind power. The compass and the astrolabe allowed seamen to know the direction in which they were heading and to use the position of the stars to guide them. There was a gradual improvement in map making.

Cartographers could depict the known world fairly accurately by 1450, although, as the map shows, there were many parts of the world they did not know. And finally, cannon gave ship crews the confidence that they could defend themselves against pirates and other enemies.

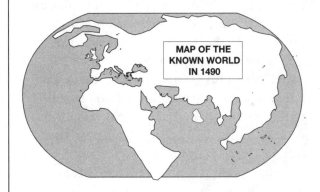

MAP OF THE KNOWN WORLD IN 1490

6   The information on the time line supports which of the following statements?

A   Portuguese inventions enabled Arabs to control the sea routes.

B   Ptolemy's maps were developed after the first printing presses appeared.

C   The Chinese used caravels to sail to East Africa.

D   Cultural diffusion helped Europeans make ocean voyages.

Portuguese and Spanish Voyages of Exploration

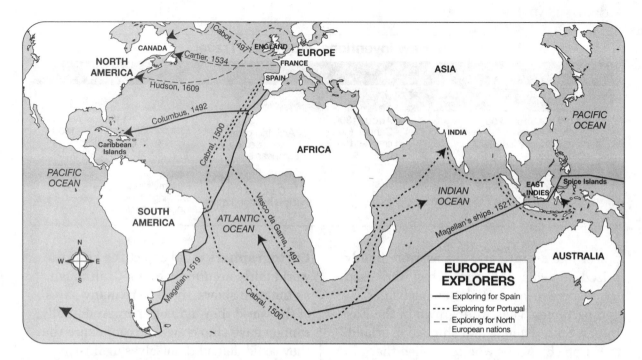

As early as 1430, **Henry the Navigator**, a Portuguese prince, had sponsored explorers who sailed down the west coast of Africa and out into the Atlantic. Trade was the goal of most Portuguese adventurers. In 1497, **Vasco da Gama** sailed to India, but failed to persuade local merchants to sell him their goods. **Pedro Cabral** was more successful. In 1500 he led 13 ships to the Indian Ocean, winning control of it by defeating a large Arab fleet. The Portuguese soon sailed beyond India to the Spice Islands. They built bases along the length of their route: in West and East Africa, in southeast Arabia, on the west coast of India, and in the East Indies. Portugal also won control of Brazil in South America.

Ferdinand and Isabella of Spain sponsored **Christopher Columbus**'s 1492 voyage across the Atlantic. His plan was to find a westward route to the East. When he reached the Caribbean Islands, he assumed he was off the coast of India—his maps showed no land mass between Europe and the East—so he called the local people "Indians." In the 1494 Treaty of Tordesillas, Spain and Portugal divided the Americas between themselves.

In 1519, **Ferdinand Magellan** set out, like Columbus, to find a western route to Asia. He, or rather his ships, succeeded. They sailed south of Cape Horn and across an ocean that Magellan named "Pacific" to the Philippines. Three years later, the survivors limped back to Spain. By sailing around the globe, they proved that the earth is round and that Columbus had reached a previously unknown New World.

7   What can you infer about Columbus's knowledge of geography from the text and the map on page 99?

_____

_____

_____

_____

_____

European Empire Building

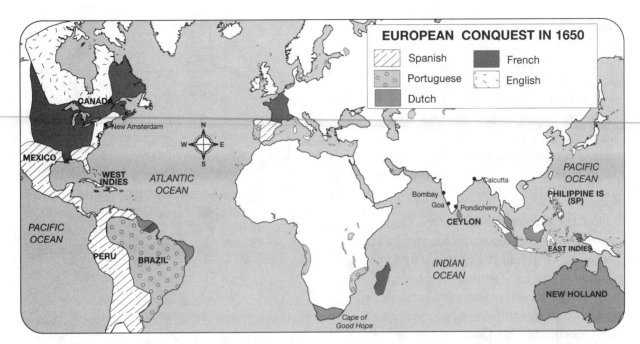

EUROPEAN CONQUEST IN 1650

Spanish monarchs wanted to expand their power and wealth and to spread the Christian religion by creating colonies in the New World. After 1492, Spain conquered many islands in the Caribbean Sea. Between 1519 and 1521, the **conquistador Hernan Cortés** conquered the Mexican Aztecs, a remarkable feat since there were only 600 men in his army. But the Aztecs were betrayed by the people they had conquered and mistreated. Moreover, Aztec arrows and spears were of little use against Spanish muskets and cannon. In 1533, another conquistador, **Francisco Pizarro**, completed the conquest of the Inca Empire on the west coast of South America. Upon the ruins of the Aztec and Inca empires, Spain built a huge and wealthy empire in Mexico and Central and South America. Year after year, the Spanish treasure fleet sailed from America to Europe loaded with precious jewels and metals.

Spain and Portugal were soon challenged by other European nations. French, Dutch, and English explorers followed Columbus across the Atlantic hoping to find a north-

west passage to the East. Failing to find one, they built trading and farming settlements in North America. **Jacques Cartier** sailed down the St. Lawrence River and claimed eastern Canada for France; a permanent settlement was created at Quebec in 1608. English colonies were founded in Virginia and Massachusetts. The Dutch built a prosperous trading center at New Amsterdam; they were even more successful in East Asia. By 1641, their East India Company had won control of the spice trade from Portugal.

8   Which of the following helps to explain why Cortés was able to defeat the Aztecs?

   A   Cortés had a large army of experienced soldiers.

   B   Guns were unknown in the Americas.

   C   The Aztecs were already fighting the Inca.

   D   The Spanish were very successful traders.

The Columbian Exchange and the Slave Trade

Spanish **viceroys** and their councils governed Spain's American empire, sending back detailed reports to Spain. As Spain expanded the area it controlled, friars traveled along with the colonists and soldiers. The friars built **missions** where Native Americans lived, worked, and were taught Christianity and European values.

In Mexico and the Caribbean Islands, Spanish nobles obtained huge ranches. Under the **encomienda** system, the crown granted landowners the right to use Indian labor. When the Spanish first planted sugar cane in the Caribbean Islands, they tried to force the local Taino people to work for them. Spaniards like **Bartolomé de Las Casas** wrote to the king complaining about the abuses in this system. The crown instituted some reforms, but it was the incredibly high mortality rate from disease and overwork, not Spanish laws, that ended the use of Indian labor.

The **Columbian Exchange** is the name given to the exchange of people, goods, and invisible items that traveled west from Europe and Africa to the Americas and east across the Atlantic. The map shows the plants and animals that were exchanged between the old world and the new. Disease was the main invisible item exchanged and Native Americans were the worst sufferers. Unlike Europeans, they had no **immunity** to diseases like measles and smallpox. **Epidemics** spread quickly through Central and North America killing off millions of people.

When the Spanish found that they could no longer rely on local labor, they turned to Africa. Thousands of African men, women, and children were captured in their homelands and shipped across the Atlantic. For 350 years, slaves from Africa worked the fields, mainly on the Caribbean sugar plan-

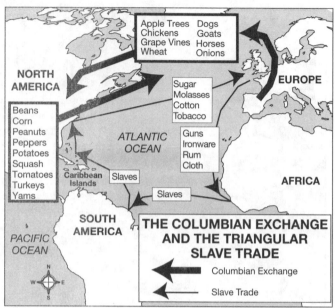

THE COLUMBIAN EXCHANGE AND THE TRIANGULAR SLAVE TRADE

tations, in Brazil, and in southern North America. Slaves were part of a **triangular trade**. Merchants carried manufactured goods from Europe to West Africa where they exchanged them for slaves. The slaves were sold in the Americas and with the proceeds, traders bought raw materials that they carried back to Europe.

9   **Describe two ways that the arrival of Europeans changed the lives of Native Americans.**

_____

_____

_____

_____

_____

_____

_____

_____

Case Studies in Absolute Rule

A Comparison of Absolute Monarchy and Democracy		
	Absolutism	**Democracy**
Nature of Power	Monarch has unlimited power	Government is based on will of people
Source of Power	Inheritance and divine right	Popular elections
Law	Monarch above the law	Everyone must obey the law
	Subjects must obey royal command without question	Citizens have right to criticize government
Religion	Monarch chooses state religion Monarch combines religious and political leadership	Citizens have freedom to worship as they wish Separation of church and state
Purpose of Government	Government exists for its own sake Subjects' role is to serve monarch	Government exists to serve people

The rise of nation states in Europe was made possible by an increase in the power of central government. In the sixteenth and seventeenth centuries, government was by personal rule, so this meant an increase in the power of the monarch. Had monarchs not had the power to decide policy, to build national armies, to impose and collect taxes, to centralize administration, and to encourage trade, it is doubtful that strong nations like France and Spain could have emerged.

Monarchs who gathered so much power into their hands became absolute rulers. They claimed that they ruled by **divine right**, deriving their authority from God and responsible to Him alone. They ignored representative institutions like the Spanish **Cortes** and the local assemblies in France.

For those who believe in the virtues of republican democracy, absolutism is never good. But in the early modern era, most individuals accepted the power of the monarch, provided it was used for the benefit of the people and the kingdom. Unfortunately, no one but the monarch could decide if his or her actions were right and just. Absolute rulers were swift to silence or limit the power of institutions such as parliaments and law courts that challenged their decisions. This allowed

them to wage costly wars that brought no benefit to their subjects but instead caused massive tax increases. Moreover, absolutism did not guarantee stable government. Many rulers were weak and incompetent and chose equally incompetent and corrupt advisors.

In the pages that follow, you will read about some of the more competent absolute rulers. As you study their actions, decide for yourself whether or not their rule benefitted their people.

10 **Describe the responsibilities of a citizen in an absolute monarchy and in a democracy.**

_____

_____

_____

_____

_____

_____

_____

_____

Akbar the Great and Mogul Rule in India

By 1206, Moslem invaders had conquered most of northern India and created a sultanate at Delhi. Gradually, Islamic traditions were absorbed by Hindu culture. This kingdom was destroyed by another Moslem invader, the ruthless **Timur Lenk**, in 1398. In 1526, a descendant of Timur Lenk and Genghis Khan named Babur established the Mogul (Persian for Mongol) dynasty which would rule India for 300 years.

Akbar the Great was Babur's grandson. In the early years of his reign, he extended his empire until it included all of northern India and much of the Deccan. Akbar was able to unify his enlarged empire and govern it effectively. Although his rule was absolute, he appointed intelligent advisors and followed their advice. His decisions were carried out by a trained civil service. Taxes were heavy, but they were imposed fairly and Akbar spent the money they brought in carefully. New roads were built and new coins minted. He spent much of his time as a judge, listening to his people's complaints and making legal decisions.

Himself a Moslem, Akbar realized that most of his subjects were Hindu. To unify his kingdom, he needed their support. There were many organizational and cultural differences between Hinduism and Islam. Moslems were monotheists; Hindus worshiped many gods. Hindus ate no beef; Moslems ate no pork. Akbar tried by various means to end the quarrels that these differences created. He married a Hindu princess. He repealed a tax that was imposed only on Hindus. He invited Taoist, Christian, Confucian, Moslem, and Hindu scholars to his court to share their beliefs. He even tried to reconcile them by creating a wholly new religion called Divine Faith.

This religion died with Akbar, but a partial blending of Islam and Hinduism did occur.

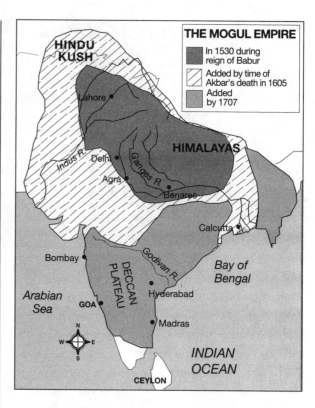

Some **untouchables** and lower-caste Hindus were impressed by Islam's idea of equality and became Moslems. Some Hindu women in northern India were encouraged or forced to adopt such Moslem practices as **purdah** (seclusion) and veiling their faces.

> "Be assured that the Hindus will never become submissive and obedient till they are reduced to poverty."
>
> A justification of his policies by the Delhi sultan Ala-ud-din in about 1300

11 How did Akbar's policies differ from those of Ala-ud-din?

_____

_____

_____

_____

_____

NOTICE: Photocopying any part of this book is prohibited by law.

The Spanish Hapsburgs: Charles V and Philip II

The Hapsburgs were blessed and cursed by the extent of their lands. **Charles V**, the Holy Roman Emperor, governed most of the Hapsburg lands shown in the map as well as Spain's possessions in the New World. The difficulty of governing such far-flung domains persuaded Charles in 1556 to divide up his empire along the lines shown in the map. His brother Ferdinand inherited the Austrian lands and the remainder went to Charles' son, **Philip II** of Spain.

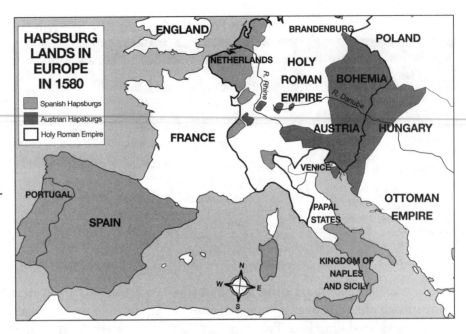

HAPSBURG LANDS IN EUROPE IN 1580

■ Spanish Hapsburgs
■ Austrian Hapsburgs
□ Holy Roman Empire

Unlike Akbar the Great, the Hapsburgs did not believe in religious toleration. They countered the spread of Protestantism in their lands by threats (in Germany) and by war (in the Netherlands). They used the Inquisition against Jews in Spain. This policy was a costly failure. German princes used religious differences to increase their independence. Jews and Protestants had been among the Hapsburgs' most hard-working subjects. Protestants in the Netherlands rebelled and the Dutch-speaking northern Netherlands broke away from Spain.

Hapsburg power intimidated other rulers. Charles spent much of his reign fighting an envious Francis I of France. Philip sent an **Armada** to punish Elizabeth of England when she challenged his supremacy; the Armada was destroyed by English ships and high winds.

Charles and Philip were conscientious and intelligent rulers, but they could not cope with all the problems they faced. Philip made all officials responsible to him alone and refused to delegate power. This made his administration very inefficient.

The Hapsburgs' worst failure was economic. Treasure ships from their American empire brought back hoards of gold and silver. Some of this money was used to finance the constant wars, but some entered the Spanish economy and caused steep **inflation**. Prices of Spanish agricultural and industrial goods rose to the point where no one could afford them; poverty and unemployment were the result.

12   What prevented both Charles V and Philip II from wielding absolute power?

_____

_____

_____

_____

_____

_____

The Reign of Louis XIV of France

1640	1650	1660	1670	1680	1690	1700	1710	1720

1643 Louis XIII dies; five-year-old becomes Louis XIV

1648 Treaty of Westphalia; France now strongest European state

1660 Cardinal Mazarin dies; Louis takes control of France

1651 Angry mob invades Louis' bedchamber

1665 Colbert becomes Minister of Finance

1668 Building of palace at Versailles begins

1667 Louis invades Spanish Netherlands; wins major Flemish cities

1682 Court moves to Versailles

1672 Louis invades Dutch Netherlands; wins Franche Comté

1685 Louis revokes Edict of Nantes; 200,000 Huguenots flee from France

1701 War of Spanish Succession

1713 War ends in French defeat; Treaty of Utrecht makes Louis' grandson king of Spain

1715 Louis dies

Unlike the Hapsburgs, **Louis XIV** had the advantage of ruling over a homogeneous and centralized kingdom. Two experiences as a youngster encouraged him to win total control over his kingdom. The first was the domination of Cardinal Mazarin who ruled France until his death when Louis was 23. The second was a revolt in which nobles and peasants demanded that the king of France be held accountable for his actions.

To escape the constant pressure of the impoverished Parisian mob, Louis moved his court to the sumptuous new palaces he built at Versailles. To break the power of his nobles, he cajoled and enticed them to attend him there, instead of serving in government positions. Their reward was freedom from taxation, the honor of taking part in court rituals, and the pleasure of such entertainments as the plays of Molière and Racine and the music of Lully and Couperin.

Louis chose his chief officials, able men like **Colbert** his finance minister and Le Tellier and Louvois his war ministers, from middle-class families. Louvois' army reforms gave Louis a fine fighting force, while Colbert's **mercantilist** policies promoted trade and industry. But Colbert failed to reform France's antiquated tax system. This system imposed a heavy tax burden on the peasants but failed to raise enough funds to pay for Louis' costly wars. These wars were Louis' undoing. He began gloriously by invading the Netherlands and capturing wealthy cities and duchies. But this aggression prompted neighboring states to form a powerful coalition against him and the last war he fought was a shattering defeat.

Like the Hapsburgs, Louis' religious policies caused him to lose many of his most productive subjects. By revoking the **Edict of Nantes** which guaranteed religious toleration, he drove the skilled, hard-working Protestant Huguenots abroad.

13 **Describe two ways in which Louis XIV increased his control over France.**

_____

_____

_____

_____

_____

_____

Peter the Great in Russia

When Peter the Great became Czar of Russia in 1689, he found that most of his subjects were illiterate and knew and cared little about the world beyond their farms and villages. Single-handedly, he tried to bring Russia out of the Middle Ages and make it into a European power. His rule was far more personal and direct than that of other absolute monarchs. He ordered Russian men to shorten their beards and wear European clothes. Russian women were told to stop secluding themselves.

One of Peter's passions was ships. He travelled around the shipyards of England and the Netherlands learning how to build them. He wanted Russia to have a port on the Baltic Sea—a "window to the West"—from which her ships could trade with Europe. Accordingly, he waged war on Sweden whose territory blocked Russia's access to the sea. In 1704 he won the land shown on the map where he built his new capital of St. Petersburg. Peter failed in his efforts to reach the Black Sea and build a warm-water port on its shores. However, he was able to persuade China to accept Russian control of Siberia.

Peter reformed many Russian institutions, bringing them more closely under royal control. He eliminated the power of the Patriarch and put the Eastern Orthodox Church under a Holy Synod (council of bishops) which reported to the government. Like Louis XIV, Peter wanted to harness the nobility to the service of the crown. In return for holding government office, they were freed from all taxes and given full control over their serfs. These wretched peasants were no longer allowed to leave their lord's service, but were bought and sold like cattle. Peter also placed the mining and metalworking industries under government control.

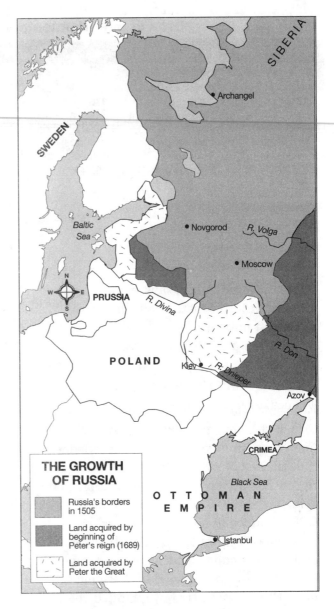

THE GROWTH OF RUSSIA

- Russia's borders in 1505
- Land acquired by beginning of Peter's reign (1689)
- Land acquired by Peter the Great

14 An absolute ruler does not share power. Peter reduced the power or freedom of all of the following EXCEPT

A the church

B the navy

C the nobility

D the serfs

Resistance to Absolutism: Growth of Parliamentary Democracy in England

Growth of Parliamentary Democracy in England

1200	1300	1400	1500	1600	1700

1215
Barons force King John to sign Magna Carta giving them right to approve new taxes & assuring freemen of right to be tried by peers

1295
Model Parliament includes nobles, bishops, smaller landowners, and town burgesses

1376
Good Parliament has House of Lords (nobles & bishops) & House of Commons (knights & burgesses)

1529–1536
Reformation Parliament breaks with Rome; makes king head of English church

1628
Petition of Right: king agrees to levy taxes only with consent of Parliament

1689
Bill of Rights requires frequent Parliaments; guarantees free speech in Parliament; gives it control over taxation

1559
Parliament creates new English church

1640
Long Parliament wins control of government

The later Middle Ages saw the development of representative institutions in several European nations. These fledgling parliaments were abolished or disregarded by absolute rulers like Louis XIV, but in a few nations they grew stronger.

Ever since the barons had forced King John to sign the **Magna Carta** (see the time line), English monarchs had acknowledged that their subjects had legal and political rights. Parliament was the institution that symbolized these rights. It began as a Great Council of nobles summoned by the king to advise him. Gradually other kinds of people—smaller landowners and town burgesses—were included in these meetings. They were elected by qualified voters and represented their interests.

Parliament changed from an occasional meeting to an institution that was summoned fairly regularly, though only when the monarch wished. But the monarch needed the Parliament, particularly the House of Commons, because it had won the right to approve all tax levies. Parliament represented the interests of many sections of the population. Its approval assured the monarch that he or she had the support of the whole nation when major legislation

was enacted. Thus it was that Edward III secured the support of Parliament when he began the 100 Years' War. Henry VIII used Parliament to separate England from the Catholic Church and to dissolve the monasteries. His daughter Elizabeth created the Anglican Church when Parliament enacted the Act of Supremacy in 1559.

15 **Using the time line and text, list three stages in the evolution of parliamentary power. Explain why each stage was important.**

1 _____

_____

_____

_____

2 _____

_____

_____

_____

3 _____

_____

_____

_____

Provided English monarchs pursued a policy that was popular with their people, Parliament was willing to foot the bill. The kings and queens of the **Tudor** dynasty (who included Henry VIII and Elizabeth I) were loved or respected. But the **Stuart** monarchs who succeeded them were less popular and less able. **James I** (1603–25) lost many friends when he lectured Parliament on his divine rights; his demands for money were ignored.

His son **Charles I** had still more strikes against him. He allowed his French queen to fill the court with Catholics. He opposed the growing Puritan movement and moved the English Church closer to Catholicism. When Parliament refused to fund a war with Spain and France, Charles forced the **gentry** (lesser nobles) to lend him money. In the **Petition of Right**, the Parliament of 1628 reasserted its right to control taxation. This persuaded Charles to summon no Parliaments for 11 years. But by 1640 England was involved in a religious war with Scotland, and the king needed new tax money to defend the country. The Long Parliament of 1640 was dominated by Puritans and enemies of the Crown. It made sure it could not be dismissed, executed the king's chief advisors, and ended illegal taxation. Within two years, supporters of the king and supporters of Parliament were at war.

By 1648, the Royalists had been defeated, and Charles was formally tried and executed. England became a republic under military rule with **Oliver Cromwell**, a great general and member of parliament, as Lord Protector. During this **Puritan Revolution**, a Puritan lifestyle was imposed on the people and religious toleration was granted to all Protestants except Anglicans. Radical ideas about religion and democracy were widespread, especially in the army.

In 1660, the people welcomed back Charles II, the son of the executed king. Parliament

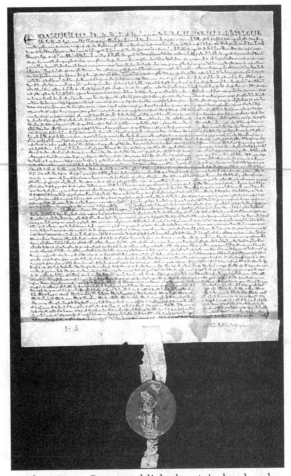

The Magna Carta established certain legal and political rights.

imposed more limits on royal rule, but still Parliament was not a permanent part of government—Charles ruled without it for five years. It was not until the **Bill of Rights of 1689**, that Parliaments were regularly summoned. Other clauses of the Bill made England a **constitutional monarchy:** Parliamentary consent was required for levying taxes and maintaining an army; laws could not be suspended; members could debate freely; and individuals were granted basic legal rights.

16   Both the Magna Carta and the Bill of Rights dealt with the issue of

A   control of the army

B   free speech

C   parliamentary power

D   the king's ability to levy taxes

Section Review: The First Global Age

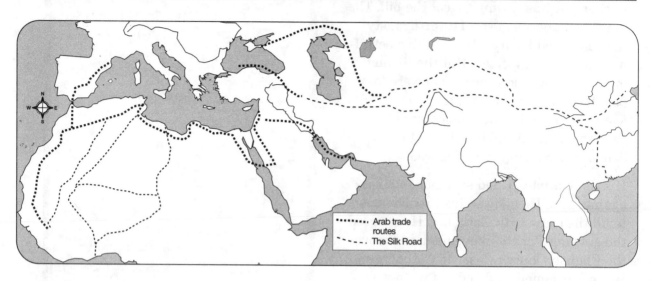

.... Arab trade routes
- - - - The Silk Road

Part A

1 The great Arab traveler Ibn Battuta spent his life journeying through Moslem lands. He visited Mecca and Baghdad and crossed the Sahara Desert to Timbuktu and the Kingdom of Mali. He also visited India, Southeast Asia, and China.

On the map, identify as many of these places as you can.

2 This is how Ibn Battuta described the people of Walata in West Africa:

The women are treated with more respect than the men, an amazing state of affairs. A man's heirs are his sister's sons, not his own sons. I have never seen such a custom anywhere else in the world except among the Indians of Malabar. But the Indians are heathens, while the people of Walata are Moslems, most careful about making their prayers, studying books of law, and memorizing the Koran. Yet their women show no shyness before men and do not veil themselves, though they go to prayers faithfully.

–Ibn Battuta

2A Do you think Ibn Battuta approved or disapproved of the role of women in Walata? Give reasons to support your answer.

_____

_____

_____

2B Based on the information that Ibn Battuta provides and your own knowledge, describe the role of women in most parts of the Moslem world.

_____

_____

_____

_____

_____

_____

Part B

1 What was one result of the Encounter between the Americas and Europe?

  1 expansion of Mesoamerican empires

  2 inflation in the Spanish economy

  3 the decline of the spice trade

  4 the spread of Islam

2 Which of the following helps to explain the strength and stability of the Ottoman Empire?

  1 avoidance of wars of expansion

  2 the development of democratic institutions

  3 an efficient bureaucracy to carry out the sultan's orders

  4 the conversion of all subject peoples to Islam

3 Which of the following is an example of the sharing of political power?

  1 The Edict of Nantes

  2 The English Bill of Rights

  3 The Middle Kingdom

  4 The Treaty of Tordesillas

> Although a prince should...initially follow the ways of kindness...as soon as he perceives opposition or rebellion, the interests of his glory and even of his subjects require that he enforce strict obedience to himself.
>
> Nothing preserves the happiness and tranquility of the provinces with greater certainty than the perfect union of all authority in the person of the sovereign.
>
> I ordered the four secretaries of state to sign nothing without speaking to me of it. Likewise the superintendent was to do nothing relative to finance without its being entered in a book that was always with me.
>
> Letter written by Louis XIV to his great grandson and heir, Louis XV, in 1715

Use the letter written by Louis XIV on the bottom left in answering the next three questions.

4 What form of government is Louis XIV describing in the second paragraph of his letter?

  1 absolutism

  2 constitutional monarchy

  3 direct democracy

  4 mixed sovereignty

5 Which other ruler who lived about 100 years before Louis XIV would have agreed with the ideas he expresses in the last paragraph?

  1 Akbar the Great

  2 Catherine the Great

  3 Elizabeth I

  4 Philip II

6 Describe the steps that Louis took to achieve the goal he describes in the first paragraph.

_____

_____

_____

_____

_____

_____

_____

_____

_____

_____

_____

13. An Age of Revolutions, Part 1: Cultural and Political Change, 1650–1825

Scientific and Political Revolution

1600	1650	1700	1750	1800

1543 Copernicus reports that the planets circle round the sun

1628 Harvey discovers circulation of blood

1632 Church bans Galileo's teachings

1687 Newton publishes theory of gravitation

1690 Locke publishes idea of government with consent of people

1733 Voltaire praises religious toleration, constitutional monarchy, & the new science

1751 Diderot publishes Enlightenment ideas in the *Encylopédie*

1762 Rousseau praises democracy in *The Social Contract*

1776 American Revolution

1789 French Revolution

1804 Haiti declares independence; beginning of revolutions in Latin American

I n this chapter we will look at some dramatic developments in the history of science and ideas and see how they affected people's thinking and behavior. Individuals began to observe the natural world more closely with the use of telescopes and microscopes. They created theories based on what they saw, theories that challenged the medieval church view of the cosmos. Even more challenging was the scientists' new approach to problem solving. Their use of observation, experimentation, and speculation rather than faith put the Catholic Church on the defensive.

These new explanations of how the physical world works were soon joined by new ideas about the nature of humanity, society, and government. Assumptions about the divine right to rule and the privileges conveyed by birth and rank were challenged by the concepts of liberty and equality. From these concepts, the philosophers of Western Europe developed new ideas about who should govern and what government should consist of. By 1770, it was only a matter of time before some troubled nation broke apart under the influence of these new ideas.

The political revolution began in North America. Colonists influenced by Enlightenment ideas and indignant that they could not elect the government that ruled them, declared their independence from Britain. Thirteen years later, the French followed suit and the armies of the French Revolution carried revolutionary ideas across Europe.

The revolutions in the United States, Europe, and Latin America overthrew the old order. But they did not immediately replace it with liberty and democracy. As you will see in Chapter 14, the forces of reaction were still too powerful for that.

The Scientific Revolution

When **Nicolaus Copernicus** of Poland began to study **cosmology**, most Europeans believed what the Catholic Church taught: that the earth was the cen-

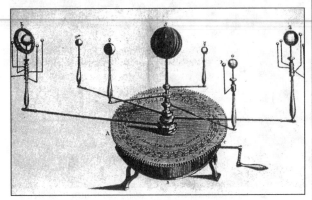

This sphere with the sun at its center illustrates Copernicus's view of the cosmos

ter of the universe. By 1500, Copernicus was convinced that the sun, not the earth, lay at the center of the cosmos and that the earth and the other planets rotated around the sun, not vice versa. **Johannes Kepler** proved this mathematically. He showed that the planets follow **elliptical** paths, not circular ones as Copernicus had thought. The Italian **Galileo Galilei** used a telescope to look at the night skies. What he saw convinced him that Copernicus was right. But when he published his ideas, the Catholic Church banned his book and forced him to recant. After this, most scientific work was done in Protestant Northern Europe where it would not be censored.

Galileo believed that physical laws govern how the universe works and these laws can be expressed as mathematical equations. The English physicist **Isaac Newton** built on Galileo's ideas. Newton realized that the same laws explain the motion of the heavenly bodies and of objects on earth. Objects attract each other; the greater an object's mass, the stronger its pull. This law of **universal gravitation** explains why the planets stay in their orbits about the sun—each one is exercising a force on the others—and also why balls thrown in the air fall to the ground. Newton also tried to describe how light travels; he thought it was composed of tiny particles—later scientists would prove that it travels by way of waves. He developed the system of mathematics called calculus to prove his theories.

None of these advances would have been possible without the **scientific method**. **Francis Bacon** taught that scientists must use this method to prove their theories. They begin by observing facts. Then they create a hypothesis—a tentative theory that may explain these facts. They submit this hypothesis to many tests. If it holds up under all circumstances, it is considered to be a proven scientific law. Bacon favored experiments. Another philosopher, **René Descartes**, preferred reason. Descartes believed that all learning is useless unless it passes the test of reason. He started with himself. Because he could experience his own mind, he knew that he existed. As he put it, "I think, therefore I am." Descartes thought reason and mathematics allow us to understand the physical world.

1   Which of the following did the Scientific Revolution make possible?

A   a more informed view of the world and mankind's place in it

B   the American Revolution

C   the calculations required to build the Maya pyramids

D   the Catholic Counter Reformation

The Enlightenment in Europe: Rethinking People and Government

Scientists demonstrated the laws that explain the *physical* world. This encouraged philosophers to believe that **natural law** would explain the workings of social, political, and economic life. These new thinkers belong to what is called the **Enlightenment**.

The Englishman **John Locke** thought that natural law explained the true nature of humanity. People, he believed, are reasonable creatures with moral values. They are born with natural rights that include life, liberty, and the right to own property. Government is a *contract* made by the people to protect these natural rights. If a government violates their rights, the people are entitled to rebel and set up another government. Locke believed the ideal form of government to be a constitutional monarchy where the ruler's power is limited by the people's rights.

The notion that society is governed by fixed laws influenced the French thinkers known as the **philosophes**. **Voltaire** mocked the church and the nobility in satires like *Candide*. Forced into exile in Britain, he praised it for its religious liberty and freedom of speech. **Montesquieu** was also impressed by British political life. He believed the best way to protect the liberty of the people against tyranny of the kind he saw in France was to separate the legislative, executive, and judicial functions of government, and assign each to a separate government branch. This principal would be incorporated into the U.S. Constitution.

Jean-Jacques Rousseau extended Locke's ideas. He believed not only that the people

Paris was the center of the Enlightenment in 1750 when Madame Geoffrin welcomed *philosophes* to her salon to discuss social inequality. However, these *philosophes* did not consider women the equal of men.

make a contract with their government, but that government is directly responsible to them. His ideal was the Athenian form of democracy where the citizenry makes the laws. In the 1770's when he wrote, most people were ruled by oppressive, absolute monarchs. Rousseau's famous book, *The Social Contract,* begins, "Man is born free; and everywhere he is in chains." He believed unjust governments should be toppled. His ideas directly challenged the power of the monarch, the nobility, and the church.

2   **Which statement about Locke and Rousseau is correct?**

   A   **Locke and Rousseau believed in unlimited governmental power.**

   B   **Locke and Rousseau opposed direct democracy.**

   C   **Locke and Rousseau rejected monarchy as a form of government.**

   D   **Locke preferred monarchy; Rousseau favored democracy.**

NOTICE: Photocopying any part of this book is prohibited by law.

The American Revolution

Educated Americans like Thomas Jefferson studied the ideas of Locke and Rousseau as young men. Applying Locke's theory of natural rights, Jefferson wrote in the **Declaration of Independence** in 1776: "Government [derives its] just powers from the consent of the governed." Jefferson was persuaded by the writings of Rousseau (and those of the Greek philosopher *Plato)* that a republican form of government is preferable to a monarchy. Jefferson's emphasis on the equality of all individuals and their rights to justice and liberty also reveals the influence of the Enlightenment.

The Declaration of Independence had a tremendous impact—not just on the development of the United States, but on the history of the whole Western world. By insisting on **popular sovereignty**—the consent of the governed—the Declaration helped ensure that the United States would become a democracy, not a monarchy like Britain. Its leaders would be chosen in free elections. By stressing that all men are created equal, it developed a goal. In the centuries to come, different groups of Americans would achieve the equality that the Declaration promised.

These two ideas—that power comes from the people and that men are created equal—set an example for peoples throughout the world. When revolution swept through France 13 years later, its leaders proclaimed a **Declaration of the Rights of Man and of the Citizen** based largely on the Declaration of Independence. And in the liberal and nationalist movements of the 19th and 20th centuries, peoples across the globe demanded freedom and independence. They, too, based their claims on the principles of democracy and equality set forth in the Declaration.

> We hold these truths to be self-evident, that all men are created equal, that they are endowed by their Creator with certain unalienable Rights, that among these are Life, Liberty and the pursuit of Happiness.
>
> That to secure these rights, Governments are instituted among Men, deriving their just powers from the consent of the governed.
>
> That whenever any Form of Government becomes destructive of these ends, it is the Right of the People to alter or to abolish it and to institute new Government, laying its foundation on such principles and organizing its powers in such form, as to them shall seem most likely to effect their Safety and Happiness.
>
> —From *The Declaration of Independence*

3 **Using this excerpt from the Declaration of Independence, describe how John Locke influenced its ideas.**

_____

_____

_____

_____

_____

_____

_____

4 **How did the American Revolution influence later revolutions?**

_____

_____

_____

_____

_____

_____

The Enlightened Despots

The term **enlightened despotism** was coined by the French philosophes. It described strong monarchies that eliminated obstacles to freedom such as censorship and encouraged trade and commerce. Historians usually use the term to describe the reigns of **Frederick the Great** in Prussia, **Maria Theresa** and her son **Joseph II** in Austria, and **Catherine the Great** in Russia.

These monarchs did indeed reform the administrative and educational systems of their nations and reduced the powers of the clergy. Joseph II abolished serfdom in Austria, appointed middle-class administrators, and gave freedom of speech to the press and freedom of religion to Protestants and Jews. Frederick the Great also followed a policy of religious toleration and created elementary schools throughout Prussia.

The career of Catherine the Great explains why many historians consider enlightened despotism to be a meaningless term. Like Frederick, Catherine corresponded with Voltaire. But she preferred to talk about enlightenment rather than to practice it. Thus she criticized serfdom while publishing a charter that guaranteed the nobility permanent control over their peasants.

The enlightened despots were interested mainly in extending the power of their governments. They were willing to enact reforms provided these reforms did not threaten their power. When Austria's bishops and nobles objected to Joseph's reforms, many reforms were repealed. When artisans began to read French Revolution pamphlets, he quickly reimposed censorship. Frederick decreed the abolition of serfdom in Prussia, but he needed the support of the aristocracy too much to force them to free their serfs. Catherine gave the philosopher Diderot a pension, but she refused to listen to those ideas that might reduce her political power.

Voltaire visits Frederick the Great

Their foreign policy showed quite clearly that these rulers preferred force and ruthlessness to reason and cooperation. Each one snatched up territory and betrayed allies, every bit as much as unenlightened rulers. Their most cynical act was to partition Poland among themselves.

5   **What lasting policies did the despots of Eastern Europe introduce that reflected Enlightenment ideas?**

_____

_____

_____

_____

_____

_____

The French Revolution: Causes and Impact

The French Revolution

1780	1785	1787	1789	1791	1793	1795

1781 Cost of fighting American Revolutionary War increases national debt	**1785-89** Cost of living rises 62% while wages rise 22%	**1788** Poor harvest; bread scarce and costly	**May, 1789** Estates General meet at Versailles	**Oct, 1789** Women march king to Paris	**1791** Church lands sold	**1792** Radicals create National Convention; universal male suffrage	**1793** King tried & executed	**1794** Execution of Danton and Robespierre
	1786 Banks refuse to lend money to government		**June, 1789** Third Estate, calling self National Assembly, vows not to disband	**Aug, 1789** Assembly abolishes feudalism; Dec.of Rights of Man	**1791** New Con-stitution		**1793** Committee of Public Safety to direct war	**1795** End of universal suffrage; five-man Directory governs France
			July, 1789 Parisians storm Bastille	**Aug, 1789** Peasant uprisings	**1791** King & queen captured as they flee	**1792** French beat foreign armies at Valmy	**1793-94** Terror; thousands guillotined	

In 1789 a revolution began in France that overthrew the **Ancien Regime**, the rule of the king, nobles, and clergy. The time line shows the principal events of this revolution. The French Revolution had deep-rooted causes, many of them economic. The government was nearly bankrupt. The wars of the seventeenth century, as well as French participation in the American Revolutionary War, had still not been paid for. The taxation system was unjust—nobles and clergy paid no taxes. It was also corrupt and highly inefficient. In desperation, Louis XVI summoned the **Estates General**. This representative body had not met since 1614. Still, Louis hoped it would agree to the levy of new taxes.

But the groups that made up the Estates General were deeply divided. The people (the Third Estate) resented the privileges of the First Estate (the clergy) and the Second Estate (the nobility). The Third Estate soon seized control and made itself into a law-making National Assembly.

Hungry mobs in Paris began to riot over the price of bread. Fearful that the king might send troops against them, they stormed the great Bastille prison to seize its supply of gunpowder, intending to use it to defend their city. Alarm and violence spread from the cities to the countryside. In a movement known as the **Great Fear**, bands of peasants burned the homes of their noble lords and destroyed the feudal documents that kept them in bondage. Back in Paris, the citizens compelled the royal family to leave Versailles and return with them to Paris.

6A Why was the French govern-ment nearly bankrupt by 1789?

_____

_____

_____

_____

6B How did financial difficulties contribute to the Revolution?

_____

_____

_____

_____

The National Assembly abolished feudalism and adopted *A Declaration of the Rights of Man and of the Citizen*. This famous document guaranteed freedom in speech and religion, and equality before the law. Some women also claimed new rights.

> Woman is born free and lives equal to man in her rights...Male and female citizens being equal in the eyes of the law, must be equally admitted to all honors, positions, and public employment according to their capacity.
>
> —Olympe de Gouges, *Declaration of the Rights of Woman*, 1791

Over the next two years, the National Assembly created a limited, constitutional monarchy. The assembly enacted laws while the king and his ministers enforced them and handled the administration. The old French provinces were replaced by 83 departments. The Catholic Church was stripped of its lands and of the right to choose its officials. Instead, priests were to be elected and paid as officials. These church reforms distressed the devout French peasantry and King Louis approved them very reluctantly. He sealed his fate when he and his family tried to escape abroad. They were recognized, marched back to Paris, and subsequently treated as enemies of France.

By 1792, the revolutionaries were deeply divided. Conservatives believed change had gone far enough. Radicals within the government were influenced by the ideas of the Enlightenment and the American Revolution and wanted to create a republic. More radical still were the citizens of Paris known as the *sans-culottes*. Foreign invasion increased the turmoil. Prussia and Austria sent troops into France to protect the royal family and to stop revolutionary ideas from spreading abroad.

War played into the hands of the radicals. They replaced the Assembly with a National Convention which swiftly abolished the monarchy and declared France a republic. The Convention introduced universal <u>male</u> **suffrage** and closed the churches. By 1793, the **Jacobins** controlled the Convention. To deal with the invading armies, they created a Committee of Public Safety to govern and organize national defense. They used a **draft** to create a citizen army that numbered 800,000 by 1794. These patriotic, well-led soldiers easily defeated the **mercenary** armies of Austria and Prussia.

Over the next two years, the Jacobins grew ever more extreme, and terror became an instrument of public policy. The king and queen were executed. As many as 40,000 people, most of them peasants and townsfolk, were guillotined. **Maximilien Robespierre** ruled as a dictator after killing off his rivals, until he, too, was sent to the guillotine. Gradually, people grew weary of terror and death, and a more moderate government (the **Directory**) took over. By 1795, the reputation of the victorious army was as high as that of the corrupt Directory was low. The time was ripe for an aggressive young general named **Napoleon Bonaparte** to seize power.

7   How did the lives of ordinary folk change during the Revolution?

_____

_____

_____

_____

_____

_____

Napoleon's Empire

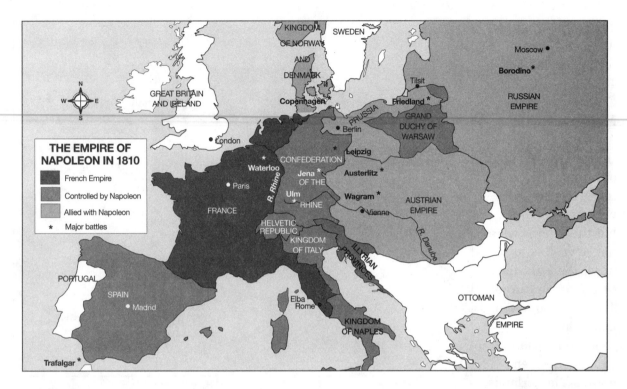

In 1804, Napoleon crowned himself Emperor of the French. He was a very able ruler. He divided France into administrative districts ruled by officials appointed by and responsible to the central government. He created a fine public education system that included schools and colleges. He reformed the tax system; now all citizens paid taxes. He introduced a new, simplified legal code known as the **Code Napoleon**. And he made peace with the Catholic Church.

In destroying the remains of feudal France, creating legal equality, and continuing religious toleration, Napoleon's reforms extended the work of the Revolution. He and his armies carried revolutionary and enlightenment ideas across Europe. They were warmly welcomed by liberals and nationalists, particularly in Italy, Poland, the Netherlands, and Germany. The absolute rulers of Central and Eastern Europe did not respond so enthusiastically.

But Napoleon was less interested in spreading revolution than in creating a strong state that he could control. This meant an end to liberty, republicanism, and democracy in France. Above all else, he was a military conqueror. He wanted to use the resources of France to help him dominate Europe. As the map shows, for a while he nearly succeeded. But by 1815, his enemies were able to overpower his weakened armies and he was finally defeated at Waterloo.

8 **In what respect did Napoleon destroy the achievements of the French Revolution?**

A **by doing away with the new education system**

B **by decentralizing government**

C **by re-establishing absolute rule**

D **by turning a peaceful foreign policy into one based on war**

The Congress of Vienna and the Balance of Power

The powers that had defeated Napoleon met at Vienna in 1814 and 1815. Guided by **Prince Metternich**, the Austrian Chancellor, they redrew the map of Europe. The victors were rewarded with new territory, but their gains were not so vast as to upset the **balance of power** in Europe. The map shows the lands won by Austria, Russia, Prussia, Sweden, and the Netherlands. Britain gained strategic naval bases around the world.

The goal of the **reactionary** monarchs of Austria, Prussia, and Russia was to keep the peace by opposing change, particularly change inspired by liberal or nationalist ideas. They made sure that the monarchs of France, Spain, Portugal, and the Italian kingdoms returned to their thrones. Austria, Prussia, and Russia, along with Great Britain, created a Quadruple Alliance. Its aim was to preserve the peace treaty and to stifle future democratic movements. Meeting at regular intervals, the allies more or less achieved their goals until the revolutions of 1848. However, they failed to suppress revolts in Latin America and Greece, where the nationalists, aided by Britain and France, won their independence.

EUROPE IN 1815

Territory changing hands following the Congress of Vienna

Arrows point to power that gained territory

NORWAY · SWEDEN · DENMARK · GREAT BRITAIN AND IRELAND · London · NETHERLANDS · PRUSSIA · PRUSSIA · POLAND · RUSSIAN EMPIRE · R. Rhine · GERMAN CONFEDERATION · Paris · FRANCE · SWITZERLAND · AUSTRIAN EMPIRE · R. Danube · ITALIAN STATES · PORTUGAL · SPAIN · KINGDOM OF THE TWO SICILIES

9A What is meant by the term the "balance of power"?

_____

_____

_____

9B In allocating lands at the Treaty of Vienna, how did the allies try to restore this balance?

_____

_____

_____

9C What kind of land allocation might have upset the balance?

_____

_____

_____

Independence Movements in Latin America

The viceroys from Spain and Portugal ruled with absolute power in Latin America. Most people had no political rights nor a voice in government. Within the ruling class, colonial-born **creoles** resented the privileges of European-born **peninsulares**. Further down the social scale, mixed-ancestry **mestizos**, Indians, and African slaves wanted to be free of their oppressive masters and to improve their living and working conditions. This situation encouraged successful independence movements across Latin American between 1804 and 1824.

The first uprising was in Haiti by African slaves led by ex-slave **Toussaint L'Ouverture**. The rebels burned the sugar plantations and by 1804 were able to declare their complete independence from France. In Mexico in 1810, a Catholic priest named **Miguel Hidalgo** led the first revolt against Spanish rule, but his Indian and mestizo followers were defeated. Mexico won independence in 1821 when Mexican creoles sided with the revolutionaries. This encouraged Spain's Central American provinces to declare their independence as the United Provinces of Central America.

The impact of the ideas of the American and French Revolutions was particularly strong in South America. Creoles like **Simón Bolívar** had been influenced by the ideals of equality and liberty. Between 1810 and 1830, he fought and won independence for Gran Colombia (present-day Venezuela, Colombia, and Panama), Bolivia, and Ecuador. José de San Martín and Bernardo O'Higgins brought freedom to Peru, Chile, and the United Provinces of La Plata (Argentina and Uruguay).

Brazil won its independence in 1822. Unlike the Spanish colonies which had to struggle for their freedom, Brazil was

INDEPENDENCE IN LATIN AMERICA, 1825

Controlled by European Nations

aided by its royal family. The king's son was proclaimed Emperor Pedro I.

> Throughout most of its history the struggle for Spanish American independence was definitely a revolt of the classes, not of the masses.
> —John A. Crow, *The Epic of Latin America*

10   What facts about Latin America's struggle for independence support Crow's point of view?

_____

_____

_____

_____

_____

_____

Section Review: Political Revolution

Part A

The documents below relate to the French Revolution. Examine each document and answer the question that follows it.

Document 1

1A What does this cartoon tell you about the cartoonist's attitude toward the three estates?

_____

_____

_____

_____

_____

1B Why might attitudes likes this lead to revolution?

_____

_____

_____

_____

_____

_____

Document 2

The National Assembly, taking into consideration that called to settle the constitution of the kingdom, to bring about the regeneration of public order, and to maintain the true principles of monarchy, nothing can prevent it from carrying on its deliberations in whatever place it may be forced to establish itself, and that in short wherever its members are gathered there is the National Assembly, resolves that all the members of this assembly will immediately take a solemn oath never to break up and to meet wherever the circumstances dictate, until the constitution of the kingdom is established and consolidated on firm foundations and that the said oath having been taken, each and every member will confirm with his signature this unshakable resolution."

—The oath taken by the Assembly on finding its Session Hall closed on June 20, 1789

2A What decision does the National Assembly take in this "Tennis Court Oath"?

_____

_____

_____

2B Why does it take this oath?

_____

_____

Document 3

I   Men are born and remain free and equal in rights...

II   The goal of every political association is the preservation of the natural and indefeasible rights of man; these rights are liberty, ownership of property, security, and resistance against oppression.

III   The source of all supreme authority lies essentially in the Nation; no body, nor individual can exercise authority which does not emanate expressly from it.

IV   Liberty consists in being able to do anything which does not harm others...

VI   The law is the expression of the general will; all citizens have the right to cooperate, personally or through their representatives, in its formation; it must be the same for everyone, whether it protects or punishes. All citizens are equal in its eyes, equally eligible for every high position, job and public service, according to their capacity...

XI   The free communication of thoughts and opinions is one of the most precious rights of man. Every citizen can therefore speak, write, and print freely...

—From *The Declaration of the Rights of Man and of the Citizen*, issued September 30, 1789

3A What were the rights of man according to this document?

_____

_____

_____

_____

3B Who or what influenced this document? Give details to explain your answer.

_____

_____

_____

_____

Document 4

4   Robespierre is the figure in this cartoon. The tombstone proclaims that all France lies beneath it. What revolutionary event does it depict? Give details to explain your answer.

_____

_____

_____

_____

_____

_____

_____

_____

Part B

The goals of the French Revolution were Liberty, Equality, and Fraternity. To what extent did the French Revolution help to achieve these goals? From the documents and your own knowledge, take a position on this question and support your point of view.

_____

_____

_____

_____

_____

_____

_____

_____

_____

_____

_____

_____

_____

_____

_____

_____

_____

_____

_____

_____

_____

_____

_____

_____

_____

_____

_____

_____

_____

14. An Age of Revolutions, Part 2: Industrialization, Nationalism, Democracy, and Imperialism, 1800-1914

In the last chapter, we learned how a scientific, cultural, and political revolution began in Europe. Now we will consider some of the consequences of this revolution.

Scientific ways of thinking made the Industrial Revolution possible. New inventions and new ways of organizing manufacturing transformed the lives of millions of people. Families moved from the countryside to the new industrial cities and worked together in

The Great Exhibition of 1851 at the Crystal Palace was Britain's triumphant announcement of the success of the Industrial Revolution

factories instead of fields. The worst abuses—child labor and overcrowding—would ultimately be corrected. But before they were, social philosophers like Karl Marx developed new social and economic theories that linked industrialization and revolution.

The Enlightenment ideas that had encouraged the French, American, and Latin American peoples to reject their governments continued to spread. They led in two directions: to democracy and to nationalism. The French Jacobins had created universal male suffrage. This goal inspired reform in Britain, Germany, and other parts of Europe. The ideal of self-determination led to the spread of nationalism across the globe. It appeared first among the subject peoples of Europe, including the Italians and Slavs ruled by Austria, the Belgians ruled by the Dutch, the Greeks and Slavs ruled by the Turks, and the Poles ruled by Russia.

During the 1800's the European peoples who had achieved their own self-government over the centuries solidified their control of large areas of Africa and Asia. Convinced of the superiority of their own cultures, they believed they were bringing new benefits to their subject peoples. But in many cases, the real goals of imperialism were economic. The industrial nations needed raw materials. They wanted to find new markets for their manufactures or to protect the markets they already had. But the same nationalism that was sweeping Europe soon spread to India and China. Colonial rule would become as unpopular in the colonies as the rule of Austria was in Italy and the rule of Russia in Poland.

Social and Economic Revolution

Changes in Agriculture

An urban middle class of merchants, crafts-people, and professionals emerged in Europe at the end of the Middle Ages. But most people still lived and worked on the land, just as their ancestors had done for centuries. They planted crops on the strips of land they owned or rented, and shared the common, unfenced land where their animals grazed. Between 1500 and 1750, these traditional methods of farming changed, particularly in England.

Some farmland had been fenced in for centuries. Landowners claimed that fenced land was more efficient. Beginning around 1550, the pace of this **enclosure movement** accelerated. Common as well as privately owned land was fenced in. A Parliament consisting mainly of landowners legalized this process. Many smaller farmers who needed to have the use of the common fields to make a living were driven off the land.

Meanwhile, landowners enhanced the productivity of the land they had enclosed. A new kind of **crop rotation** was introduced in which turnips were grown on exhausted soil to add nutrients. This meant that farmers could keep *all* their fields in production. **Jethro Tull** bred animals selectively to enhance their strength or size. A drill was developed that allowed farmers to plant seeds in an orderly rather than random fashion.

These agricultural changes allowed farmers to produce a food surplus. They began to grow crops for the marketplace as well as for their families. Not only did they grow more food, but its quality was better. Women began to marry earlier and have more children. Before 1700, only one person in two reached the age of 21; with improved nutrition, more children survived to adulthood. These factors led to the tremendous population increase shown in the graph.

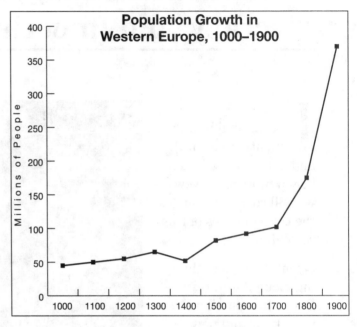

1A By how much did Europe's population increase between 1750 and 1850?

_____

_____

1B What agricultural changes help to account for this increase?

_____

_____

_____

_____

_____

_____

_____

_____

The Industrial Revolution Begins in Britain

Even before the Industrial Revolution began, there was plenty of industry in Britain. Thousands of spinners (most of them women), weavers, **fullers**, and dyers worked at home turning locally produced wool into cloth. For centuries, iron ore had been **smelted** with charcoal to produce pig-iron. Charcoal was becoming scarce, but there was plenty of coal to replace it.

An abundance of important raw materials and skilled workers helps to explain why the Industrial Revolution began in Britain. The enclosure movement drove many people off the land creating potential industrial workers. An increase in agricultural output meant that there was enough food to feed them. Britain was a stable, orderly nation with fine roads, canals, and (unlike France) an absence of internal tolls. Also, it had many wealthy merchants and landowners who were willing to invest their capital in commercial and industrial growth.

The Revolution began with inventions that enhanced productivity in the textile industries. Traditional methods couldn't keep up with the increased demand for cotton and wool textiles. New machines were able to turn out more and better quality yarn and cloth. This machinery was too big for home use, so factories were built where workers labored under the watchful eye of managers. At first, the factories used water power to drive their machines. After **James Watt** designed a steam engine, steam power was used instead.

New technologies improved the quality of cast and wrought iron. In 1856, **Henry Bessemer** developed a cheap method of converting pig iron into high-grade steel. Textile machinery was made from iron and steel. So were the railroads that could carry coal, iron, and textiles much faster than roads or canals.

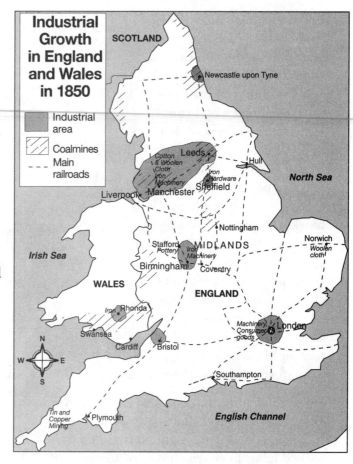

Industrial Growth in England and Wales in 1850

These changes in mining, metal making, and cloth making speeded up change in other industries. Railroads were so successful in England that road use declined sharply.

2　List two reasons why the Industrial Revolution began in Britain.

_____

_____

_____

_____

3　In which parts of England and Wales was industry located?

_____

_____

Industrialization Spreads Beyond Britain

Britain kept its industrial lead until 1870. She exported capital and technical support while her factories supplied the world with textiles, machinery, and rails. Even so, the U.S. was able to develop a textile industry by the 1830's with the help of smuggled British trade secrets and a huge domestic market. American factories used new techniques to speed up production. One of them was the use of interchangeable machine-made parts. Another was the assembly line: as a product advanced along a conveyor belt, each worker performed a specialized task.

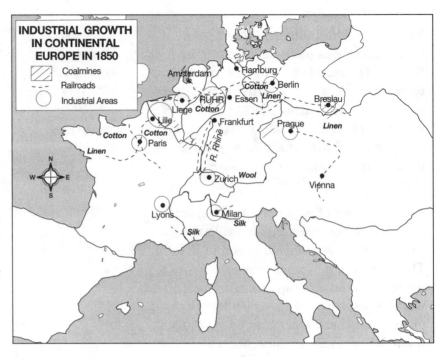

INDUSTRIAL GROWTH IN CONTINENTAL EUROPE IN 1850

After 1850, other nations also challenged Britain's industrial supremacy. Belgium had large deposits of coal and iron and a skilled labor force which it used to develop a metalwork industry. France had a long tradition of textile making, particularly of luxury fabrics like silk and linen. The government backed this industry and also supported mining and railroad construction.

German states began to industrialize in the 1840's. They imported British machinery and capital to construct coal, iron, and textile industries and railroads. After Germany was unified in 1871, industrial growth took off. Internal customs barriers were abolished. A uniform system of money was introduced. Railroad, mail, and telegraph systems linked the different states. German industry was the first to apply some major scientific discoveries. New coal-based dyes were used in its textiles. Other discoveries led to the development of chemical fertilizers. In 1886, Gottlieb Daimler built a gas-based internal combustion engine that could power cars and boats. Another German engineer named Rudolf Diesel built an oil-driven engine that could run larger equipment.

4A What were some of the reasons the areas shown in the map experienced industrialization?

_____

_____

_____

_____

4B What do you think were some of the reasons industry developed so slowly in other parts of Continental Europe?

_____

_____

_____

_____

_____

128

Mercantilism and Laissez Faire Economics

Prior to the Industrial Revolution, most European governments were mercantilist. They encouraged and regulated trade and commerce. In particular, they supported manufacturing which they considered more profitable than selling raw materials. They protected their domestic industries behind a wall of high **tariffs**. Mercantilists believed that the world's supply of riches and resources was limited, so nations had to compete to win what was available.

Eighteenth-century philosophers had challenged mercantilism. They believed that natural laws govern economic as well as scientific and social activity. In his work *The Wealth of Nations*, **Adam Smith** put forward the doctrine of *laissez-faire.* He argued that governments should stop regulating economic life and leave the market to its own devices. He believed that the economy should be governed by the forces of **supply and demand**. Businesses compete to buy raw materials as cheaply as possible. They <u>pay</u> their workers as little as possible, and they <u>sell</u> their goods for as much as possible. Consumers search for the <u>best quality</u> goods at the <u>lowest prices</u>. Smith thought this self-interested behavior would lead to business expansion, the hiring of more workers, and the general public good.

Two other British economists, Thomas Malthus and David Ricardo, agreed with Smith that the government should not regulate the economy. But in other respects, they disagreed with him. Malthus believed poverty will always be with us because populations grow faster than the food supply. Ricardo believed that growing populations mean more competition for jobs and lower wages for the working class.

In some respects, both Smith and Ricardo were right. Industrial economies continued to expand, creating new jobs for their growing populations. On the other hand, it took decades before industrial workers saw a real rise in their wages. And many laborers were laid off during economic downturns.

**The Irish Potato Famine:
A Case Study in *Laissez Faire* Economics**

Between 1781 and 1841, the population of Ireland increased from five to eight million. Most Irish people were peasant farmers and the tenants of absentee English landowners. They paid their rents by exporting grain and living on potatoes. But in 1845, a deadly fungus killed much of the potato crop. The following year the whole crop was destroyed. Wheat was still shipped to England. With little else to eat, and a government relief effort that was quite inept, a million people starved to death and another million emigrated. Private charities were responsible for the lives that were saved.

5A Use the principles of supply and demand and the information in the passage above to identify a crop that was in great demand in England in 1845.

_____

5B "The Irish Potato Famine revealed the shortcomings of *laissez faire* capitalism." Using *laissez faire* principles, explain why the English government did not aid the starving Irish.

_____

_____

_____

_____

_____

Industrialization and Ideology

There were many responses to industrialization. In England, **evangelical** reformers like Michael Sadler and Lord Shaftesbury pushed successfully for laws to limit the hours that women and children could work in factories and mines. **Robert Owen** was an early socialist. As a mill owner, he did not oppose industrialization, but he wanted the poor to share in its benefits. Owen set up a model community in Scotland where workers helped to run the textile mill.

The most influential response to industrial capitalism was that of the philosophers **Karl Marx** and **Friedrich Engels**. They saw it as a terrible misfortune for the working class and dismissed Owen's socialism as unscientific and **utopian**. Marx and Engels argued that all aspects of society: its customs, its beliefs, its art, and its laws, are based on economic factors. The most important factor is the control of production. The ruling class controls production. The labor force doesn't want to be controlled and this leads to class struggle.

Karl Marx the founder of modern socialism and communism

In 1848, Marx and Engels published their theories in the *Communist Manifesto.* Later in *Das Kapital,* Marx developed his theory of historical change. He argued that history is divided into four stages.

Having left feudalism behind, industrial Europe was in the fourth, capitalist, phase. But this was only temporary. In a revolutionary uprising, the **proletariat** or working class would seize control from the **bourgeoisie** or middle class. It would create a new **communist** society where the people would own everything, private property would not exist, and the government and state would wither away.

The course of the Industrial Revolution did not bear out Marx's predictions. By 1900, Western European governments had introduced universal suffrage. Once they could vote, workers lobbied for further economic and social reforms. Influenced by Marxist ideas, many wanted to redistribute the wealth of the landed and middle classes. They wanted major industries to be nationalized. But they worked for change *within* the system as **democratic socialists**.

Many years after Marx wrote, a communist revolution swept through Russia (see page 152). Its leaders imposed on the nation their version of communism, but it was not the communism Karl Marx had predicted.

6   **Why, according to Karl Marx, is revolutionary struggle a consequence of industrialization?**

_____

_____

_____

_____

_____

_____

_____

_____

Urbanization and Changes in Social Classes

Industrialization attracted millions of people to the growing cities. Industrial areas grew up almost overnight in the English Midlands, the Scottish Lowlands, the plains of northern France, the German Rhineland, the American Northeast and Midwest, and northern Italy. Before 1800, one Briton in five lived in a city. By 1914, this figure had reached 80 percent. Between 45 and 60 percent of the American, German, and French people had become city-dwellers.

The new cities housed rich and poor, but the poor bore the brunt of widespread crime and disease. Richer citizens often moved to the cleaner, roomier city outskirts where new suburban communities emerged. In the inner ring were the artisans' small homes and the workers' row houses, several stories high, and jammed together close to the factories. A family of 10 might live in a single room.

The new industrial cities grew rapidly without planning or government regulation, and conditions were appalling. City leaders began to improve their cities in the late 1800's. Sewers were installed and garbage collected. Building codes reduced overcrowding, and new police and fire departments created safer streets.

Industrialization caused Europe's middle class to expand. In the past, bankers and merchants were its wealthiest members. Now they were joined by factory and mine owners. Below the top rank, managers and clerks now kept company with professionals and shopkeepers. This middle class was reform minded, ambitious, thrifty, hard working, and also selfish, callous, materialistic, and smug. The roles of middle class men and women became sharply differentiated. Men's energies were focused on the workplace, women's on the home and family.

The working class was divided into skilled craftspeople and unskilled factory workers and miners. For the unskilled, working conditions were atrocious. Hours were long, and work was unhealthy and dangerous. Families—men, women, and children—labored together. Politically unorganized, they rarely protested.

Skilled workers included tailors, printers, and builders. Better educated than factory workers, they were the center of political and economic protest. Their old guilds served as a model for trade unions. They struggled for political reform and against the industrialization that threatened to take over their crafts.

> In the center of this street there is a gutter into which potato parings, the refuse of vegetable and animal matter of all kinds, the dirty water from the washing of clothes and of the houses are all poured, and where they stagnate and putrefy…all the lanes and alleys of the neighborhood pour their contents into the center of the main street…Families live in the cellars and kitchens of these undrained houses.
>
> **—A Parliamentary Report on London housing**

7A **What have you learned that helps explain the terrible conditions described in this report?**

_____

_____

_____

7B **Why had these conditions improved by 1900?**

_____

_____

_____

Revolution, Reaction, and Reform

Western Europe, 1815-1848

Europe 1815–1848							
1815	1820	1825	1830	1835	1840	1845	1850

1815
Congress of Vienna; creation of Quadruple Alliance

1818
France admitted to Alliance

1820–23
French troops crush Spanish revolt

1819
Carlsbad Decrees; censorship in Prussia

1821
Austria crushes revolts in Italy

1821-29
Greeks win independence

1825
Decembrist revolt in Russia crushed

1830
Revolution in France; constitutional monarchy

1830
Belgians declare independence

1831
Russia crushes Polish revolt

1831
Austrians crush Italian revolution

1832
Reform Act in Britain; middle class wins vote

1848
Revolution in France; Louis Napoleon president of Republic

1848
Uprisings in German cities; liberal reforms

1848
Austria abolishes serfdom

1848
Venice wins independence; becomes a republic

Between 1815 and 1848 European politics were dominated by two trends: **liberalism** and nationalism. Liberalism was a reform movement that favored democracy and individual freedom. Its roots were in the economic and philosophical ideas of the Enlightenment. Nationalism had been carried from France across Europe by the soldiers of the French Revolutionary War. It found an eager audience among the peoples ruled by foreign powers.

Liberalism and nationalism were vigorously opposed by monarchs and their aristocratic supporters who feared (correctly) that these ideas challenged their power and wealth. As the time line shows, the reactionary rulers of Austria, Russia, and Prussia tried to suppress liberal and nationalist revolts wherever in Europe they occurred.

Unlike the Eastern empires, Britain and France had traditions of democracy and revolution. This made them better able to absorb demands for reform. It also made them more sympathetic to nationalist movements in other parts of Europe. These nations helped the Greeks and Belgians to win their independence.

Democracy expanded in Britain. The **1832 Reform Act** enfranchised middle class males and gave previously unrepresented cities the right to elect members to Parliament. In the 1860's and 1870's new political parties used their reform programs to compete for votes. The Liberal Party was led by **William Gladstone** and the Conservative Party by **Benjamin Disraeli**. It was during this period that Britain conferred **dominion** (self-governing) status on the colonies of Canada, New Zealand, and Australia to which many Britons had migrated.

There were revolutions in France in 1830 and again in 1848. When Charles X tried to impose censorship and autocratic rule in 1830, the people of Paris drove him from the throne and replaced him with the constitutional monarch, Louis Philippe. When Louis refused to extend the franchise, he, too, was driven from the throne and the rebels proclaimed France a republic in 1848.

The 1848 Revolution spread rapidly across Europe. As the time line shows, there were uprisings against absolute rule in German, Austrian, and Italian cities. But after their initial unity, the rebels divided along class and ethnic lines. All these revolts were crushed and many of the liberals who had participated in them migrated to the United States.

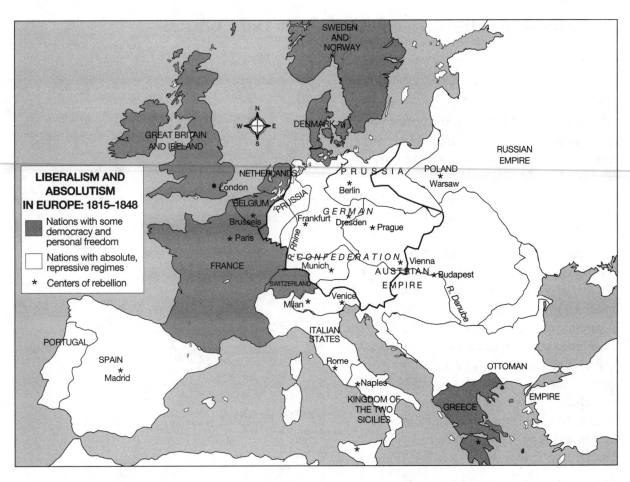

LIBERALISM AND
ABSOLUTISM
IN EUROPE: 1815–1848

Nations with some
democracy and
personal freedom

Nations with absolute,
repressive regimes

★ Centers of rebellion

The map shows those European states with some democratic government and those where the power of the monarch was absolute. It also shows areas where absolute rule was challenged.

8A List three instances where reform or revolution triumphed.

_____

_____

_____

8B Explain why any one of these movements was successful.

_____

_____

_____

_____

9A List three instances during this period where the forces of reaction triumphed.

_____

_____

_____

9B Explain why each of these three rebellions failed.

_____

_____

_____

_____

_____

_____

_____

_____

The Triumph of Authoritarian Government in Latin America

Most Latin American nations won their freedom from Spain and Portugal in the 1820's, but self-rule brought neither peace nor stability. Bolívar had hoped that the new states might create a unified nation like the United States. But geographical barriers like the high Andes Mountains and the Amazon rain forest made trade and transportation difficult and limited contact between regions. These factors, along with border disputes, power struggles, and local rivalries, encouraged **regionalism** (loyalty to smaller geographic areas). A total of 18 nations were established in Latin America. Bolívar's creation, Gran Colombia, split into Colombia, Venezuela, and Ecuador. Argentina and Uruguay were carved from the United Provinces of La Plata. And Costa Rica, El Salvador, Nicaragua, Honduras, and Guatemala emerged from the United Provinces of Central America.

The newly independent nations became republics and most wrote constitutions modeled on that of the United States. But unlike the former British colonies, Spain's ex-colonies had no experience of self-government. A long tradition of absolute rule prevented the emergence of democracy. In many of the new nations, **caudillos** (military dictators) seized power. They ignored the constitutions that called for elections and stayed in power with army support.

The rigid social divisions of colonial times continued. The creole elite refused to share power with mestizos, blacks, and Indians. Government policies favored the land-owning upper classes and ensured that the rest of society remained landless and oppressed. The Catholic Church also owned huge tracts of land and sided with the creoles in opposing liberal reforms.

The privileged few who owned the region's vast resources allowed them to be exploit-

LATIN AMERICA: 1825-1906

Colonies owned by foreign powers

ed by Europeans. Raw materials were exported as cash crops in exchange for manufactured goods. Nations became dependent on one or two commodities, as Haiti was on sugar. When prices fell, the national economy slumped. Even so, a few nations formed stable governments and expanded their economies. Brazil's rubber and coffee plantations stimulated foreign trade. Many European immigrants grew rich as cattle ranchers in Argentina.

10 **Which factor helps to explain why democracy did not develop in Latin America?**

A the lack of trained troops to maintain national borders

B the lack of a middle class

C the relative lack of poverty

D the weakness of the Church

Absolutism and Expansion in Russia

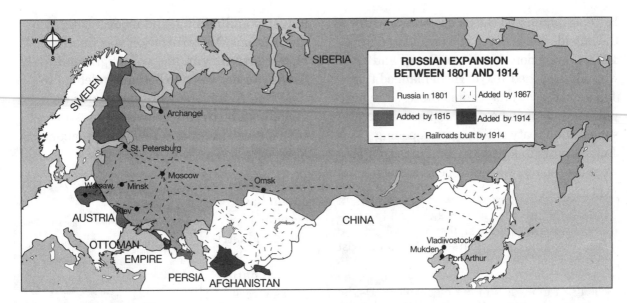

Russia expanded rapidly in the nineteenth century. It obtained vast new territories by conquest and treaty from China in the east, from Turkey, Persia, and the Moslem khanates in the southwest, and from Sweden and Poland in the west. Even so, Russia's defeat by France and Britain in the Crimean War (1854–56) revealed how backward and poorly organized she was.

Absolutism and repression colored Russia's domestic policies. An uprising in 1825 of young Russian officers infected with the spirit of the French Revolution was swiftly suppressed. There was a brief period of reform during the reign of **Alexander II**. In 1861, the tsar issued an **emancipation decree** freeing the serfs who farmed the nobles' huge estates. Half the nobles' land was given to peasant **mirs** (villages). No longer bound to their lords, but with no land of their own, many peasants moved to the cities. There they joined a growing body of unskilled, under-employed, and resentful laborers. Alexander also introduced some self-government in rural areas. He liberalized the press laws, introduced jury trials, reorganized the army, reduced the use of the secret police, and built more schools.

But these reforms did not satisfy the radicals who preached anarchy, revolution, and terror. Alexander was assassinated and succeeded by his despotic son, Alexander III. In an attempt to unite the empire, Alexander launched **pogroms** against its non-Russian peoples, particularly the Jews.

Meanwhile, Marxist ideas were winning support among the **intelligentsia**. After Russia was again badly defeated—by Japan in 1905—humiliation, rising food prices, and an opposition to czarism led to revolution. Tsar Nicholas II yielded to demands for a law-making **Duma**, but he soon dissolved it.

11   **Which factor best explains the triumph of reaction in Russia?**

A   the efficient use of terror to suppress opposition

B   the intelligence and skill of its tsars

C   the long period of Mongol rule that prevented Western ideas from reaching Russia

D   the thriving economy which made the people content

The Modernization of Japan

In 1636, Japan had cut off all contact with the outside world. Over 200 years later, in 1853, Commodore **Matthew Perry** and his warships reached Tokyo. He demanded that Japan trade with the United States. The next year the shogun who ruled Japan reluctantly signed the Treaty of Kanagawa opening Japan's ports to foreign trade. Trade treaties were also signed with European nations.

> If we try to drive them away, they will immediately begin hostilities, and then we shall have to fight. In time, the nation will incur vast expense, and the people [will be] plunged into misery. Rather than allow this, as we are not the equals of foreigners in the mechanical arts, let us have relations with foreign countries, learn their drills and tactics, and it will be not too late then to declare war.
>
> **View expressed by those Japanese leaders who favored signing the Treaty of Kanagawa**

The shogun was overthrown by a group of senior samurai in 1868. The young emperor in whose name they seized power was called the **Meiji** (enlightened one). The samurai who were the real rulers of Japan were also known as Meiji. They enacted a series of reforms that turned Japan from a feudal aristocracy into a modern state. They persuaded great landowners to exchange their lands for high government office. By imposing universal military service, they reduced class differences and encouraged nationalism. Under the influence of Western culture, the Meiji adopted a constitution that empowered the emperor to appoint a prime minister and to disband Parliament. They also created a civil service based on talent.

To make Japan economically competitive with the West, the Meiji visited European factories and hired Westerners to teach industrial skills to the Japanese. They created a huge demand for industrial goods by building up the military, investing in heavy industry and mining, and modernizing communications. Modernization was financed by the government, not by foreign capital—Japan did not want to become indebted to the West. A universal system of education and a high birth rate provided industry with a plentiful, cheap, and skilled labor force.

By 1890, Japan had become a world industrial power. Since its own natural resources were meager, it looked for overseas sources of minerals and metals.

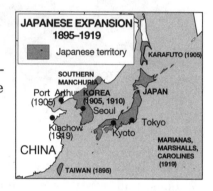

JAPANESE EXPANSION 1895–1919
Japanese territory
KARAFUTO (1905)
SOUTHERN MANCHURIA
Port Arthur (1905)
KOREA (1905, 1910)
Seoul
JAPAN
Kiachow (1919)
Kyoto
Tokyo
CHINA
MARIANAS, MARSHALLS, CAROLINES (1919)
TAIWAN (1895)

Japan won control over Taiwan and Korea following a war with China. In 1902, it signed a naval alliance with Britain. In the Russo-Japanese War of 1905 it won Port Arthur and southern Manchuria from its humiliated opponent. In World War I, Japan fought on the allied side and was rewarded with some of Germany's Pacific colonies.

12 Why might those Japanese who favored the Treaty of Kanagawa support industrialization?

_____

_____

_____

_____

_____

_____

Global Nationalism

The Unification of Italy and Germany

Until the mid-nineteenth century, Italy and Germany consisted of independent states and cities. Patriots inspired by nationalist fervor worked to unite these areas.

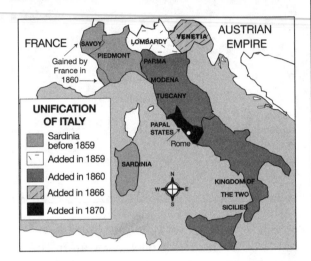

The Italian people were divided by dialect, by trade barriers, and by poor transportation. The strongest opponents of Italian unification were Austria, which controlled Lombardy and Venetia, the kings of the Two Sicilies, and the Popes. The passionate nationalist **Giuseppe Mazzini** led an unsuccessful effort to expel foreign rulers from Italy in 1848. Eleven years later, the more prudent **Count Cavour**, minister to King Victor Emmanuel II of Sardinia, fostered a rebellion in Lombardy. A joint French and Sardinian army defeated Austrian troops. Meanwhile, in the southern Kingdom of Two Sicilies, **Giuseppe Garibaldi,** another charismatic leader, marched his red-shirted followers to victory and the king fled. Victor Emmanuel's kingdom expanded to include all of Italy excepting Nice, Savoy, and the Papal States. Nice and Savoy were given to **Napoleon III** of France for his military help. The Papal States became part of Italy in 1871.

Prussia played the same role in German unification that Sardinia had played in Italy:

Otto von Bismarck, Prussia's prime minister, was Germany's Cavour. Prussia was a well-governed nation with a strong army. The king and his minister determined to impose a Prussian-dominated unity on the German states. In 1864, they fought Denmark and won the disputed province of Schleswig. In 1866, Prussia fought a lightning war with Austria. The peace settlement gave it the Duchy of Holstein and control over the foreign policy of the north German states. In 1870, Prussian defeat of France in the Franco-Prussian War removed the last obstacle to unification. In 1871, 25 German states, including Alsace Lorraine, were united under William I of Prussia, who became kaiser (emperor) of Germany.

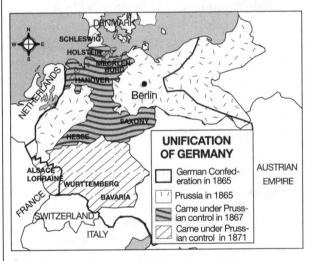

13 **Use the letters to create a time line showing the sequence of Italian and German unification.**

A **Sardinia absorbs Lombardy.**

B **Alsace and Lorraine become German states.**

C **Prussia wins Schleswig.**

D **Mazzini's uprising fails.**

Nationalist Struggles in the Ottoman and Hapsburg Empires

Unification can create unity in a region; it can also create disunity. The empires of Austria-Hungary and Ottoman Turkey contained many different nationalities. Until the spread of nationalism, these ethnic distinctions did not pose any particular problem. But after the French Revolution, the empires' nationalist groups began to press for free speech and representation.

PEOPLES OF AUSTRIA-HUNGARY AND THE OTTOMAN EMPIRE IN 1875

Austria regained control of its empire after the revolution of 1848, but nationalist challenges did not disappear. In 1867, Hungarian nationalists forced the emperor **Franz Josef** to divide his empire into a dual monarchy of two separate but equal states, both headed by him. Hungarian ambitions were satisfied, but those of the empire's Slavic peoples, the Poles, Czechs, Slovaks, and Serbs, were not. Nationalist tensions were intensified by social struggles. In Hungary, the oppressed Slav peasants challenged their Magyar landlords. In Bohemia, Czech industrial workers struggled against their German managers.

By 1875, the Ottoman Empire was known as the "Sick Man of Europe." It was only a shadow of the great power it had once been. A reform decree issued in 1856 gave equality to all citizens, but it failed to impress non-Turkish groups. They wanted complete independence. Outside Europe, Turkey had already lost Algeria, Egypt, and Arabia. Within the Balkans, Greece had won its independence, and Russia had seized Turkish lands on the Black Sea. It was to halt further Russian expansion at Turkey's expense that Britain and France fought the Crimean War. In 1875, the Turks brutally suppressed revolts by the subject peoples of

Serbia, Bulgaria, and Romania. Russia, as champion of the Slavs, declared war. In the resulting peace treaty, it won control of Bulgaria. The other European powers protested at this increase in Russian power and gathered in 1878 at the Congress of Berlin to revise the treaty. Part of Bulgaria became independent as did Serbia and Romania. Austria-Hungary won the right to occupy the provinces of Bosnia and Herzegovina. Between 1908 and 1913, the Balkan states drove Turkey from the peninsula, apart from a small area near Istanbul. Their independence inspired and unsettled Slavs who remained <u>inside</u> Austria-Hungary.

14 **In what way did the nation of Serbia create a problem for Austria-Hungary?**

_____

_____

_____

_____

_____

The Mexican Revolution and Socioeconomic Nationalism

The Mexican Revolution

1875	1910	1915	1920	1925	1930

1876
Porfirio Díaz becomes President of Mexico

1911
Madero wins presidential election; ousts Diaz; overthrown by Victoriano Huerta

1910
Revolution erupts across Mexico led by Zapata, Villa, and Carranza

1915
Carranza wins presidency with U.S. help

1916
Villa raids New Mexico; U.S. troops enter Mexico chasing him

1917
U.S. troops withdrawn

1917
Carranza's liberal constitution

1920
Carranza killed; General Obregón becomes President

1919
Zapata keeps fighting for land reform; Zapata murdered

1929
Formation of the Party of the Mexican Revolution

Like other Latin American nations, Mexico was ruled by military dictators for most of the nineteenth century. During the 35-year presidency of **General Porfirio Díaz**, Mexico used foreign capital to build railroads and factories. But most Mexicans remained underpaid, landless **peons**.

In 1911, **Francisco Madero,** a rich liberal landowner, overthrew Diaz. But he failed to give the people what they most wanted: "land and liberty!" Revolutions burst out in different parts of Mexico. Two charismatic leaders, **Emiliano Zapata** and **Pancho Villa**, led vengeful and violent armies across Mexico demanding radical reforms.

In 1915, America intervened to help Venustiano Carranza become president. An angry Pancho Villa crossed the U.S. border and killed several Americans. In retaliation, U.S. troops entered Mexico on an unsuccessful mission to seize him, provoking strong anti-Americanism among the Mexican people. In 1917, Carranza introduced a liberal constitution that guaranteed civil liberties. It also proclaimed that the government could confiscate lands and distribute them to peasant villages. But Carranza was slow to implement these radical land reforms. So Zapata continued his revolutionary struggle until his murder in

1919. In a revolt the following year, Carranza was overthrown and replaced as president by **General Álvaro Obregón**. Obregón ended the civil war and began the land reforms promised by the constitution.

The Party of the Mexican Revolution was formed in 1929 by pro-revolution factions. They aimed to make permanent the stability Obregón had brought and to eliminate military rule. The party still rules Mexico.

15A What socioeconomic issues helped to bring about a revolution in Mexican?

_____

_____

15B What role did nationalism play?

_____

_____

15C How did socioeconomic and nationalist issues get linked up?

_____

_____

Imperialism

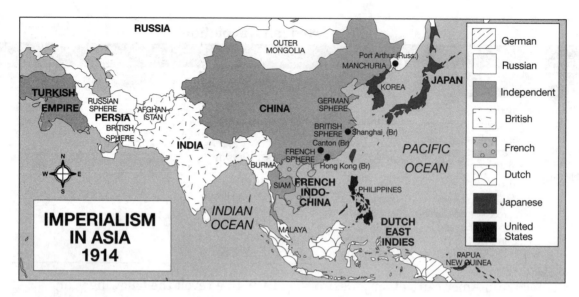

Imperialism means the domination of one country by another. A country under the political control of another nation is known as a colony. Sometimes imperialism involves social or economic but not political control.

Imperialism has existed almost as long as civilization. Ancient Egypt and Rome were imperialist powers just as much as Britain and France. Europe's first imperial age began in the sixteenth century when Spain, Portugal, and the northern European states brought the Americas under their control. Their empires were largely lost between 1776 and 1825. But imperialism survived in a different form. Britain, France, and the Netherlands had prized their colonies for their commercial possibilities. Now they set up trading posts around the world, importing raw materials from tropical areas and exporting manufactured goods. Economic imperialism expanded after the Industrial Revolution. More and more nations wanted colonial raw materials. More and more nations had manufactures to sell.

After 1870, the colonizing powers began to secure their markets by imposing political control. Thus began a race to win colonies. This competition was increased by intense nationalist rivalries. Conflicts between European powers were fought out in the tropics as struggles for colonial possessions. The possession of colonies came to be considered a badge of prestige.

Most of this new imperialism was directed at Africa and Asia. By 1914, about 95% of Africa consisted of European colonies; Egypt was a British **protectorate**. In Asia, India, the East Indies, and Indochina were colonies while large areas within Persia and China were European **spheres of influence**. Imperialism was not limited to European nations. Russia, Japan, and the United States had also carved out empires for themselves.

Unlike most earlier imperial powers, the European colonizers ignored local customs and traditions. Convinced of the superiority of Western civilization, they believed their mission was to bring their moral values and the Christian faith to the native peoples. They rarely permitted local self-rule.

Imperialism varied from one colonial power to another. For instance, France, unlike Britain, wanted to export its culture and to incorporate its colonies into France. But in all cases, imperialism created local resentments that grew stronger over time.

British Rule in India

After its rulers abandoned their policy of religious toleration, the Mogul Empire was weakened by internal conflict. Hindus, Muslims, and Sikhs fought each other as did native princes. This allowed French, Dutch, and British merchants to build forts and trading posts across India. By 1763, Britain, aided by its princely allies and its armies of *sepoys* (native troops), had defeated and expelled its rivals. The British East India Company spent the next 100 years expanding its territory and its commerce.

In 1857, the sepoys rose in revolt when they heard a false rumor that their rifle bullets were greased with pork and beef fat—a problem for both Moslems and Hindus. The revolt, known in India as the Great Rebellion and in Britain as the Indian Mutiny, became a massive popular uprising. It took the East India Company a year to regain control of India. It succeeded with the help of Sikh troops and through the loyalty of the princes and maharajahs with whom it was allied. To punish the mutineers, the British killed thousands of Indians, creating a lasting bitterness.

In 1858, the British government abolished the East India Company and took control of India. Policy was now created in London and carried out by a viceroy whom the crown appointed. The part of India under British rule was known as the **Raj**. Outside the Raj, the maharajahs continued to rule their princedoms, but Britain gained more and more control over them. The British governed India through a civil service. At first, all its officials were British. Later an Indian elite (paid at a far lower rate) was added. By 1900, 4,000 Britons and half a million Indians ruled a population of 300 million.

Britain created a powerful, unified state based on a single system of law and language (English). It built roads, railroads,

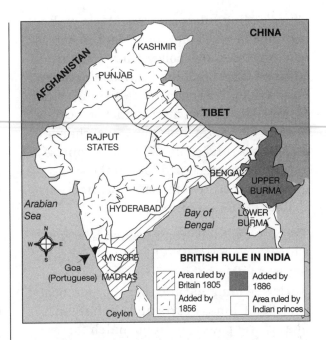

and a modern communications system. Schools and universities were opened. Industry and agriculture were developed to meet the needs of a world market, but not the needs of India's people. Millions starved to death when farmers had to grow cotton to supply Britain's textile mills rather than wheat. And so, despite the stability and order it brought, British rule grew very unpopular. It disregarded the customs, religion, and languages of the diverse people it ruled. It excluded Indians from top government posts. It flooded the country with its cheap, machine-made goods, driving Indian artisans out of business and into debt.

16 **Classic imperialism follows these stages: trade war, economic influence, and political control. Explain how British rule in India followed this pattern.**

_____

_____

_____

European Spheres of Influence in China

China's Ming rulers cut off contacts with the outside world and their Manchu successors continued this policy. Until 1839, trade between China and the European nations was limited. This changed as a result of the Opium War. British merchants had begun to smuggle opium into China in exchange for tea, silk, and china. When the Chinese government intervened to stop the smuggling and destroyed imported opium, Britain demanded compensation.

The war that followed revealed how far China, once a great technological innovator, had fallen behind. Britain was the world's leading naval power; her gunboats attacked Chinese ports and China's antiquated weapons proved no match for British firepower. Britain seized several coastal cities. The Treaty of Nanking gave Britain the island of Hong Kong, the right to set the tariffs that the Chinese could levy, and the right of British subjects in China to live under British law.

Widespread economic discontent and the unpopularity of the Manchu emperor led to the **Taiping Rebellion** (1850–64). The rebellion was put down with the help of foreign troops. In return, France and Britain won another concession: the emperor agreed to let the Chinese emigrate. (They were used as labor to build railroads in the U.S. and South Africa.)

By the 1890's, Europeans were no longer content to have trading rights in coastal towns. Each nation claimed its own sphere of influence where it enjoyed exclusive trading rights. Intervention by the United States prevented the outright partition of China. But China's sovereignty had already been damaged by the many concessions it had made. The angry Chinese organized secret societies to expel all foreigners and punish Chinese Christians. In 1900, a group known as the **Boxers** attacked foreigners across northern China. An international army of Europeans, Americans, and Japanese suppressed the rebellion. For their help, they demanded and received a large sum of money and permission for their troops to remain on Chinese soil.

A   The Great Powers were unable to carve up China as they had Africa. The Europeans were able to wring such concessions as Hong Kong, trading, and special privileges from the weak empire.

   —*Western Civilization*, by Marvin Perry et al.

B   Trade with China is our only object; conquest there would be as dangerous as defeat, and commerce never prospers when force is used to sustain it.

   — *Letter from the British Home Secretary to the Governor General of India, 1840*

17A Which quote is a primary source?

_____

17B What information in that quotation supports your conclusion?

_____

_____

_____

17C Do the events described on this page support the position held by the British Home Secretary?

_____

_____

_____

_____

In 1908, the old Manchu empress died; her heir was a small child. With the dynasty so weakened, nationalist revolutionaries prepared to seize power. They included soldiers, students, workers, and court officials. Their leader, **Sun Yat-sen**, wanted to modernize China using **"The Three Principles of the People"**: nationalism, democracy, and livelihood (improved living standards).

Sun had been educated in the West and this, along with the Western ideas he advocated, won him the support of the Western powers. In 1911, a revolution swept through China and in the following year, Sun became the first president of the republic of China.

18 In the cartoon shown above, China is represented by a dragon, and the European powers by various other animals. Summarize the meaning of the cartoon.

_____

_____

_____

_____

_____

_____

_____

Europeans Scramble for Africa

Apart from South Africa's **Boer** farmers, most of the white people in Africa before 1880 were traders or missionaries. By 1900, Africa had been partitioned among the European powers in the manner shown in the map. There were several reasons for this scramble for Africa: traders in West Africa and missionaries in East Africa demanded government protection; quarrels and rivalries among the European powers led them to grab colonies to enhance their prestige; many Europeans believed it was the "White Man's Burden" to spread their "superior" religion and culture among the "heathen" Africans. Whatever their initial motives, the European powers soon found that there was great profit to be made from Africa's raw materials, especially the precious gold and gems of South Africa.

European rule had some benefits. Roads and railroads were built and harbors were improved. Western medicine brought hospitals, improved sanitation, and better disease control. New crops were grown and fertilizers increased crop yields. But European rule also had a negative impact. Africa was divided into colonial states that ignored ethnic and cultural boundaries. A European sense of superiority led the colonial powers to despise traditional African culture and to weaken tribal ties. Africans were forced to labor long hours for low pay in the fields and mines, and their civil and human rights were ignored.

The first major resistance to colonial rule came from the Zulus of southern Africa. Boer farmers had migrated from British-controlled Cape Colony to set up independent republics on land claimed by the Zulus. At first the Zulus under King Cetywayo beat Boer troops. But the Zulu empire was destroyed by better-armed British troops. The Sudanese led by their Moslem leader, the Mahdi, waged a holy war against the

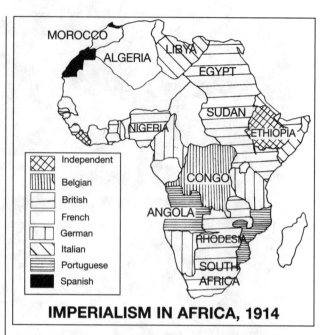

IMPERIALISM IN AFRICA, 1914

British but were defeated at Omdurman in 1898. Ashanti uprisings in West Africa were also defeated by European troops.

When gold and diamonds were found in Boer territory, British settlers moved in and conflicts developed between them and the Boers. A bitter war began in 1899 that took the British three years to win.

19 **Decide what percentage of Africa was independent in 1914 and what percentages were held by the 7 colonial powers. France's share has been filled in. Complete the chart and label each slice of the pie.**

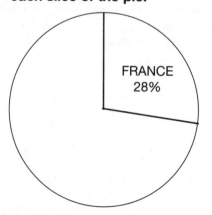

144

Section Review: The Nineteenth Century

Part A

1 What was one consequence of the agricultural revolution?

  1 Britain began to import grain.

  2 The common areas available for animal grazing were expanded.

  3 The quantity and quality of cash crops increased.

  4 The need for agricultural laborers increased.

2 Karl Marx is to communism as Robert Owen is to

  1 imperialism

  2 impressionism

  3 mercantilism

  4 socialism

3 The Great Rebellion in India, the Boxer Rebellion in China, Pancho Villa's expedition to New Mexico, and the Balkan War of 1912 were the direct result of

  1 imperialism

  2 industrialization

  3 enlightenment

  4 socialism

4 What was the most important issue in the Mexican Revolution of 1910-1920?

  1 civil liberties

  2 land reform

  3 racial discrimination

  4 women's suffrage

5 One similarity between the authoritarian governments of Russia and Latin America is that both

  1 encouraged civil but not political liberty

  2 held power only because they enjoyed the support of the army

  3 relied on the support of the land-owning upper class

  4 supported the development of domestic industries

6 What role did Napoleon III of France play in the unification of Italy and Germany?

  1 He supported both.

  2 He opposed both.

  3 He supported Italian unification and opposed German unification.

  4 He supported German unification and opposed Italian unification.

7 What did British imperialism in Africa have in common with the Japanese occupation of Korea in 1905?

  1 Both involved the desire to expand trade and obtain raw materials from overseas.

  2 Both involved expansion of the slave trade.

  3 Both stemmed from the desire to control more industrially advanced regions.

  4 Both were undertaken in order to provide more territory for a rapidly expanding population.

Part B

Question 1

Shade the major industrial regions that had developed before 1900 on this map.

Label five places (countries, regions, or cities) that were particularly involved in industrialization.

Create a key to explain the symbols you use.

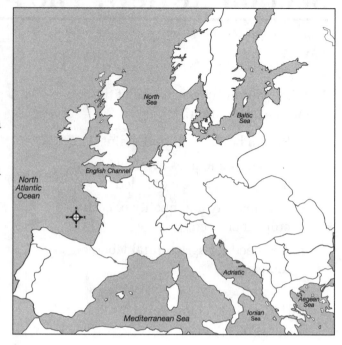

Question 2

A   In 1831 the cost of living was 11 per cent higher than in 1790, but over this span of time urban wages had increased, it appears, by no less than 43 per cent.

—The Industrial Revolution, by T.S. Ashton

B   From 1842 to 1848 I should [could] not average 9 shillings per week wages; outdoor labour was bad to get then and wages were very low. I have been a woolen weaver, a comber, a navvy on the railways and a [quarryman]…[so I may claim some knowledge] of the state of the working classes.

—The struggles of an Old Chartist, by B. Wilson

Which quotation is a primary source?

_____

What information in that passage supports your conclusion?

_____

_____

These two writers hold opposing points of view. How would you summarize the differences between them?

_____

_____

_____

_____

_____

Part C

<u>Statement</u>: The development of global nationalism in the nineteenth century created widespread political instability.

<u>Directions</u>: Write a five paragraph essay that supports and develops the above statement. You must cite three instances of nationalism.

_____

_____

_____

_____

_____

_____

_____

_____

_____

_____

_____

_____

_____

_____

_____

_____

_____

_____

_____

_____

_____

_____

_____

_____

_____

_____

_____

_____

15. Crisis and Achievement, 1914-1945: War, Revolution, and Totalitarianism

Nationalist rivalries caused two terrible wars between 1914 and 1945. The European powers fought each other to a standstill in World War I. In the process they lost a whole generation of young men. Unfortunately the treaties that ended the war failed to lead to a lasting peace.

The weakened powers of Western Europe sought safe solutions to their problems for the next 20 years. They offered little resistance to the demands of a resurgent Germany. Besides being physically, economically, and emotionally exhausted, they were also terrified of the "Soviet menace." Communists had seized power in Russia in 1917 and Fascists took control of many European nations in the years that followed. The traditions of democracy and liberalism were coming under attack from the right and left. Totalitarian governments banned all political opposition and pried into people's lives in a fashion not seen before. The Western democracies viewed communism as a greater threat than fascism. At least Fascists respected property rights; Soviet Communists had followed Karl Marx in abolishing private ownership.

Edvard Munch painted *The Scream* back in 1893, but the agony it expresses has come to symbolize the first half of the twentieth century.

Recovery from the devastation of total war was thwarted by economic disaster. Many nations experienced severe inflation in the post-war years. Hardly had this subsided when a terrible economic depression hit the United States and spread across the non-Communist world. Nations realized how vulnerable their economies were to global crisis. Japan reverted to its old tradition of self-sufficiency, but with a difference. Itself weak in natural resources, Japan decided to conquer those regions that had the resources it wanted.

This fateful decision linked with Adolf Hitler's increasing aggressiveness in Europe made war inevitable. Germany first provoked war with Britain and France and then invaded Russia. The U.S. was soon attacked by Japan and brought into the war. The Second World War was even more global than the first. Civilians again participated in the war effort. An uneasy alliance under the leadership of Churchill, Roosevelt, and Stalin ultimately defeated the Axis powers. The full horror of the war only became known in 1945 when Hitler's death camps were liberated, and two major Japanese cities were destroyed by nuclear explosions.

World War I

The Causes of the War

The event that triggered World War I was the assassination of Franz Ferdinand, Austria-Hungary's heir to the throne, by Gavrilo Princip, a Bosnian terrorist. Princip belonged to a group of Slav nationalists with links to Serbia. Austria decided to punish Serbia.

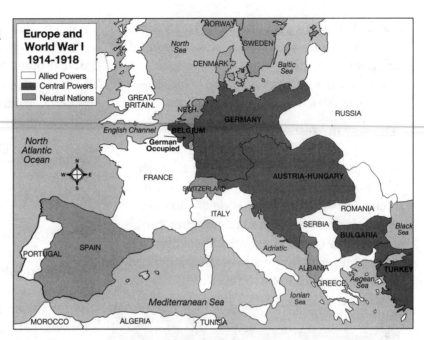

Germany was allied militarily with Austria. Fearing that nationalist pressures might cause her ally to disintegrate, Germany encouraged Austria to take strong action. Austria issued an **ultimatum** that Serbia was bound to refuse. When it did, Austria declared war on Serbia.

Russia saw itself as a friend and ally of the Slav peoples. In the past it had failed to act aggressively on their behalf. Now Tsar Nicholas felt he must come to Serbia's aid. When he mobilized his troops, Germany declared war. France was allied with Russia, so Germany declared war on France, too. Britain was allied with France and Russia. When a German army invaded Belgium en route to France, Britain also declared war.

The alliance system was not the cause of World War I, but it broadened what might have been a local conflict into a European war. If we look at who was allied with whom, it will help us understand the war's underlying causes. France had been hostile to Germany since she lost Alsace-Lorraine in 1870; she also feared the might of the German army. Russia, as protector of the Slavs, was clearly a threat to Austria-Hungary. Britain and Germany were colonial, commercial, and naval rivals. Germany feared that the Franco-Russian alliance would encircle and throttle it.

Tensions mounted in the years before the war; there were numerous incidents that might have led to conflict. As rivalries intensified, the allies co-ordinated their military plans. Pro-war propaganda convinced many Europeans that war was inevitable and just. At its outbreak, most people expected it to be brief and glorious.

1   **Which underlying conflict do you think was most responsible for the outbreak of war? Give details to support your answer.**

_____

_____

_____

_____

_____

_____

_____

How the War Was Fought: Strategies and Technology

World War I was given its name by President Wilson because it involved nations from all over the world. Most of the action took place in Europe, but campaigns were also fought in Africa and the Middle East.

The war in Western Europe was static. The armies faced each other across lines of trenches that stretched from the English Channel to the Alps. The state of military technology dictated this style of warfare. Cannon, mortars, and machine guns could mow down ranks of advancing soldiers. The tanks and armored vehicles that could protect troops were not available until late in

Allied troops fight while hiding in trenches.

the war. Even so, generals periodically ordered men "over the top" (of their trenches) to attack the enemy. A typical result was the 60,000 casualties received by British troops on the first day of the Battle of the Somme. A more mobile war was fought in Eastern Europe where German troops decisively defeated Russia's ill-equipped armies.

Planes were used mainly for reconnaissance, but submarines were used effectively by Germany to destroy ships carrying food and other supplies to the allies. It was the unrestricted use of submarines that brought the U.S. into the war. When German subs sank four U.S. merchant ships, the U.S. Congress declared war. For the allies, the arrival of two million fresh American soldiers more than made

FOOD WILL WIN THE WAR
You came here seeking Freedom
You must now help to preserve it
WHEAT is needed for the allies
Waste nothing

up for Russia's withdrawal from the war in March, 1918. An exhausted Germany signed an armistice eight months later.

The war involved civilians as well as the fighting forces. The military needed huge amounts of guns, bullets, uniforms, transport, and food and medical supplies. With men away fighting, factories and farms were staffed largely by women. Propaganda such as this U.S. poster encouraged personal sacrifice along with hatred of the enemy.

2   **What was most responsible for the heavy casualty figures on the Western front?**

   A   the backward state of medicine which made it incapable of treating gunshot wounds

   B   the difficult terrain on which the armies had to fight

   C   the inability of technology to shield human flesh against firepower

   D   the skill of the opposing generals

The Treaty of Versailles Creates New National Boundaries

The empires of Russia and Austria-Hungary disintegrated towards the end of the war: Russia was rent by revolution, and the German kaiser and the Hapsburg emperor both abdicated. The victorious powers met at Versailles under the leadership of British Prime Minister **Lloyd George,** French Premier **Clemenceau**, and U.S. President **Wilson**. They proceeded to dismember the eastern empires. The republics of Czechoslovakia and Yugoslavia were carved out of Austria. Germany was forced to repudiate the Brest Litovsk Treaty she had signed with Russia. Poland, Finland, and the Baltic States won their independence from Russia. Other smaller parcels of land were given as rewards to the victors. Germany was stripped of its colonies, which went largely to Britain and France. She was disarmed and made to pay **reparations** (damages) for allied losses. Allied troops occupied the Rhineland, her industrial heartland.

President Wilson had published **Fourteen Points**. This was a peace plan based on national self-determination, arms control, the avoidance of punitive damages, and an end to secret alliances. These principles were largely ignored. The new states were just as multi-national as the old empires. Yugoslavia, for example, contained Serbs, Hungarians, Bosnians, Croats, and Slovenes. In imposing such harsh terms on Germany, the Western powers were creating future problems for themselves.

The allied victory was also a disaster for the Ottoman Empire, which had been allied with Germany. Britain had supported Arab independence movements during the war. But when peace came, Turkey's Arab lands were placed under British and French control. The Turkish general **Kemal Atatürk** expelled Greek troops from Turkey itself in 1922. After the sultan abdicated, Atatürk created a secular, westernized republic which he ruled until he died in 1938.

3   Post-World War I Poland was formed from three pre-World War I empires. Which ones? (Refer to map above.)

_____

_____

_____

Revolution and Change in Russia

Lenin and the Revolutions of 1917

The Soviet Union: from Revolution to World War II

1915	1920	1925	1930	1935	1940

1917, March
Street riots; Tsar abdicates; provisional government

1917, Nov.
Lenin and Bolsheviks seize power

1918
Peace with Germany

Comintern formed

Tsar & family murdered

1918–22
Civil War

1922
Stalin general secretary of Communist party

1921–28
The New Economic Policy (NEP)

1924;
Lenin dies; Stalin rules

New constitution for U.S.S.R. (new name for Russia)

1928
Stalin ends NEP; starts first Five-Year plan

1929–35
Collectivization of agriculture

1931–33
Kulaks resist collectivization and are exterminated

1936–38
Stalin uses show trials to purge opposition including old Bolsheviks; millions more disappear

1939
USSR & Germany sign pact of non-aggression

1941
Hitler invades Russia

Unlike the states of Western and Central Europe, Russia in 1900 was still a nation of lords and peasants. There had been some industrial development in the large cities, but the middle class was small. Power remained in the hands of the tsarist government and, in times of trouble, its troops. Russia's 1905 Revolution had failed, in part, because the army remained loyal to the tsar. But by 1917, Russian soldiers had lost their faith in a government that sent them to die in a hopeless war. Short of food and fuel, the citizens of Petrograd (St. Petersburg) rioted in March, 1917. When his troops refused to fire on the crowds, Tsar Nicholas abdicated.

Power passed to members of the Duma who formed a provisional government under the leadership of the socialist **Alexander Kerensky**. But the government did not withdraw from the war nor carry out reforms as promised. The Petrograd Soviet of Workers' and Soldiers' Deputies became a focus for more radical revolutionaries. The **Bolshevik** leader **Lenin** hastily returned from exile and his supporters, even though they were a tiny minority party, soon won control of the Soviet. In November, the Bolsheviks seized key points in the city and overthrew the provisional government.

The Bolsheviks, who now called themselves Communists, created a socialist state based in part on the ideas of Karl Marx. Private property was abolished, land was distributed among the peasants, and workers won control of their factories.

In 1918, Lenin signed a peace treaty with Germany surrendering a vast amount of territory. Although most Russians accepted these terms, moderate and royalist opponents of Bolshevism did not. Civil war broke out between these Whites, and the Communist Reds. By 1921, Lenin had won control over a ruined nation.

4   Review the description of Marxist ideology on page 130 and then explain why Marx would have been surprised by the Bolshevik Revolution.

_____

_____

_____

_____

_____

Lenin and Stalin Create a Totalitarian State

During the civil war, Lenin began to create the Soviet state that survived until 1991. He brought the nation's industries under state control and created a vast and inefficient bureaucracy to run the nation. Although he proclaimed a **dictatorship of the proletariat**, it was the Communist party, not the workers, who held power. Russia controlled the non-Russian Soviet republics just as the tsars had done.

In 1921, Lenin announced a New Economic Policy which permitted people to own and run small farms and businesses; major industries remained under state ownership. Lenin's successor, **Josef Stalin**, ended the NEP. All industry and agriculture came under state control again. In 1928, he announced a Five-Year Plan to build up heavy industry. Despite mistakes, and a shortage of consumer goods, the plan was fairly successful. Stalin followed with a program to collectivize all farmland. Farms would be run by government managers and worked by the peasants. The **kulaks**, the most prosperous peasants, resisted vigorously but futilely. Millions of them died, both in resisting this change and from starvation—the **collective farms** failed to grow enough grain to feed the population.

Stalin's rise to power had been challenged by **Leon Trotsky**. Trotsky believed in permanent revolution and strongly supported the **Comintern** that Lenin had created to guide revolutionary movements across the globe. Stalin, however, preferred to build "socialism in a single country." As general secretary of the Communist party, he controlled the bureaucracy and was able to outfox his rivals. In 1929 Trotsky was exiled.

Twelve years later he was murdered at his home in Mexico City by Soviet agents.

During the 1930's, Stalin attacked other enemies, real and imagined. Millions of old Communist Party members (called Bolsheviks) were arrested and sent to Siberia or shot. During this horrendous **purge**, Stalin used **show trials** to charge his enemies with treason and other crimes. Under psychological pressure, most of them pleaded guilty.

Stalin made the Soviet Union into a **totalitarian** state. With the government, civil service, and industry under tight control, he turned his attention to controlling the minds of his people. Using the threat of terror and a secret police force, he created a citizenry that did not dare to oppose his will. The arts were also brought under party control. All books were censored: artists or writers who criticized the government simply disappeared. A new style of **socialist realism** depicting heroic working people began to dominate the arts.

5   How did the Soviet state resemble or differ from the communist state envisioned by Karl Marx?

_____

_____

_____

_____

_____

_____

_____

Between the Wars

The League of Nations and an Uneasy Peace

The Allied Powers between the World Wars

1920	1925	1930	1935	1940

1919 Treaty of Versailles; League of Nations formed

1921-22 Washington Naval Conference; naval arms race slows down

1921 Southern Ireland becomes an independent nation

1926 Britain paralyzed by general strike

1925; Locarno Pact; France, Belgium, & Germany agree not to change their borders

1928 Kellogg-Briand Pact; nations agree to settle disputes by peaceful means

1929 Wall Street crash; worldwide economic depression

1931 Statute of Westminster creates British Commonwealth of Nations

1936 Socialist Leon Blum forms government in France

1938 Munich Agreement between Britain, France, & Germany

1939 Hitler invades Poland; Britain & France declare war

President Wilson failed to achieve most of his aims at Versailles, but he did persuade the European powers to create a **League of Nations** to act as an international peace-keeping body. However, the U.S. Senate decided to avoid further foreign entanglements and refused to ratify the Versailles Treaty or allow the U.S. to join the League. Without America, the League was probably doomed from the start. During the 1920's, there did seem to be a new spirit of reconciliation in Europe. But the power of the League was tested in the 1930's and it failed. League members refused to put aside their economic interests for the greater good, so the League could not resist acts of aggression in Europe, Asia, and Africa.

France and Britain emerged from the war crippled by debts. Both nations had sold many assets to finance the war and borrowed large sums from the United States. Britain's industries were outdated and the nation lost many of its overseas markets to aggressive Japanese and U.S. competitors. Factories and mines closed and the resulting unemployment led to a bitter general strike in 1926.

France was in even worse shape after the war. Its industry was in chaos, and its government nearly bankrupt, and half its young men were dead. France lacked a strong two-party system, so governments changed frequently. Extremist parties of the right and left challenged democratic government. To stop future German invasions, France built a massive line of fortresses known as the Maginot Line along her northern border.

> A general association of nations must be formed …[to give] mutual guarantees of political and territorial integrity to great and small nations.
>
> —From *The Fourteen Points*, 1918

6A What did this proposal lead to?

_____

6B Who do you think made it?

_____

6C Give one reason why the body that resulted from this proposal failed to achieve its ends.

_____

_____

_____

Nationalist Responses to Colonialism in Asia

Europe's colonial empires (apart from that of Germany) remained intact at the end of World War I. Many colonial troops had fought for their "mother country," and the colonies had hoped to be given some self-government as a reward. In 1917 the British government had specifically promised India home rule. Moreover, the colonies had listened when President Wilson proclaimed that subject peoples have the right to self-determination. But when the war ended, the European powers showed no signs of letting go of their profitable colonies. So colonial nationalists began a fight for home rule or independence.

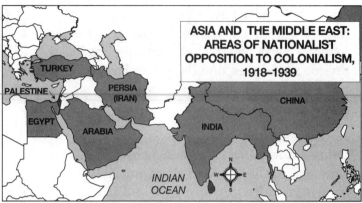

India's nationalist movement was led by the **Muslim League** and the **Indian National Congress**. Their members soon realized that Britain would not honor its promise. In 1919, Britain enacted new laws which enabled it to arrest nationalists and hold them without trial and to outlaw large meetings. When 10,000 Indians gathered for a political meeting at Amritsar, British troops fired on the crowd and killed and wounded 1,600 people. **Mohandas Gandhi** emerged as a nationalist leader. He taught his followers to use non-violent protest and **civil disobedience** in their fight for self-rule. After his release from a British jail in 1930, Gandhi staged new boycotts and protest marches. By 1935, millions of Indians opposed British rule. In response, the British Parliament created a constitution giving control of agriculture, education, and public health issues to India's provinces. By 1939, the independence movement had split in two: **Mohammed Ali Jinnah's** Muslim League wanted a separate Muslim state while **Jawaharlal Nehru's** Hindu-dominated Congress Party wanted a united India.

China was now a republic, but it continued to be torn apart. Warlords battled for supremacy. One of them, **Chiang Kai-shek**, defeated his rivals with Soviet aid and formed a government in 1925. His reforms fostered economic growth but did little to help China's peasants. The Communist party gained peasant support by redistributing land. When Chiang tried to destroy the party, thousands of peasants joined **Mao Zedong's** Communist Red Army. In 1934, Mao and his army fled from Chiang's encircling troops. Their **Long March** covered 6,000 miles and thousands died, but Mao and a small band survived. Meanwhile, Japan had invaded Manchuria. By 1939 it controlled most of eastern China, and Mao and Chiang withdrew to the west.

7   The movements led by both Mao Zedong and Mohandas Gandhi both

A   gained their support mainly from the wealthy

B   were based on ideology and nationalist goals

C   were influenced by democratic and liberal ideology

D   were intended to split their countries into two parts

Nationalist Responses to Colonialism in the Middle East

When World War I ended, the Ottoman Empire was stripped of its Middle East possessions. Syria and the Lebanon were made French **mandates**, and Palestine, Jordan, and Iraq came under British control.

Palestine was the scene of conflict between Jewish and Arab nationalists, both of whom claimed it as a homeland and a holy place. Jews and Arabs had lived there amicably for centuries, but between 1890 and 1914, fugitives from Russian pogroms swelled the Jewish population. They were encouraged by **Zionism**, a belief that Jews should build a nation in Palestine where they had lived centuries before. Britain had promised nationhood to both sides: to the Arabs for their help in the wartime struggle against the Turks and to Jews in the Balfour Declaration of 1917. When Palestine came under British control, Britain failed to resolve the tense situation. Jewish immigration to Palestine increased even more in the 1930's as a result of **Nazi** persecution, and soon there were frequent clashes between the two groups.

Egypt had been occupied by British troops since 1882. Nationalist uprisings forced Britain to grant limited independence in 1922. In 1936 it withdrew all its troops, apart from those in the Suez Canal zone, and Egypt gained full independence.

Persia was nominally independent, but Britain and the Soviet Union shared controlling interests in its oil fields. In 1921, the shah was overthrown by **Reza Khan**, an army officer who wanted to eliminate foreign influences. Like Kemel Atatürk in Turkey, Reza introduced many Western ideas and fashions: he built schools and hospitals and upgraded transport and communication systems. Later on Reza made himself shah and changed the nation's name to Iran.

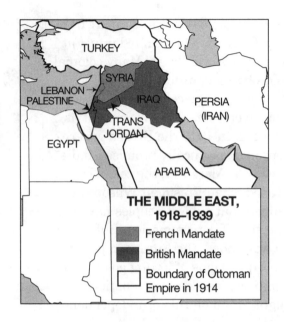

THE MIDDLE EAST, 1918–1939

- French Mandate
- British Mandate
- Boundary of Ottoman Empire in 1914

I am an Arab. I believe Arabs constitute one nation. This nation's sacred right is to be sovereign in her own affairs. Her ardent nationalism drives her to liberate our homeland, uniting all parts…

Statement made at the Arab Students Congress in the postwar period

---

8A **Had this speaker's wishes been granted, which of the nations shown on the map would have been affected? (Information on page 76 may help you.)**

_____

_____

_____

8B **Which of the non-Arab nations shown on the map had full control over their own affairs in 1918 and which did not?**

_____

_____

Economic Depression and its Consequences

After World War I, economic expansion continued in Japan. and the United States. By contrast, the economies of Germany and Italy, like those of Britain and France, were in ruins.

Italy had been on the winning side, but it seemed like a defeated nation. Its war veterans could find no work. There were food shortages and rising prices. Violent strikes spread through its industrial areas and peasants seized the land on large estates. The middle and upper classes expected a communist revolution. **Benito Mussolini** used these chaotic conditions to seize power.

As a defeated nation, Germany had the additional problem of paying a multi-billion dollar reparations bill. When Germany defaulted on its debt, France occupied the industrial Ruhr Valley and seized its income. The German government printed more and more money to pay its bills. This merely created stupendous inflation which wiped out many families' savings.

Germany's economy recovered during the late 1920's. But in 1929, the **Great Depression** began in the United States. Seeing their economy collapse, American investors hurriedly withdrew the capital they had invested in Europe. Germany was dependent on U.S. loans and was especially hard hit; unemployment skyrocketed. The Nazi party grew in size as **Adolf Hitler** promised German workers that he would restore prosperity and end unemployment.

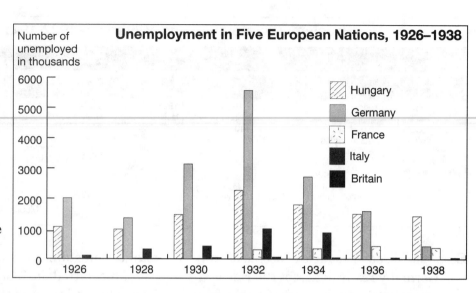

Unemployment in Five European Nations, 1926–1938
Number of unemployed in thousands
Hungary / Germany / France / Italy / Britain

The Depression also had a major impact on Japan. Millions of workers lost their jobs, revealing how sensitive Japan was to the world economy. This, in turn, enabled Japan's military leaders to gain approval for their plan to build a Pacific empire. This empire, they argued, would make Japan more self-sufficient. It would yield oil, metals, and grain while providing markets for Japanese manufactures and space for its growing population.

9A Which two nations shown in the graph had the most dramatic fall in unemployment between 1926 and 1938?

_____

_____

9B What did these nations have in common?

_____

_____

_____

_____

Fascism and Militarism in Europe and Japan

Fascism, Dictatorship, and Militarism, 1922-1941

1920	1925	1930	1935	1940

1922 Mussolini and fascists march on Rome; king makes him prime minister

1923 Hitler jailed after Munich putsch; writes *Mein Kampf*

1924 Mussolini becomes dictator of Italy

1931 Japan conquers Manchuria

1933 Japan withdraws from League of Nations

1933 Hitler becomes chancellor of Germany

1935 Anti-Jewish Nuremberg Laws in Germany

1936 Hitler invades Rhineland

1935 Italy invades Ethiopia

1936 Spanish Civil War begins; Franco becomes dictator

1937 Japan invades China; Nanking massacres

1938 Hitler invades Sudetenland; Munich Agreement

1939 Hitler invades Poland; World War II begins

1941 Japan bombs U.S. fleet at Pearl Harbor

Economic disaster made the people of Italy and Germany ready to accept the rule of a strongman who promised relief. Other factors were also responsible for the rise of fascism in these two nations. Democracy had come late and had not yet developed deep roots. The greatest fear of their middle classes was revolution from below—the Communist party had many supporters in both nations. Fascism, unlike Soviet totalitarianism, did not abolish private property.

In both nations, the people felt cheated by the Versailles settlement. As a victorious ally, Italy considered itself entitled to gain more territory. Germans were angered and humiliated by the terms of the treaty. They were required to accept responsibility for starting the war; they were saddled with a huge reparation bill; their richest industrial area was occupied; and many areas with German populations had been taken away. So while some Italians opposed Mussolini and a few Germans opposed Hitler, a vast majority supported them.

Fascist parties obtained office legally in both nations, but once in power, they eliminated their opposition. Rival parties were banned, censorship was imposed, and legislative bodies lost their power. Mussolini became dictator in Italy in 1924. Democracy survived in Germany until 1933 when Hitler came to power and began to build a totalitarian state. Jews were the chief target of his hatred; in 1935 the Nuremberg Laws stripped them of their civil rights. Hitler also attacked labor unions and the Christian church.

Fascists also seized control of Portugal and Spain during this period. **General Franco** led a right-wing, nationalist revolt against Spain's anti-Catholic republican government. The struggle developed into a civil war in which Franco was aided by Italy and Germany. Despite support from Stalin, the loyalist pro-government forces were defeated. Following his victory, Franco ruled as dictator until his death in 1979.

10　**Which groups of Italians and Germans would have opposed the rise of Hitler and Mussolini and why?**

_____

_____

_____

_____

_____

_____

_____

A hallmark of fascist leaders was their stress on nationalism and violence. Hitler flooded German radio, its press, and its movies with propaganda stressing military might. He rebuilt the German army and helped the German economy to recover by ordering planes, tanks, and weaponry. Mussolini solved Italy's unemployment problem by building up its armed forces. He promised Italians that he would make Italy the great power that it had been in Roman times.

Convinced that a colony would enhance Italy's world status, Mussolini invaded Ethiopia in 1935. In 1936, he signed the **Axis** pact of alliance with Hitler. Until 1939, Hitler's policy was to unite lands occupied by German-speaking peoples with Germany. In 1936, he invaded the Rhineland. Hearing no protest from France or Britain, he invaded Austria in 1938 and absorbed it into Germany (the **Anschluss**). Later that year his troops seized the German-speaking Sudetenland from the Czechs.

The leaders of France and Britain wanted to avoid war at all cost. Their people would not tolerate another war like World War I. In 1938, Britain signed the **Munich Pact** which allowed Hitler's conquests to stand. Today this policy is seen as **appeasement** —a failure to stand up to bullying—but then it was wildly popular. It did not work. Hitler soon seized the whole of Czechoslovakia. France and Britain finally began to rearm. And when Hitler invaded Poland in 1939, they declared war.

Japanese militarism was made possible by Japan's constitution which made army leaders responsible to the emperor, not to the parliament. During the prosperity of the 1920's, the civilian government was in power. But once the Depression struck, the military took over (see page 157). To create

Hitler used the massive Nuremberg rallies to arouse military ardor and national pride among the German people.

a Pacific Empire, Japan invaded iron and coal rich Manchuria in 1931. Then in 1937 its forces moved into northern China. 200,000 citizens were executed during the capture of the Chinese capital of Nanking. By 1939, war with China had diminished Japan's supplies of oil, rubber, and metals, and she began to eye Southeast Asia where these resources were plentiful.

11 **France and Britain did not oppose Hitler sooner because**

A their people rejected war as a means of solving problems

B they couldn't afford to rearm

C they had formed an alliance with him

D they supported his policies

12 **Which development helped make the other three possible?**

A the occupation of Manchuria

B the Anschluss

C the weakness of the League of Nations

D the invasion of Ethiopia

World War II

War in Europe

Hitler secured his eastern border by signing a pact with Stalin in 1939; both men promised not to attack the other. This allowed Hitler to conquer Poland, then France and most of Europe, and North Africa. By 1941, Britain, ably led by **Winston Churchill**, was the only opponent he had not defeated.

The tide began to turn against the Nazis when they invaded the Soviet Union in 1941. Millions of soldiers on both sides died in huge battles in or around the Russian cities of Leningrad, Moscow, and Stalingrad. Eventually, the German advance came to a halt.

After the United States entered the war on the allied side in 1941, its weapons, food supplies, and manpower proved decisive. Even so, the well-led and well-equipped German troops held off the allies for three-and-a-half more years.

Since 1942, Stalin had been demanding that the Western allies open a second front to take the pressure off Russia. In 1944, allied troops landed on the beaches of Normandy in northern France. Slowly they fought their way through France and into Germany while Russian troops advanced from the east. In May, 1945, the war in Europe ended in victory for the allies and defeat for Germany.

World War II: Europe in 1942

- ☐ Allied Powers
- ▨ Neutral Nations
- ▨ Occupied by Axis Powers
- ▨ Axis Powers

13 Which of the following turned out to be a disaster for Hitler?

- A the annexation of Czechoslovakia
- B the invasion of Russia
- C the Munich Pact
- D the Nazi-Soviet Pact

14 Which event came first?

- A the defeat of France
- B the invasion of Poland
- C the invasion of Russia
- D the U.S. entry into the war

War in Asia

In 1940, Japan made a fateful decision. **President Roosevelt** had halted U.S. fuel and metal shipments to Japan. Without these supplies, Japan was hampered in its war with China. It decided to advance into Southeast Asia where supplies were abundant, risking war with the U.S.

The United States had followed an isolationist policy since 1918. The nation remained neutral after World War II began, even though it sent large amounts of aid to Britain. Then on December 7, 1941, Japanese planes unexpectedly attacked and destroyed much of the U.S. fleet at **Pearl Harbor** in Hawaii. The United States immediately declared war on the Axis powers. Japanese armies rolled through Indochina, Malaya, and the East Indies. In the Philippines they swiftly defeated U.S. and Filipino troops in the battle of Bataan.

The war in Asia now turned to the sea. In several huge battles, the U.S. won control of the Pacific. Then its troops under General **MacArthur** began to leapfrog across the Pacific islands towards Japan. These land battles involved much hand-to-hand fighting, and casualties were high. The Japanese fought on, even after the war in Europe ended. When **Harry Truman** became President in 1945, he decided to drop an atomic bomb on the Japanese city of **Hiroshima**. This was a tough decision— one atomic bomb could kill 100,000 people, most of them civilians. President Truman believed that American troops would suffer huge losses if they tried to invade Japan. He hoped the bomb would end the war quickly.

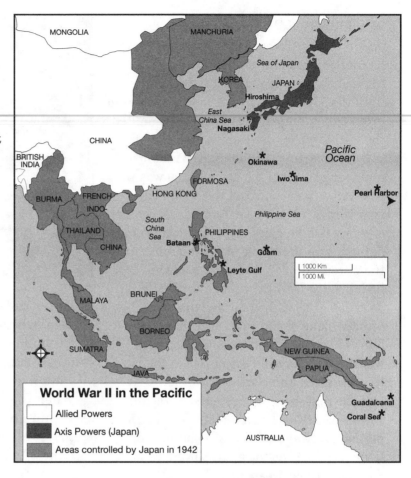

World War II in the Pacific
- Allied Powers
- Axis Powers (Japan)
- Areas controlled by Japan in 1942

Three days after Hiroshima was bombed, another atomic bomb was dropped on Nagasaki. Japan surrendered 24 days later and the war in the Pacific was over.

15 In 1943, allied forces began to island hop from Guadalcanal towards Japan. By 1945 they had reached Okinawa. Which islands do you think they captured along the way?

_____

_____

_____

_____

The Legacy of Total War

World War II was fought on land and sea and in the air. Technology determined how its battles were fought. German submarines came close to controlling the Atlantic Ocean until the Allies developed a convoy system to protect their ships. Surface ships dominated the Pacific where battleships and aircraft carriers maneuvered themselves into firing and flying range of the enemy. This was the first war where control of the air was decisive. German bombers destroyed the centers of many British cities until Royal Air Force fighters won the Battle of Britain and drove them from the skies. Allied **saturation bombing** of German cities was equally destructive, though it showed that air attacks alone would not defeat the enemy. Tanks had become an essential aspect of warfare and played a major role in the battles in Russia and North Africa. Germany was the first power to use missiles (against Britain in 1945). The use of nuclear weapons permanently altered warfare and international relations as the great powers raced to develop nuclear weaponry.

Once again war was fought on the home front as well as the battlefield. Munitions factories began to operate around the clock and unemployment finally disappeared. Women replaced men on the assembly line; this changed the attitudes of many women about their traditional role in society.

Prisoners at the Buchenwald concentration camp in Germany

Hitler had a vision of a German "master race" which would rule Europe, enslaving or eliminating Slavs, Jews, Gypsies, and other "subhuman" peoples. In 1939, most Jews lived in the cities of Eastern Europe. When the war began, they were confined within **ghettos** or labor camps from which they were taken to work in factories and mines. Then, in 1942, Hitler adopted a policy known as the "final solution." Jews were to be exterminated. Men, women, and children were moved to death camps at Auschwitz and other sites where they were gassed. Over six million Jews together with huge numbers of Slavs and Gypsies died in the **Holocaust**.

16 How did technology affect the outcome of the war?

_____

_____

_____

_____

_____

_____

Women welders contribute to the Allied effort.

Section Review: World War and Economic Depression

Part A

The documents below relate to socialism, nationalism, and World War I. Examine each document and answer the question that follows it.

Document 1

An international proletarian movement...can only grow out of the existence of independent nations.

—Friedrich Engels, 1882

1 What did Engels perceive as a positive feature of nationalism?

_____

_____

_____

Document 2

Wars can only come about so long as the working class either supports them enthusiastically, because it considers them justified and necessary, or at least accepts them passively. But once the majority of the working people comes to the conclusion...that wars are nothing but a barbaric, unsocial, reactionary phenomenon, entirely against the interests of the people, then wars will have become impossible, even if the soldiers obey their commanders.

—Rosa Luxembourg at her trial in 1914 for urging German workers not to fight against Russian workers

2 What did Rosa Luxembourg believe would prevent national rivalries from leading to war?

_____

_____

_____

Document 3

The tasks of the proletariat in these countries (Austria-Hungary, Russia, and the Balkans)...cannot be achieved unless it champions the right of nations to self-determination. In this connection the most difficult but most important task is to merge the class struggle of the workers in the oppressing nations with the class struggle of the workers in the oppressed nations.

—Lenin, *Theses on the Socialist Revolution and the Right of Nations to Self-Determination, 1916*

3 Which groups did Lenin hope would join together and for what purpose?

_____

_____

_____

Part B

"Many socialists are nationalists and vice versa."

Discuss this statement in the light of socialist attitudes towards nationalism in the years before the Russian Revolution.

_____

_____

_____

_____

_____

_____

_____

_____

_____

_____

_____

_____

_____

_____

_____

_____

_____

_____

_____

_____

_____

_____

_____

_____

_____

Part C

Base your answers to questions 5 through 10 on the speakers' statements and your knowledge of world history

Speaker A: Only an adequate large space on this earth assures a nation freedom of existence…We must hold unflinchingly to our aim…to secure for the…people the land and soil to which they are entitled.

Speaker B: You ask what is our policy? I will say: it is to wage war, by sea, land, and air, with all our might and with all the strength that God can give us: to wage war against a monstrous tyranny, never surpassed in the dark, lamentable catalogue of human crime.

Speaker C: The fighting in Southern Europe is not the Second Front, but all the same, it is something like the Second Front…Naturally, only a real Second Front—which is now not so far away—will greatly speed up victory over Nazi Germany, consolidating still further the comradeship-in-arms of the Allied States.

Speaker D: As commander-in-chief of the Army and Navy I have directed that all measures be taken for our defense. Always will we remember the character of the onslaught against us. No matter how long it may take us to overcome this premeditated invasion, the…people…will win through to absolute victory.

5   These quotations are taken from the speeches and writings of Winston Churchill, Adolf Hitler, Franklin Roosevelt, and Josef Stalin. Identify each speaker.

Speaker A _____ B _____ C _____ D _____

6   Which speaker offers an argument for territorial expansion?

1   Speaker A

2   Speaker B

3   Speaker C

4   Speaker D

7   Which speaker's country was least affected by the Great Depression

1   Speaker A

2   Speaker B

3   Speaker C

4   Speaker D

8   Which speaker waged war against the other three?

1   Speaker A

2   Speaker B

3   Speaker C

4   Speaker D

9   What steps had Speaker C taken that enabled his state to wage war effectively?

1   building a great empire

2   abandoning an isolationist policy

3   annexing his oil-rich neighbor

4   implementing the Five-Year Plans

10 Who were responsible for the "monstrous tyranny" that Speaker B describes?

1   the Communists

2   the capitalists

3   the imperialist powers

4   the Nazis

11 Which nation was responsible for the onslaught that Speaker D describes?

1   Germany

2   Italy

3   Japan

4   the Soviet Union

16. The Twentieth Century Since 1945: Conflict, Crisis, and Change

Until 1990, the period after World War II was dominated by a struggle for supremacy between the power blocs headed by the Soviet Union and the United States. This struggle pitted two different economic systems and two different ideologies against each other, both of them trying to win support around the globe. Both nations spent vast sums on the development of technology that would put them first in space and first in nuclear capability. Indeed, overspending in this area helped bring about the Soviet collapse.

The headquarters of the United Nations in New York City. The UN has had some success in resolving international conflicts, provided they did not touch on the special interests of the superpowers.

The wealth of the United States gave it a powerful weapon in Europe and Japan. U.S. aid helped these regions to rebuild their shattered economies. In the process, it strengthened their commitment to democracy. Communist ideology had great appeal for the oppressed and for radical thinkers. This allowed the Soviet Union to win support among the new African and Asian nations, in Latin America, and among European workers and intellectuals.

The most spectacular economic recovery occurred in the defeated nations of Germany and Japan. By 1980, their industrial output was second only to that of the United States and the quality of their goods was often superior. Unlike their economic revival, the foreign policy of these two nations was low-key. Punished and shamed for their wartime aggression, both were reluctant to rebuild their military strength. Ideologically and diplomatically, Germany and Japan committed themselves firmly to the West.

This was a period of vast change in Africa and Asia. By 1980, nearly all the world's former colonies had won their independence. This transition was achieved fairly peacefully—the colonizing nations were too weakened by World War II to offer much resistance. The wars that did occur in these regions were more likely to grow out of local power struggles. Conflicts in the Middle East and in Southern and Southeast Asia were often intensified by ideological differences, economic rivalry, and superpower involvement. One nation that did succeed in expelling all foreign influence was China. Mao Zedong made his nation into a Communist state along Soviet lines. The economic policy of his successors has brought it closer to the West. Whatever its orientation, China has undoubtedly become a great power.

The Cold War

The Emergence of Two Superpowers

During the course of the war, the "Big Three," Churchill, Roosevelt, and Stalin, held meetings at Yalta and other sites to decide strategy and to plan for the postwar world. As the war neared its end, the rivalry between the Western allies and Stalin became more important even than defeating Hitler. Two **superpowers**, the United States

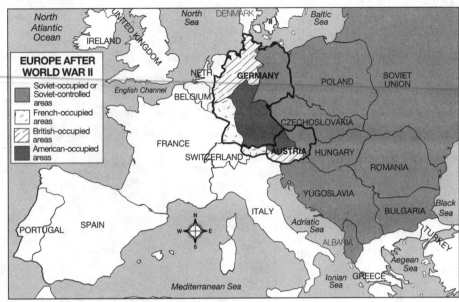

and the Soviet Union, were far more powerful than any other nation. With different forms of government and different political agendas, relations between the two nations deteriorated sharply in 1945.

The Soviets adopted extremely aggressive policies in Europe. When the war ended, allied armies occupied Central Europe and Soviet troops controlled Eastern Europe. Germany and Austria were divided into the occupation zones shown on the map. In the east, the Baltic States of Lithuania, Latvia, and Estonia were absorbed into the Soviet Union. The nations of Eastern Europe remained theoretically independent, but Russian troops remained and by 1948, Soviet-dominated Communist governments were installed everywhere but Yugoslavia.

The Western allies were angered by Stalin's refusal to hold elections in Eastern Europe as he had promised at Yalta and the world became divided by what Winston Churchill termed an "**iron curtain**." On one side were the Soviet Union and its satellites, and on the other, the Western democracies led by the United States.

1 On the time line below, using the labels A through D, place the events in the list in chronological order in the boxes provided.

A Germany's surrender ends the war in Europe.

B Roosevelt, Stalin, and Churchill reach agreement at Yalta.

C Soviet troops occupy Eastern Europe.

D Stalin refuses to hold elections in the nations of Eastern Europe.

Standoff in Europe

The superpowers never fought each other directly, but there were many conflicts during the **Cold War** which found the two nations supporting opposite sides.

The United States developed a policy of **containment** directed against the spread of communism and Soviet power. In 1947 Greece and Turkey were under internal and external Communist pressure. President Truman declared his support for the two countries by announcing that the U.S. would aid free peoples threatened by aggression.

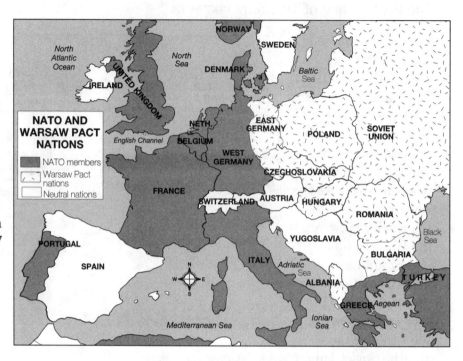

Another confrontation occurred in 1948. After the war, Berlin, the former Nazi capital, as well as Germany itself, was divided into allied zones. Berlin was surrounded by Soviet-occupied Germany. Stalin wanted complete control over the city and began blocking rail and road routes into West Berlin. Truman ordered a massive airlift. The airlift ended in 1949 when Stalin backed down and ended the blockade. The Western allies then united their occupation zones to form an independent West German state. The Soviets responded by creating the German Democratic Republic. Berlin remained a divided city. In 1961, the East German government (with Soviet support) build a concrete wall across the city to stem the flood of refugees from east to west.

In 1949, the United States, Canada, and ten European nations formed **NATO (**the North Atlantic Treaty Organization). An attack on a NATO member would cause the other members to come to its aid. Four U.S. Army divisions were stationed in Europe. The Soviets responded by creating a defensive alliance, the **Warsaw Pact**, in 1955. It soon became clear that the Pact was also intended to increase Soviet control of Eastern Europe. In 1956 Soviet troops stationed in Hungary suppressed a national uprising. In 1968, Soviet troops invaded Czechoslovakia where a liberal regime had come to power.

2   **Using your own knowledge of history and the information you have just read, explain what the Truman Doctrine was and give an example of it.**

_____

_____

_____

_____

_____

_____

Rivalries Across the Globe

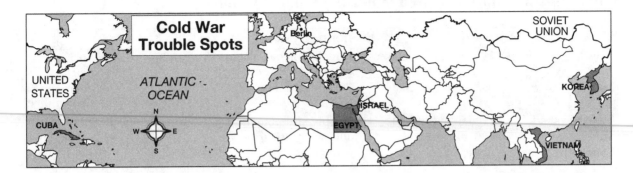

In 1950, the Cold War became a global struggle. The Soviet Union had detonated its first atomic bomb, and a nuclear arms race began. The U.S. and the Soviet Union, began to stockpile massive quantities of nuclear weapons, although neither nation ever launched a nuclear attack since the attacker would be destroyed in the process.

After World War II, the Japanese colony of Korea was divided into two nations—a pro-West South and a Communist North. North Korean troops invaded South Korea in 1950. The United Nations agreed to send a force to drive out the invaders. This force of mainly U.S. and South Korean troops was led by General Douglas MacArthur. At first it was pushed back. Then it launched a brilliant land-sea assault that forced the invaders to retreat all the way to the Chinese border. Mao Zedong, the Chinese leader, considered this a serious threat. He sent a huge army against MacArthur's troops which were driven back into South Korea. In 1953 a truce was declared and Korea remained a divided nation.

In 1956 the Cold War spread to the Middle East. Egypt's President **Nasser** wanted to build a dam to capture the power of the River Nile. When the U.S. refused to loan money to build it, Nasser seized the British-controlled Suez Canal. Britain, France, and Israel attacked Egypt and were condemned by the UN for their aggression. Swift action by U.S. President **Eisenhower** prevented

further trouble and the allies pulled back. But Soviet engineers and money built the Aswan High Dam and the Soviets began supplying arms to Mideast nations.

The struggle between the superpowers played an important role in the development of the new nations of Africa and Asia, and in Latin America. When power was disputed among different factions, the Soviets aided one side and the U.S. the other. In some cases, a superpower was one of the combatants. The Cold War reached the Western Hemisphere in 1959 when the communist **Fidel Castro** seized power in Cuba. In 1962, the Soviet Union began erecting missiles in Cuba aimed at the U.S. President **Kennedy** demanded that the missiles be removed and set up a naval blockade of the island to keep out Soviet ships. The Soviets backed down and removed their missiles on the condition that the U.S. promised not to invade Cuba.

3　**Did superpower involvement cause regional conflicts to escalate? Use one region to illustrate your answer.**

_____

_____

_____

_____

Global Economic Issues, 1945-1990

Communism, Capitalism, and Other Economic Systems

Economic Systems				
	Who owns businesses	How businesses decide what to make or sell	Technology	How prices are decided
Market System	Private individuals	Supply and demand	Advanced	Competition among suppliers
Mixed System	Private individuals and government	Supply and demand and government	Advanced	Competition or set by government
Command System	Government	Government	Advanced or developing	Set by government
Traditional System	Families or communities	Custom	Old	By custom; barter

The Soviet Union and other communist nations had **command** economic systems. In the command model, economic decisions are made by the government. After Stalin cancelled the New Economic Policy and introduced the Five Year Plans, the Soviet bureaucracy controlled the economy. Stalin and his successors imposed command economies on their East European satellites. Instead of setting their own economic priorities, these nations had to focus on meeting Soviet needs.

Command systems do not suffer from severe economic fluctuations. Governments generally provide full employment and keep prices low. But these economies are inefficient. Decision-makers usually want to build up basic industry and military strength, so very few resources are allocated to the production of consumer goods, and those produced are often of poor quality. There may also be severe shortages of food. It was the shortage of consumer goods and basic foods and declining living standards that convinced the Russian and East European peoples in the 1980's that their command economies were not working.

Most European nations in the post-war era had **mixed economies**. They were regulated by the government, but they were also controlled by free market forces. For example, the government usually owned railways, airlines, utilities, and some heavy industry. But the rest of the economy was privately owned and run. Recent years have seen a trend towards the **privatization** of the industries that used to be state-owned, particularly in France and Britain.

Although there is some government regulation of the U.S. economy, it was and remains mainly a **market** (capitalist) system based on the *laissez faire* theories of Adam Smith. The laws of supply and demand dictate what is produced. This results in a wide variety of well-made consumer goods, usually at reasonable prices. But these laws do not always lead to a smoothly operating marketplace. **Recessions** are common. **Inflation**—a widespread rise in prices—is another problem for market economies. The depression of the 1930's persuaded many Europeans and Americans that command systems worked better than capitalist ones.

4   The basic ideals of a command economy may be summarized as:

A   all society benefits from economic competition

B   state control of the economy promotes the well-being of the many, not the few

C   the state must let the economy take care of itself

D   the state must protect domestic industries

170

Case Studies of Economic Growth in Developing Regions

Between 1880 and 1955, the European powers created in their African colonies economies based on the export of crops and minerals. Even so, most Africans still belonged to traditional economies, growing food for themselves and their families as their ancestors had done. African economies depended on one or two **cash crops**. This left them at the mercy of fluctuating world prices: if prices plunged, a nation lost its income. Since independence, many African leaders have tried to diversify their nations' economies by developing industry and commerce. But a lack of capital, skilled workers, and transportation systems has made this difficult. Foreign aid has often been spent on feeding the hungry rather than on building telecommunications and highways.

Between 1945 and 1980, Latin American economies prospered. There was a strong demand for its coffee, timber, beef, oil, and minerals. Foreign capital improved regional **infrastructures**. Industrial output of steel, electricity, and machinery increased tenfold. Then between 1980 and 1988, the region's Gross Domestic Product fell steadily. The main reasons for this slowdown seems to have been government corruption and the greed of foreign banks (the region's economies were offered more loans than they could absorb). Instead of being invested in productive undertakings, much of this loan money was siphoned off by corrupt military rulers and their cronies. Heavy foreign borrowing created huge debts and high inflation. When the International Monetary Fund (IMF) along with U.S. and European banks began applying heavy pressure on Brazil and other nations to repay their loans, the funds simply weren't there. The banks then required Latin America's debtor nations to enact major economic reforms as a condition of extending further loans. The reforms bit deeply into social programs and caused widespread unemployment.

In India as in Africa, the growth of industry had been discouraged during the colonial era. Since 1947, India's leaders have worked hard to modernize the nation's economy. Local ores are used in India's steel industry. But most Indians continue to raise crops such as tea, cotton and sugar cane. Progress is hampered by the high birth rate. Better irrigation methods have increased agricultural output. So has the **Green Revolution** which introduced farmers to new, high-yield seeds. These changes have enabled India to feed its surging population, but at the price of diverting attention away from industrial growth to food production.

Yearly Per Capita GDP of Latin American Nations (in dollars)			
	1960	**1970**	**1980**	**1988**
Chile	1,845	2,236	2,448	2,518
Argentina	2,384	3,075	3,359	2,862
Uruguay	2,352	2,478	3,221	2,989
Brazil	1,013	1,372	2,481	2,449
Paraguay	779	931	1,612	1,557
Bolivia	634	818	983	724
Peru	1,233	1,554	1,716	1,503
Ecuador	771	904	1,581	1,477
Colombia	927	1,157	1,595	1,739
Venezuela	3,879	4,941	5,225	4,544
Guyana	1,008	1,111	1,215	995
Surinam	887	2,337	3,722	3,420
Mexico	1,425	2,022	2,872	2,588
Guatemala	1,100	1,420	1,866	1,502
Honduras	619	782	954	851
El Salvador	832	1,032	1,125	995
Nicaragua	1,055	1,495	1,147	819
Costa Rica	1,435	1,825	2,394	2,335
Panama	1,264	2,017	2,622	2,229

5 **What has made it hard for developing nations to industrialize?**

_____

_____

_____

Economic Growth in East Asia: Japan and the Pacific Rim

In 1945, Japan came under the economic, military, and political control of American occupying forces. Here, as in Europe, the U.S. wanted to promote economic recovery. It redistributed land and broke up some of the *zaibatsu*, the giant combines that controlled industry. About 3.5 billion dollars were invested in the Japanese economy. The Japanese government worked closely with business corporations to expand industry. By 1980, Japan's economy was second only to that of the United States. Its TVs, VCRs, and CD-players dominated world markets and it had a 29% share of the worldwide automobile market. Economic expansion slowed down in the 1990's. Some felt Japan had entered a period of recession.

For most of the 1980's and 1990's, the **Pacific Rim** nations of South Korea, Hong Kong, Singapore, and Taiwan were big success stories as large producers of electronics, computers, and telecommunications equipment. Then in 1997, Pacific Rim nations ran into economic difficulties. Some of them then devalued their currencies to make their exports cheaper. They hoped this would allow them to undercut other countries in world markets. But it intensified their already fierce trade rivalry and in some cases led to further economic problems.

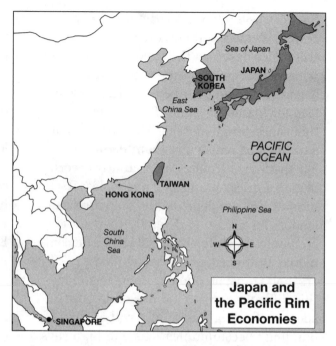

Japan and the Pacific Rim Economies

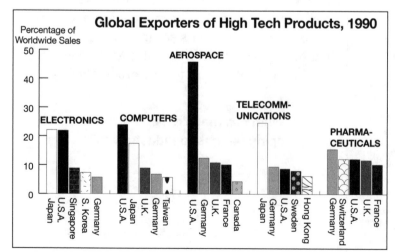

Global Exporters of High Tech Products, 1990

6   **How might co-operation help the economies of the Pacific Rim ?**

A   by allowing Japan to set economic policy for the region

B   by boosting trade within the region through the elimination of trade barriers

C   by eliminating competition between Japan and the United States

D   by allowing these nations to cut prices again by another currency devaluation

7   **The graph suggests that Asian manufacturers have had the largest share of which hi-tech market?**

A   automobiles

B   computers

C   electronics

D   telecommunications

Economic Recovery and Steps Towards Union in Europe

European nations, both winners and losers, came out of World War II with their economies in shambles. Fearing that this situation could lead to upheaval, the U.S. decided to provide financial aid. This program, known as the **Marshall Plan**, was a huge success. It allowed all of Western Europe to rebuild its economies with Germany becoming the leading industrial nation in Europe.

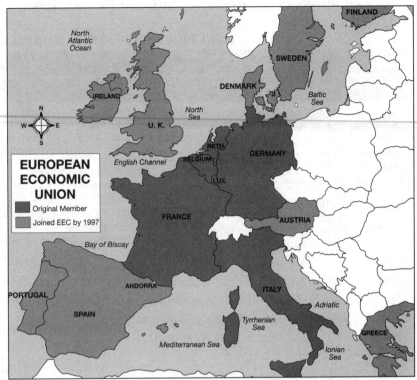

EUROPEAN ECONOMIC UNION
- Original Member
- Joined EEC by 1997

After the war, the nations of Western Europe led by France and Germany decided to put the past behind them and work towards unity. Their first goal was to achieve economic union. In 1957, the six nations shown on the map signed a treaty creating the **European Economic Community** (EEC) or Common Market. The member nations abolished tariffs among themselves and adopted a series of common economic policies. By 1995, membership had expanded to 15 nations. Today 60 per cent of all trade by EEC nations passes within the EEC. In 1999, 11 member nations began the process of changing over to a single European currency, the euro. A central European bank began operations. The hope is that economic union will make more efficient the economies of all involved.

Encouraged by the success of economic cooperation, EEC members moved towards political union. A European Parliament elected by the citizens of member nations meets regularly. A permanent civil service handles economic and administrative functions. In 1992, EEC members united politically to form the European Union.

8   In 1957, the founders of the EEC hoped that membership would move the European states to "an ever closer union." Has this goal been achieved? Explain your answer.

_____

_____

_____

_____

_____

_____

_____

_____

_____

_____

_____

The Chinese Communist Revolution

Mao Zedong's Economic and Cultural Revolution

The Chinese Revolution and its Aftermath

1950	1960	1970	1980	1990	2000

1949
Mao's troops beat Chiang's nationalists; Chiang forms Republic in Taiwan

1950–53
China aids North Korea

1953–58
Five-Year Plan; state to control industry & agriculture

1958–60
Great Leap Forward; co-ops merged into huge communes; millions starve

1960
Alliance with Soviets ends

1964
China explodes atom bomb

1966
Mao launches Cultural Revolution

1968
Mao ends Cultural Revolution

1972
Pres. Nixon visits China

1971
U.S. withdraws opposition & China admitted to UN

1976
Mao dies; Deng gains power

1979
China & U.S. form diplomatic ties

1977
Deng introduces economic reforms (Four Modernizations)

1989
Tiananmen Square massacre

1997
Deng dies; Jiang Zemin gains power

1997
Jiang allows state industries to sell stock

1997
Hong Kong reunited with China

In 1949, China's long civil war ended in victory for Mao Zedong and the Communists. Mao won over the people by his promise to reform land ownership, to end corruption, and to rid China of foreign meddling. The Communists modeled their regime on that of their Soviet allies. They set up two parallel organizations: the Communist Party and the government. Mao headed both. The party set policy; the government carried it out.

In 1950, China's landlords were dispossessed of their land—the million or so who resisted were killed. This land was divided up among the peasants. But then, during the first five-year plan, these small holdings were combined into collective farms of about 250 households each. In the Great Leap Forward, the collective farms were combined into communes containing about 25,000 people each. Peasants were organized into military-style units. Working, eating, sleeping, and child-rearing became communal activities. The people hated this regimented lifestyle, and years of crop failure caused famines that took 25 million lives.

The first five-year plan centralized planning for industry as well as agriculture. It nationalized all private companies and set production targets for steel and other goods.

It had modest success. But poor planning hampered further industrial growth.

During the early 1960's Mao took a back seat and new leaders issued incentives to encourage hard work. Mao decided that these changes weakened the revolutionary spirit. To regain control and revive the revolution, he encouraged youngsters to leave school and form military units called Red Guards. Their task was to search out individuals who criticized the government or had special privileges. This movement is known as the **Cultural Revolution**; it disastrously disrupted industry and agriculture and was ended in 1968.

9 **The Chinese had many needs. Which needs did Mao satisfy and which did he fail to satisfy?**

_____

_____

_____

_____

_____

_____

Deng Xiaoping Introduces Limited Reforms

China's foreign policy had changed radically under Mao. In 1960, the Sino-Soviet alliance came to an end. The two powers were competing to control the spread of communism among developing nations. This split allowed relations between China and the U.S. to improve. President Nixon visited China in 1972. In 1979 the two nations established diplomatic ties.

After Mao died in 1976, **Deng Xiaoping** emerged as China's new leader. Deng supported the economic growth that Prime Minister **Zhou Enlai** had introduced after the Cultural Revolution. Deng introduced a plan known as the **Four Modernizations**. To increase food output, communes were replaced by family-run farms that used land leased from the state. The government took some produce as rent; families could keep or sell the remainder. Managers were given the power to make industrial plants more efficient; they could use supply and demand to determine production levels. Individuals were allowed to own small businesses and private property. Foreign investment and technology were welcomed; foreigners could even set up their own businesses in special economic zones.

Deng's reforms were a tremendous success. The economy grew and the standard of living rose. New ideas entered China through the newly opened doors to the West. Chinese students learned about democracy and demanded political freedom and civil rights for the Chinese people. In 1989, they held massive demonstrations in Tiananmen Square in the heart of Beijing. A million sympathizers joined them. But when they began to demand that Deng resign, the hard-liners took control. Tanks fired on the crowds killing and wounding many. The pro-democracy movement was crushed.

Deng Xiaoping and Jimmy Carter meet to sign diplomatic agreements.

10 Why was Deng willing to introduce the West's capitalist system but not its human rights?

_____

_____

_____

_____

_____

11 How did the dynastic idea of a mandate from heaven (see page 81) influence the way Deng handled student demonstrators?

_____

_____

_____

_____

Collapse of European Imperialism

Independence Movements and Independence in Africa

For decades, nationalism had been widespread among Africa's European-educated officials and businesspeople. After World War II nationalism became a mass movement. The colonial powers were too weakened by the war to offer any serious resistance to the independence movements.

In 1945, only four African nations were independent. By 1994, the whole continent was governed by Africans of non-European descent. The first nations to win their independence were in North Africa. The Gold Coast was the first Sub-Saharan nation to win its freedom. In 1957, **Kwame Nkrumah** led a general strike which persuaded the British to grant independence. The nation was renamed Ghana. For some nations, Nigeria for example, independence was achieved smoothly. For others, it was won only after violent struggle.

South Africa was the last nation to achieve black self-rule. Before 1994 it had been ruled by Dutch-descended Afrikaners. They imposed a policy of **apartheid** on the country. Races were legally segregated. Blacks were denied many rights of citizenship and were moved to rural areas. Under global pressure, President **de Klerk** and his government abolished apartheid and freed the jailed nationalist leader, **Nelson Mandela**. In 1994, black Africans were elected to two-thirds of the seats in the legislature, which then elected Mandela as President.

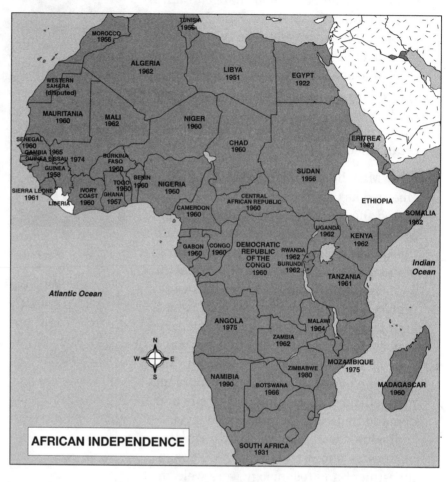

AFRICAN INDEPENDENCE

Independence did not solve Africa's problems. Some nations have thrived, but many more have experienced civil war, corrupt dictatorships, and economic decline (see Chapter 17).

12A According to the text, which African nation was independent in 1945 but ruled by people of European origins?

_____

12B How did this nation's black citizens come to participate in government?

_____

_____

_____

176

India: Independence and Partition

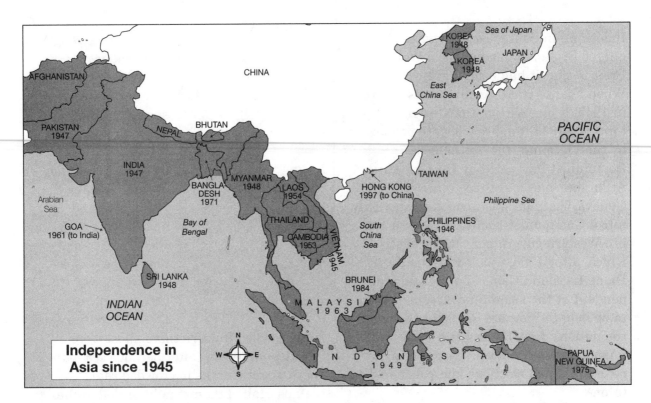

Independence in Asia since 1945

In 1947, the Indian subcontinent won its independence from Britain. Ali Jinnah had insisted that Moslems have their own state, so India was partitioned into two nations: India in the center with Pakistan to the west and to the east in what is now Bangladesh. Burma (Myanmar) and Ceylon (Sri Lanka) became independent the following year. Many Hindus found themselves in Pakistan while many Moslems remained in India. This led 12 million people to migrate amid horrendous violence. Millions of Moslems still live in India and religious tensions remain high.

Jawaharlal Nehru was India's first prime minister. He introduced a Western-style government based on universal suffrage, religious freedom, social equality, and the abolition of caste. The Indian economy successfully combined government-run industry with private enterprise. Nehru led the developing nations in practicing **nonalignment** with either of the super-powers.

Religious and political conflict remained a problem. In the 1980's, Sikh separatists demanded independence and assassinated Prime Minister **Gandhi** (Nehru's daughter).

Relations between Pakistan and India remain unstable. Both nations want to control Kashmir and tensions increased after first India and then Pakistan exploded nuclear devices in 1998.

Other developments in the region: After fierce fighting, Bangladesh split off from Pakistan (1971). In 1983, an endless war erupted in Sri Lanka with Hindu Tamils fighting against the ruling Buddhist Sinhalese.

13 Apart from Pakistan, which nation that used to be part of British India is a Moslem state?

A Bangladesh

B India

C Myanmar

D Sri Lanka

Turmoil and Tragedy in Southeast Asia

Indochina in Southeast Asia was conquered by Japan during World War II. Prior to that it had been a French colony. When France tried to reassert its control in 1945, it met with nationalist resistance. In 1954, the French were defeated by the Vietminh (the Vietnamese Communist Party) led by **Ho Chi Minh**. At an international peace conference in Geneva, Vietnam was divided temporarily into a Communist-dominated North and a pro-Western government in the south which, after 1955, was led by Ngo Dinh Diem. Laos and Cambodia became independent at the same time. Elections were to be held in Vietnam in 1956 to decide the nation's fate. Diem was a weak, unpopular leader. With U.S. backing, he refused to hold elections and ruled as dictator.

U.S. policy in Southeast Asia was based on the **domino theory**—if one nation fell to communism, it was held that its neighbors would follow. Accordingly, when Communist guerrillas (the **Viet Cong**) began to win wide support in South Vietnam, the U.S. entered the conflict. First, it approved of Diem's murder and replacement. Then it sent advisers to Vietnam. In 1964, North Vietnam allegedly fired on two U.S. destroyers. President **Lyndon Johnson** used this incident to persuade Congress to agree to send American troops to Vietnam.

By 1968 there were half a million American soldiers in Vietnam; heavy U.S. bombing raids were routine. North Vietnam began to send troops and supplies (some supplies came from China and the U.S.S.R.) south along the Ho Chi Minh trail. Superior numbers and modern technology were no match for guerrilla tactics and the dedication of the Communist troops. When the Viet Cong launched the Tet Offensive, Americans back home realized that their troops had failed

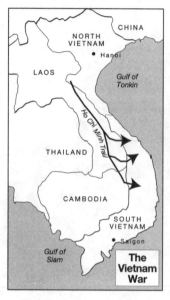

The Vietnam War

to dent the strength of its enemy. Opposition to the war began to spread. In 1973, there was a cease-fire and the last U.S. troops left Vietnam. Two years later, the North attacked again. The South was defeated and the nation was re-united under Communist rule. Over 1.5 million refugees fled from Vietnam. Most were **Boat people** who, after perilous sea journeys, spent months in crowded refugee camps. Half of them finally settled in the United States.

The war had spread to other parts of Indochina. U.S. planes bombed Cambodia in 1969 to destroy Viet Cong bases and halt the southward flow of supplies. The bombing worsened the conflict between pro-U.S. forces and the Cambodian Communists led by Pol Pot. After Pol Pot's victory, he tried to remake the nation into an agricultural society and ordered everyone to leave the cities and towns. Famine, disease, and government-sponsored genocide followed this upheaval and one-third of the population died. Vietnamese intervention led to the overthrow of Pol Pot in 1975.

14   **Did the outcome of the Vietnam War support the domino theory? Provide support for your answer.**

_____

_____

_____

Conflict and Change in the Middle East

The Creation of Israel and the Arab Response

Israel and its Neighbors, 1947–1998

1948	1958	1968	1978	1988	1998

1948–9
Defeat of Arab attack on Israel

1947
UN splits Palestine into Arab & Jewish states

1949
700,000 Palestinians homeless; many move to refugee camps in Jordan

1956
Suez crisis; Israel invades Egypt; UN troops patrol Israeli-Egyptian border

1967
Six Day War; Israel wins Sinai, Golan, Gaza, & West Bank

1967
Palestinian refugees flee West Bank; PLO gains support

1973
Yom Kippur War; Egypt & Syria invade Israel; attacks repulsed with U.S. aid; Arabs ban oil exports to Israeli allies

1978
Sadat & Begin sign Camp David accords; Egypt recognizes Israel which gives up Sinai

1982
Israel invades Lebanon & destroys PLO bases

1993
Israel & PLO recognize each other; agree to future self-rule for West Bank Palestinians

1994
Israel and Jordan sign peace treaty

1996–98
Terrorism by militant Palestinians; Israeli troop reprisals

After 1945, the Middle East nations that remained under European control won their independence. The last to do so was Palestine. Britain, which was responsible for the region, was unable to reconcile the conflicting promises it had made the Jews and Arabs who lived there. The UN solved the problem in 1947 by dividing Palestine into two states, one Jewish and the other Arab. Neighboring Arab states rejected this solution—they argued that Arabs had lived there for centuries, whereas Jews were recent arrivals—and immediately attacked the new state of Israel. Israel fought off its attackers. Although Jordan now occupied the West Bank of the Jordan River, and Egypt had seized the Gaza Strip, Israel had survived and won part of Jerusalem. Over 700,000 Arab Palestinians fled and became refugees in neighboring Arab states.

Over the next 24 years, there would be three more wars between Israel and its neighbors. Egypt, Syria, and Jordan, often with financial backing from Saudi Arabia, military aid from the Soviets, and emotional pressure from the homeless Palestinians, tried to destroy Israel. Israel with U.S. military and financial support, fought for its life. After its victory in the Six-Day War, Israel seized territory from its attackers: the Golan Heights from Syria, the Sinai Peninsula from Egypt, and the West Bank from Jordan. There followed decades of diplomatic activity among the Mideast nations and the United States. The U.S. wanted to help Israel restore friendly relations with its neighbors. The Arab states wanted Israel to return their territories.

By the 1990's, the issues had changed. The **PLO** (Palestine Liberation Organization), led by Yasir Arafat, pressed for self-rule for Arabs in Gaza and the West Bank. A tentative agreement was reached in 1993, but Palestinian terrorism and Israeli reprisals continue to threaten the peace.

15A What issues have troubled relations between Israel and its neighbors?

_____

_____

15B What efforts have been made to resolve these issues?

_____

_____

Arab Nationalism, Oil Production, and Regional Conflict

Since 1945, the history of the Middle East has been dominated by the region's role as an oil producer, by Arab nationalism, and by the influence of **Islamic fundamentalism** (the latter topic will be explored in the next chapter). In 1945, the Arab states shown on the map formed an Arab League to unify the Arab nations and to oppose a Jewish state. In 1956, President Nasser emerged from the Suez crisis as leader of the Arab world. In 1958, Syria and Egypt merged as the United Arab Republic under his fiercely anti-Western leadership. The region became polarized after Nasser-inspired Arab nationalism spread to Iraq, Jordan, and Lebanon. Feeling threatened, King Hussein of Jordan and Lebanese Christians sought and received aid from the U.S.

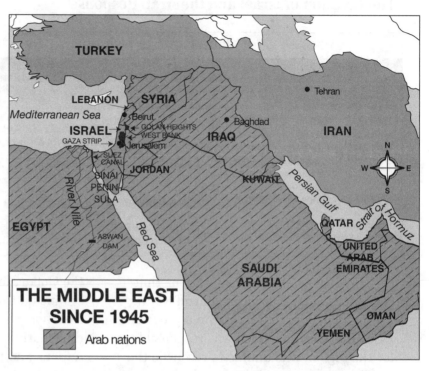

Two major non-Arab Middle East states were also allied with the West. Iran grew closer to the West after Shah Pahlavi returned to power with support from the U.S. Since 1952, Turkey had been a member of NATO and other anti-Soviet alliances.

The West had signed very favorable agreements with the region's oil producers. But by 1970, the Persian Gulf states had gained control of their oil resources. They founded the Organization of Petroleum Exporting Countries (**OPEC**) to coordinate oil production. During the Yom Kippur War, OPEC cut back on oil production and banned oil shipments to Israel's allies. This created a global energy crisis that caused oil prices to soar and created high inflation. Prices had fallen sharply by 1986, but oil profits still bring great wealth to oil-producing states.

In 1979, the Shah of Iran fled and power passed to the **Ayatollah Khomeini**. He created a republic based on Islamic values. When Iran tried to export its religious revolution to neighboring Iraq, a border dispute became an eight-year war. After it ended, **Saddam Hussein** of Iraq invaded oil-rich Kuwait in 1991. Coalition forces led by the U.S. defeated him in the brief **Gulf War**.

16 **Explain the factors that have made it difficult to resolve the conflicts in the Middle East.**

_____

_____

_____

_____

_____

_____

_____

The Collapse of Communism, 1989-1991

The Breakup of the Soviet Union

The Dissolution of the Soviet Union

1980	1985	1990	1995	2000

1979 Soviets invade Afghanistan

1985 Gorbachev new General Secretary of Communist Party

1986 New policies of glasnost & perestroika

1988 Elections for Congress of People's Deputies

1989 Soviets leave Afghanistan

1990 Lithuanian Parliament declares independence

1990 Yeltsin elected President of Russia

1991 Union Treaty gives republics more self-government

1991 Failed coup; collapse of Communist Party; Gorbachev resigns as Gen. Secretary

1991 Republics declare independence; form Commonwealth of Independent States; Gorbachev resigns as President

1994–96 Russia fights breakaway Chechnya

1992 Yeltsin ends price controls

1995 Russia to hold all ex-Soviet nuclear weapons

1998 Russia defaults on international loans

By 1986, the Soviet system had become inefficient and corrupt. The nation was involved in a draining war in Afghanistan. It could no longer afford to compete in an arms race with the United States. A new President **Mikhail Gorbachev** introduced a policy of **glasnost** (openness). People were allowed more freedom of expression, dissidents were released from jail, and Soviet Jews were allowed to emigrate. This was followed by **perestroika**, an attempt to rebuild the economy. Factory managers were given more freedom and some private enterprise was permitted.

The slow pace of economic reform encouraged criticism (which was now legal). Rival leaders like **Boris Yeltsin** emerged. At the same time, a wave of nationalism swept through the non-Russian Soviet republics. The Baltic States declared their independence in 1990. But hard-line conservatives were opposed to reform and feared that the U.S.S.R. would disintegrate. Gorbachev tried to appease them, but this only antagonized radical reformers like Yeltsin. In 1991, the hard-liners staged a coup which failed when Yeltsin and key army units remained loyal to Gorbachev. Shortly after this, the Communist Party collapsed and the remaining Soviet republics declared their independence, Gorbachev resigned as General Secretary and as President.

The Soviet Union was replaced by a loose confederation called the Commonwealth of Independent States. Yeltsin, as President of Russia, became the most powerful figure in the region. He began to convert Russia to a market economy. Price controls were ended, inefficient factories were closed, and many state-owned industries passed into private hands. But these changes caused a rise in prices and unemployment. Production fell, government was lax, and crime and corruption soared. The nation remains unstable.

17 **What internal factors were most responsible for the collapse of the Soviet Union. List them in descending order of importance.**

_____

_____

_____

_____

_____

Independence and Change in Central and Eastern Europe

The Soviet-dominated states of Eastern Europe faced the same problems as the Soviet Union. Their inefficient factories produced basic goods but little for the consumer, their land was polluted, and their governments extremely unpopular.

Already there had been signs of rebellion. The Polish trade union Solidarity led by **Lech Walesa** staged a massive strike in 1980. Hungary had introduced some democratic reforms. In 1989, Gorbachev made two moves that told the old Communist leaders to expect no help from the Soviets. First, he halved the number of Soviet troops in Eastern Europe. Second, he declared "no external force [should] interfere in the domestic affairs of socialist countries."

Against this background, the Communist regimes in Czechoslovakia, Poland, East Germany, Hungary, Romania, and Bulgaria toppled one by one in 1989. There was little violence except in Romania. Amid ecstatic celebration, the Berlin Wall was torn down. Germany was reunited as its eastern half was absorbed by capitalist, democratic West Germany. The playwright **Vaclav Havel** became president of Czechoslovakia which split into the Czech Republic and Slovakia in 1993.

The burden of out-dated industries, huge debts, and worthless currencies has created turmoil in all the East European states. Some nations have re-elected Communist

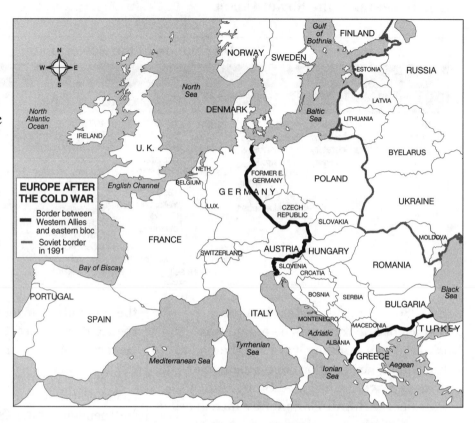

EUROPE AFTER THE COLD WAR
— Border between Western Allies and eastern bloc
— Soviet border in 1991

governments. Poland, Hungary, and the Czech Republic have the strongest industries and seem most likely to become economically prosperous democracies. Their ties with the West were reinforced by the decision to admit them to NATO in 1999.

18 Which member of the old Eastern bloc is most likely to prosper in the future and why?

_____

_____

_____

_____

_____

_____

_____

Revolution and Conflict in Latin America

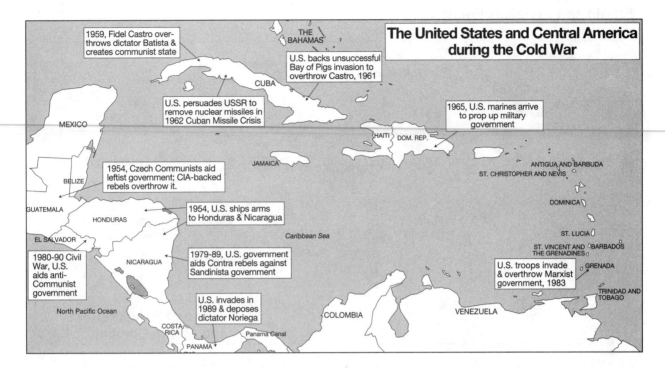

The United States and Central America during the Cold War

1959, Fidel Castro overthrows dictator Batista & creates communist state

U.S. backs unsuccessful Bay of Pigs invasion to overthrow Castro, 1961

U.S. persuades USSR to remove nuclear missiles in 1962 Cuban Missile Crisis

1965, U.S. marines arrive to prop up military government

1954, Czech Communists aid leftist government; CIA-backed rebels overthrow it.

1954, U.S. ships arms to Honduras & Nicaragua

1979-89, U.S. government aids Contra rebels against Sandinista government

1980-90 Civil War, U.S. aids anti-Communist government

U.S. troops invade & overthrow Marxist government, 1983

U.S. invades in 1989 & deposes dictator Noriega

THE BAHAMAS · CUBA · MEXICO · HAITI · DOM. REP. · JAMAICA · ANTIGUA AND BARBUDA · ST. CHRISTOPHER AND NEVIS · BELIZE · DOMINICA · GUATEMALA · HONDURAS · ST. LUCIA · EL SALVADOR · Caribbean Sea · ST. VINCENT AND THE GRENADINES · BARBADOS · NICARAGUA · GRENADA · TRINIDAD AND TOBAGO · North Pacific Ocean · COSTA RICA · COLOMBIA · VENEZUELA · Panama Canal · PANAMA

Since 1945 many parts of Latin America have had political upheavals, most of them stemming from the poverty of the peasants and urban poor. Communism promised to redistribute the wealth and this gave it great appeal among the poor. The threat of revolution increased middle- and upper-class support for right-wing, military governments.

In 1946 Argentina elected Juan Peron President. He set about establishing a fascist-style dictatorial regime. Initially it had wide support as he raised industrial wages, nationalized foreign-owned industries, and built schools and hospitals. His wife **Eva** inspired the devotion of millions of Argentinians. After her death and amid severe economic decline, Perón lost power (1955) but then staged a brief comeback in the 1970's. By the 1980's a harsh military dictatorship had taken power; 20,000 citizens simply disappeared. Silent protests staged by the mothers of the missing gained worldwide attention, and eventually Argentina returned to democracy.

Central America and the Caribbean Islands saw the most turmoil during this period. The map shows the occasions upon which the U.S. or Communist powers intervened in the region. **Fidel Castro** seized power in Cuba in 1959 and introduced a Communist-style **authoritarian** government. His support for revolutionary movements in Latin America and his close alliance with the Soviet Union attracted the enmity of the United States. The **Sandinista** government of Nicaragua was one of the groups that Castro aided. Their left-wing policies aroused the hostility of the U.S., which supplied massive aid to an opposition force known as the **Contras**.

19 The amount of conflict in Central America declined in the 1990's. What do you think are some of the reasons for this?

_____

_____

_____

Tensions in the 1990's

Ethnic and Religious Conflict

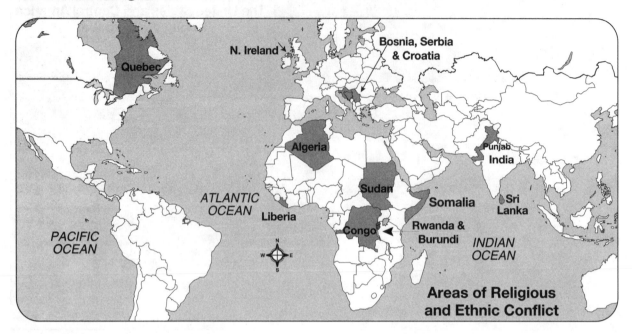

Areas of Religious and Ethnic Conflict

Overpopulation in the developing world often worsens already existing ethnic tensions. It sometimes drives thirsty, starving populations to migrate to neighboring lands where they are rarely welcome.

Such ethnic tensions have led to deadly results in many parts of East Africa since 1980. In Somalia in the 1980's, rival clans were struggling for control of the government when drought struck. Fighting prevented food supplies from reaching the hungry. Ethnic rivalry led to violent conflict among the surging populations of Rwanda and Burundi during the '90's. The Hutu-led government of Rwanda encouraged the killing of countless numbers of their Tutsi countrymen and then was overtaken by a Tutsi-led rebellion. Half a million people were killed and two million fled to Congo (formerly Zaire) and other neighboring states. The 1.2 million refugees who were camped in Congo faced mass starvation when ethnic conflict erupted there, too, and hundreds of thousands returned to Rwanda. Soon the conflict between the Tutsis and Hutus spread to Burundi and surfaced again in civil wars in the Congo.

There has also been widespread economic and political unrest in North Africa. In Algeria, a military-led government has been fiercely challenged by militant Islamic groups, infuriated by the fact that the military refused to accept the victory of Islamic parties in national elections. Islamic terrorists adopted tactics involving the indiscriminate killing of whole communities of neutral men, women, and children.

Sri Lanka is another area with a high birth rate that has been torn by decades of ethnic strife. The island republic is inhabited by 18 million people, most of whom are Buddhist Sinhalese; a minority are Hindu Tamils. Resentment of Sinhalese control has led the Tamils to mount a guerrilla war in which 40,000 Tamils have died and many more have fled to India. To the north, on the densely populated Indo-Ganges Plain, Sikh separatists want to expel Hindus from Punjab and make it a Sikh state. Tensions remain high in the area.

Conflict usually has multiple causes. Africa's ethnic struggles were made worse by population pressure, but they also had historical roots. The boundaries drawn by the colonial powers rarely took account of tribal areas. Instead, different tribes, often those with a tradition of rivalry and conflict, were combined into one nation.

In other parts of the world, population pressures were not an issue; regional conflicts had their roots in history. Religious conflict has torn Ireland for centuries. Until the 1600's, most Irish were Catholics. Then the English government encouraged colonists, particularly Scots Protestants, to settle there. Tensions between the two faiths continued into this century. Beginning in the 1970's, Catholics and Protestants in Northern Ireland began fighting a guerrilla war. The British army tried, with modest success, to keep the warring parties apart. Peace efforts were unsuccessful—neither side trusted the other—until 1998 when a new peace accord was supported by all the major parties.

Most Canadians are English speakers, a result of British control of Canada from 1763 to 1926. Britain had won control of Canada from the French, and Quebec Province is still dominated by a French-speaking majority, many of whom want independence. Although other Canadians oppose this move, the referenda held in Quebec showed that separatists are close to obtaining the majority they need.

In parts of Eastern Europe, the collapse of authoritarian Communist states allowed their multi-ethnic peoples to go their own way. Yugoslavia's main ethnic/religious groups—Roman Catholic Croats, Eastern Orthodox Serbs, and Moslem Bosnians— had lived for centuries in mixed communities. But when first Croatia and soon thereafter Bosnia declared independence, deadly fighting broke out. The Serbs, supported by the Serb-led government in what

remained of Yugoslavia, at first took over sections of Croatia. They were eventually defeated by the Croats and large numbers expelled as refugees. In Bosnia, Serbs, Croats, and Moslem Bosnians all fought desperately against each other. The Serbs took over large chunks of the country and began the process of **ethnic cleansing**, expelling or murdering the Moslems under their control. UN peace-keeping troops arrived in 1995, and Bosnia was subdivided largely along ethnic lines. But the ethnic conflicts of the area continue. The latest outbreak was in the Yugoslav province of Kosovo where Yugoslav Serbian troops attempted to ruthlessly suppress a rebellion by Moslem Albanians. Pressure from the U.S. and the UN tried to bring stability to the area, with unclear results.

A different kind of racial conflict exists in many European nations which used to be ethnically homogeneous. Since the 1950's large groups of Indians, Pakistanis, West Indians, Turks, and Algerians have settled in northern Europe. Some immigrants were guest workers who provided unskilled labor. Some had lived in Europe's colonies. Although laws ban discrimination, racial prejudice makes these immigrant communities widely unpopular.

20 **What do the causes of the ethnic conflicts in Ireland, Sri Lanka, and Bosnia have in common?**

_____

_____

21 **How would you characterize the ethnic conflicts in both Rwanda and Bosnia?**

_____

_____

Other Hot Spots Across the Globe

Iraq under Saddam Hussein became an outcast nation. After its attempts to take over Kuwait were repulsed in the Desert Storm War, it was forced to allow UN weapons inspectors to enter the country. In 1998 it threw the inspectors out and intensified its belligerent policies. Tension remains high.

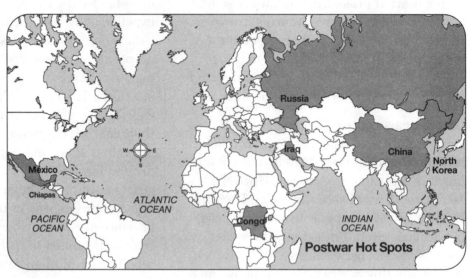

Postwar Hot Spots

Mexico's economy has had many ups and downs. For years it has had to fight inflation. In the early 1990's it had to borrow large sums from the U.S. to stay afloat— all of it was repaid. While NAFTA, the free-trade agreement with the U.S. and Canada, has spurred economic growth, the country's poor have not always benefitted. In 1994 the people of the southern province of Chiapas began an ongoing rebellion, complaining about poverty and mistreatment by the government.

North Korea isolated itself as a doctrinaire Communist state. Unable to cope with an agricultural disaster in the 1990's, it sought outside aid to keep millions from starving and allowed some contacts with South Korea, the U.S., and other countries. But its large army and attempts to build nuclear weapons continued to make it a threat to its neighbors.

Since turning away from communism, Russia has had to face a whole new set of problems. Government mismanagement linked with business corruption has hampered economic growth. The standard of living has fallen. The government has failed to resolve such major problems as crime, poverty, unemployment, and pollution. If law and order collapse, a new authoritarian regime could seize power.

China's economy has grown in great leaps, but its growth has been uneven. Most new industry is located on the coast where millions of peasants from the interior have migrated in search of work. It remains to be seen whether there will be new demands for political freedom and how the government will handle them.

Much of Africa has been beset by revolutions and counter-revolutions with continual warfare. Typical is the Congo where guerrilla forces under Laurent Kabila seized control from a totally corrupt government in 1997. The new rulers seemed just as bad as the old ones and before long a new revolution broke out with both sides heavily supported by different neighboring countries.

22 Which of these hot spots do you think is most likely to explode into violent conflict and why?

_____

_____

_____

17. Global Connections and Interactions

In this final chapter, we will review current trends and issues from a global perspective. The most unfortunate aspect of the current era is the increased divergence between the developing and the industrial worlds. The rich are getting richer and the poor are getting poorer. Poverty has prompted a vast migration of people into the industrial world. Within developing nations, poverty and the hope of a better life has encouraged many families to leave the countryside and move into the cities. But the cities have few jobs to offer, and vast squatter camps build up on their outskirts. A principal reason for poverty is population pressure. The birth rate in developing nations is very high. Farmers need more land to feed their families. This has encouraged them (and others) to cut down millions of acres of forest and to replace trees with crops. Unfortunately, forest soil is rarely rich. Moreover, large-scale deforestation affects the world's climate. So does the pollution created by the burning of fossil fuels; for this, the industrialized world is largely responsible.

Many developing nations have begun to industrialize—some with marked success. India and China have been major industrial powers for decades. Mexico and some South American nations are increasing their already large manufacturing output. But there is little industry in Sub-Saharan Africa, and its nations continue to export their raw materials. Many of the ex-colonies still maintain ties with the nations that used to rule them. But these relationships have created cultural connections rather than economic prosperity.

On the other hand, the industrialized world *is* prospering. Science and technology constantly generate new kinds of products. Medical research is producing medicines that allow those who can afford them to live longer and more pain-free lives. Capitalist competition occasionally brings downturns—for instance, the Pacific Rim in 1998. But businesses are mindful that they now operate on a global basis and that a recession in one area can cause problems across the world. For this reason, there is a good deal of cooperation among the wealthiest nations to help their ailing trading partners.

Since the collapse of Communism, the Western powers, especially the United States, have been dominant in world political and economic affairs. They have tried to export their democratic values along with their goods, particularly in the direction of China. Some of the nations that have industrialized in recent years feel a pull between modern, Western ideas and customs, and their own traditional ways. The Japanese have managed to combine the two. But in the Islamic world, the West's materialism and the role it assigns to women challenge fundamental Moslem attitudes.

Social Trends

Population Pressure and Poverty

In 1990, the world's population was 5.3 billion people. This figure is expected to double by 2025. Ninety-five percent of this growth will occur in the developing nations of Africa, Southeast Asia, and Latin America, and in India and China. Europe's population increases by 0.22 percent per year; Africa's increase is three per cent. There are two reasons for this difference. First, families in nations with a high standard of living generally have small families. Second, improved health care in developing nations is reducing infant mortality rates while the birth rate remains high. The only brakes on population growth in Africa and parts of Asia are hunger and the AIDS epidemic.

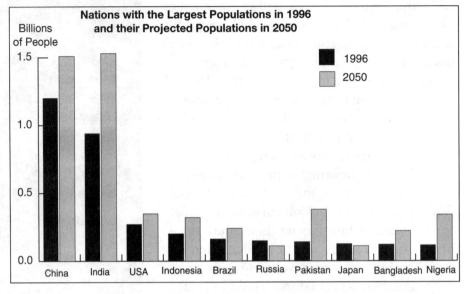

Nations with the Largest Populations in 1996 and their Projected Populations in 2050

To maintain a nation's overall size, each woman needs to give birth to 2.1 children. But women in many developed nations are having fewer children than this—Italian women, for example, have on average 1.5 children. This means that the populations of developed nations contain an increasing number of elderly. About 18.3 percent of Swedes are over 65. By contrast, the developing nations have far younger populations—in the poorest African nations, only two or three percent of the people are over 65. In most Arab countries, four out of 10 people are under 15 years old.

Old people and the very young tend to consume more resources while placing greater demands on their nations' social and health-care services. The earth and its resources cannot sustain the demands that come from the billions of new babies born in the developing world and from the stable but "greedy" populations of the industrialized world (for example, the United States with four per cent of the world's people consumes one-quarter of its oil).

1 What kind of problems will face those nations with the largest projected population growth?

_____

_____

_____

_____

_____

_____

_____

_____

_____

Urbanization

Most nations with growing populations are **agrarian**. When the available farmland cannot feed the increasing number of mouths, young people often migrate to the cities. At present there are 1.4 billion people living in the urban areas of developing countries; there will be 4.1 billion by 2025. Latin America will be the most urbanized area in the world with nearly 85 percent of its people living in cities. More than half the people of Africa will be city-dwellers. In 2000 there will be 20 cities with populations of over 11 million—16 of them in developing nations.

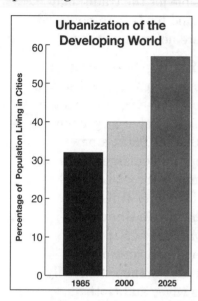

Urbanization of the Developing World

Percentage of Population Living in Cities

1985 · 2000 · 2025

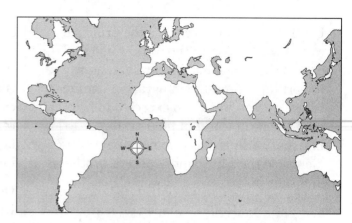

We tend to think of great cities as centers of wealth, creativity, and culture. But unless massive amounts are spent to improve their infrastructures, the megacities of Latin America and Asia will be centers of poverty and social collapse. Population density alone will make it impossible for these cities to provide the housing, sanitation, transportation, and communication systems that we associate with urban life. There are 143,000 people per square mile in Lagos, Nigeria; in New York this figure is 11,400. How will the citizens of Lagos get fed, especially during times of famine? Where will the billions of new city dwellers find jobs?

2A On the map, show the location of at least five of the cities included in the graph below.

2B In which continent are the majority of the graph's ten cities located?

_____

_____

2C What can you say about the rate of growth from 1971 to 1991 of megacities in Japan and the U.S. versus Latin America?

_____

_____

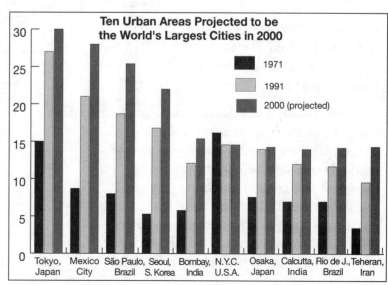

Ten Urban Areas Projected to be the World's Largest Cities in 2000

- 1971
- 1991
- 2000 (projected)

Tokyo, Japan · Mexico City · São Paulo, Brazil · Seoul, S. Korea · Bombay, India · N.Y.C. U.S.A. · Osaka, Japan · Calcutta, India · Rio de J., Brazil · Teheran, Iran

The Status of Women: Tradition and Change

Until the twentieth century, the principal role of women across the world was to take care of the home and family. There were important exceptions: in agrarian communities, women were also expected to help with the farm work. In industrialized nations, working-class women might work alongside their husbands, fathers, brothers, and sons in factories and workshops.

A Suffragist

By 1900, women on many continents were pressing for change. In Europe and North and South America they had already won the right to be educated. Now they wanted to extend their rights as citizens. In particular, most, though not all women, wanted to be able to vote and campaigned hard for the **suffrage**. Most men vigorously resisted this demand. It was only after women had successfully replaced them in factory and farm jobs during World War I that this resistance cracked. By 1930, most women in the West could vote. They had also gained more cultural and social freedom. Many women smoked for the first time. During the 1920's, dress styles were more casual: it was now permissible for women to wear make-up and short skirts.

After the Russian Revolution, the Communist Party promised "to liberate women from all the burdens of antiquated methods of housekeeping" by providing nurseries and central laundries. The need to combine family responsibility with work kept women out of management positions in the party and bureaucracy. But the ideal of sexual equality remained alive. Women's

experience under another Communist regime—Mao's China—was similar. The law made them equal with men, and state-run nurseries were created to care for their children while they worked. However, they remained responsible for the traditional household chores and top government and industrial jobs were not open to them.

During World War II, women once again worked in armaments factories and served in a supporting role in the military. In the USSR they even saw combat as ground soldiers and pilots. By the 1960's, a new women's movement had emerged. Its aim was to win economic and social as well as legal and political equality. It began in France where **Simone de Beauvoir** labeled women *The Second Sex*. Betty Friedan and other American women attacked the idea that women could only find fulfillment as wives and mothers. Women's groups in the West engaged in **consciousness-raising** sessions to explore their attitudes towards relationships, work, and the family.

3   **Describe two ways that the role of women differs in traditional societies and in modern, industrialized societies.**

_____

_____

_____

_____

_____

_____

_____

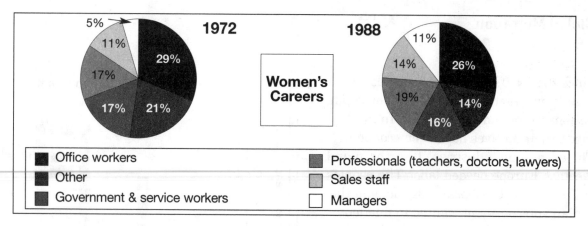

Women's Careers

1972 — 29%, 21%, 17%, 17%, 11%, 5%

1988 — 26%, 14%, 16%, 19%, 14%, 11%

- ■ Office workers
- ■ Other
- ■ Government & service workers
- ■ Professionals (teachers, doctors, lawyers)
- □ Sales staff
- □ Managers

The women's movement has won itself enemies as well as friends in the West. Many men have found themselves at odds with some **feminist** attitudes. A pocketbook issue has been the fear that women might steal men's jobs. Some female homemakers were upset when feminists claimed that women needed a life outside the home. The women in ethnic minorities have claimed that the movement has ignored their needs. Certainly women's and men's roles have changed since 1966. Men now handle many family tasks that used to be considered "women's work." Many more women have joined the work force, and, as the graph shows, many of them have moved into careers previously dominated by men. But even today very few women have moved into top management.

Women have moved away from personal freedom towards traditionalism in the fundamentalist Islamic nations. They must wear black chadors that cover them from head to toe. They are encouraged to have large families, further stimulating population growth. An Iraqi poster proclaims: "Bear a child, and you pierce an arrow in the enemy's eye." A Westerner might want to tackle widespread poverty with a massive

Adult Female Literacy Rate in Selected Nations (Islamic states in italics)	
Yemen Arab Rep.	*3%*
Burkhina Faso	6%
Afghanistan	*8%*
Sudan	*14%*
Honduras	58%
Singapore	*79%*
Thailand	88%
Canada	93%
Chile	96%
Hungary	98%

education program. But where Islamic fundamentalism is strong, the education of females is unthinkable. And with few exceptions, most Islamic women accept the restrictions imposed on them.

Use the graph to answer the next two questions.

4   In 1972 the largest group of women

   A   held jobs labeled "other"

   B   held office jobs

   C   were managers

   D   were saleswomen

5   Which group of women workers had the largest <u>percentage</u> growth from 1972 to 1988?

   A   government workers

   B   managers

   C   office workers

   D   saleswomen

6   Singapore's high level of female literacy probably reflects the fact that it

   A   has a high birth rate

   B   has a rural economy

   C   is economically prosperous

   D   is not an Islamic nation

Global Migration

Since the 1950's there has been a large-scale movement of peoples from developing nations to the industrial world. In most cases, their motives have been economic. The expanding industries of Northern and Western Europe needed labor. The peoples of Turkey, the Caribbean, Algeria, and the Indian sub-continent wanted to find jobs and improve their living standards. Some migrants like the Turks and Italians who moved to Germany and Scandinavia were "guest workers" providing unskilled labor. Sometimes this migration followed the path of old colonial relationships: West Indians, Indians, and Pakistanis settled in Britain and Algerians settled in France.

Prior to these migrations, the European host countries had been largely homogeneous ethnically. Although their laws banned discrimination, racial prejudice made immigrant communities unpopular in many areas. In Germany, millions of ethnic Germans from the east moved west. This provoked fear among West Germans that jobs would become scarcer and their living standards would decline.

Political as well as economic factors have affected immigration to North America. Until 1965, U.S. immigration policy favored Northern and Western Europeans. New laws set quotas by hemisphere instead of by country and doubled the number of immigrants who could enter the country each year. The wars and revolutions of Southeast Asia and Latin America created thousands of refugees who were allowed to enter the U.S. outside the quota system. As the graph shows, most U.S. immigrants now come from Asia (mainly from Vietnam, China, the Philippines, and Korea) and the Western Hemisphere. Hispanics are the fastest growing ethnic group in the nation.

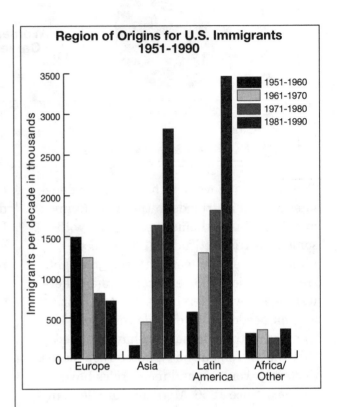

Region of Origins for U.S. Immigrants 1951-1990

The ethnic conflicts in Rwanda and Burundi have led to a massive migration of people. Two million refugees fled to Congo and other neighboring states. When civil war broke out in the Congo many of these refugees returned to Rwanda.

7 Which of these statements is supported by the graph?

A Asian and Latin American immigration rose sharply between 1981 and 1990.

B Changes in U.S. immigration policy boosted immigration from Africa.

C The number of U.S. immigrants of European origin remained fairly constant between 1951 and 1990.

D The U.S. welcomed "guest workers" until 1965.

Modernization and Tradition in Japan and the Islamic World

In 1840, Japan and the Arab-occupied parts of the Ottoman Empire were traditional, pre-industrial societies. Power remained in the hands of feudal lords or tribal leaders. By the end of the twentieth century, both areas had seen massive change. Japan is a fully industrialized democracy. The Arab nations are self-governing and they have been extensively modernized by the introduction of transportation and communication systems. Japan has blended its customs with Western influences fairly smoothly, but change has been a source of tension and conflict in the Arab world.

Modernization has not destroyed Japanese culture. Rather, the Japanese have built a business environment that reflects their values. Japanese corporations stress co-operation rather than individualism and competition. Workers are encouraged to take pride in their companies and this loyalty is rewarded by job security. Until very recently, Japan's largest companies guaranteed lifetime jobs to their workers. Strikes are rare and so is absenteeism.

The response of the Islamic world to socio-economic change has varied from one region to another. Many Moslems are antagonistic to democracy, *laissez faire* economics, global communication systems, open intellectual inquiry, and social change—movements that have characterized the culture of industrial nations over the past 100 years. Like Latin America and Sub-Saharan Africa, many Islamic states are experiencing a huge population growth which puts great pressure on already scarce supplies of food and water. Four out of ten Tunisians and Algerians and one in five Egyptians are unemployed. These hundreds of thousands of out-of-work individuals see no economic future for themselves; instead they are attracted to religious leaders who

A shopper in the oil-rich state of Oman

stress Islamic pride and identity.

But there is great wealth as well as bitter poverty in the Moslem world. The oil-rich nations of the Persian Gulf and North Africa have created modern states that use the latest technologies. In some states like Iraq, the government is led by secular rulers. In others, such as neighboring Iran, Islamic fundamentalists govern the country. These nations are still wrestling with the difficulty of combining their religious beliefs with the economic pressures of the 1990's.

8 **Would you expect to find more tension between tradition and modernization in wealthier or poorer Islamic states? Why?**

_____

_____

_____

_____

_____

_____

_____

Economic Trends

Decision-Making in Developing Economies

Since 1960, the leaders of the developing economies of Africa, Latin America, and Asia have pushed hard to industrialize their economies. At the beginning of this period, most of their people were poor farmers. The money to finance industrialization had to come from the export of raw materials—in Africa, coffee, peanuts, cotton, cocoa, and palm oil still account for over 80% of all exports. But crop prices are highly volatile and may not yield enough revenues to finance industrialization. So these nations turned to foreign sources of capital. (Another consequence of gearing up economies to export cash crops is that farmers may be unable to grow enough food to feed expanding populations.)

The push to industrialize encouraged many people to move to the cities to find work. But these nations lacked efficient phone systems and there were few decent roads or railroads. Without a communication and transportation infrastructure or a skilled work force, economic growth has been slow. In addition, many developing nations have been plagued by non-economic problems. Civil wars are frequent and corruption is widespread. Famine and disease have destabilized the economies of many African nations. By 1985, the sub-Saharan nations were 130 billion dollars in debt. To break their dependence on foreign investment, some of them formed regional associations. For example, several West African states, including Nigeria, created an organization that barters goods for oil.

There has been far more industrialization in the nations of North Africa than south of the Sahara. Oil-rich Arab nations have helped their poorer neighbors to expand their economies. One beneficiary was Egypt which has built hydroelectric plants on the

International food aid for war-torn Ethiopia

Nile to expand crop irrigation. But these improvements may not keep pace with population growth—Cairo with 12 million citizens is now Africa's biggest city.

The world's most indebted nations are in Latin America. Mexico was rescued from bankruptcy by a multi-billion dollar U.S. loan. In 1998, the IMF agreed to help Brazil restructure its debts provided its government enact major economic reforms. These reforms bit deeply into social programs and caused widespread unemployment. They also failed to solve Brazil's severe economic problems.

9   What problems have made it particularly difficult for a people like the Ethiopians shown in the picture to industrialize?

_____

_____

_____

_____

_____

The Global Economy

The political and economic stability that followed World War II led to a huge surge in industrial output in the West. Growth in service industries like insurance, banking, tourism, and advertising was even greater than that in the manufacturing sector. This expansion inevitably led to an increase in world trade. Multinational corporations have played an important role in this global economic expansion. Competing with each other for market share, they produce goods across the world, wherever labor is cheapest. Aided by the revolution in communications and financial technology, they have created a global market for services and goods.

This worldwide exchange of goods and services has created what is known as global interdependence. Nations and peoples depend on each other to supply what they do not produce themselves—one nation specializes in the manufacture of electronic goods, confident that another will supply it with food and raw materials.

Optimists argue that economic globalization means that consumers can buy the best products at the lowest prices without government restrictions. But, as the graph shows, global economic growth has benefitted those who live in developed nations far more than the inhabitants of developing nations.

Even in developed nations, many people are alarmed by the consequences of globalization. Some European governments fear that the internationalization of manufacturing

and finance makes them less able to control their nations' affairs.

Corporations used to maintain close ties with the communities in which they were located. Today nations, regions, and cities compete with each other to attract new manufacturing facilities or to prevent existing plants from relocating. Prosperity in one region often means decline in another. Many skilled blue-collar workers have lost their jobs when their companies relocated production to nations where labor costs were lower.

10 **Auto workers have for the most part felt threatened by the globalization of the world's economies. Why?**

_____

_____

_____

11 **Global interdependence is possible only if nations**

A **are self-sufficient**

B **eat all the food they grow and consume all the goods they make**

C **fight regular trade wars**

D **supply each other with the goods each needs**

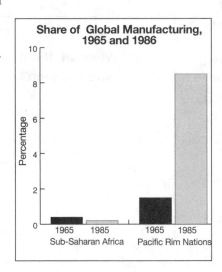

Share of Global Manufacturing, 1965 and 1986

NOTICE: Photocopying any part of this book is prohibited by law.

195

Environmental Issues

Deforestation and Desertification

The population explosion has led to massive **deforestation**. Trees are being cut down to make room for grazing and road building. Recently, tropical forests have been cleared at the rate of one per cent per year in Latin America, 0.8 per cent in Africa, and 1.2 per cent in Asia. Population pressure in developing countries has led to the loss of wetlands as well as forests. Grazing and growing areas are over-used.

Drought has made matters worse for the people who live in Sub-Saharan Africa. Several years of low rainfall have turned land that was once fertile into desert. The West African grassland region of Sahel has been particularly affected. Population pressure has combined with drought to increase ecological damage: rivers have been polluted and lakes die. It is estimated that since 1950, the world has lost one-fifth of its topsoil, one fifth of its tropical rain forests, and tens of thousands of plant and animal species.

It is hard to see how local pressures on the environment can be reduced. The herders of East Africa, for example, need the grazing lands for their cattle. But the number of cattle has doubled since 1950. The grasslands deteriorate, the soil disappears, and the cattle herders face starvation. In the rain forest of Indonesia, the government is responsible for much of the tree clearance. It claims that the land must be used to grow rice, coffee, and other crops. In Brazil, peasants as well as government agencies cut down trees. Tree loss is followed by soil erosion. Rain forests often grow in thin soil; without trees to anchor this soil, it may blow away and the land turn into desert.

Unrestrained *industrial* activity has also led to environmental disaster. The factories of Soviet-dominated Eastern Europe killed or poisoned many of the region's fish and forests. Similar damage occurs today in the

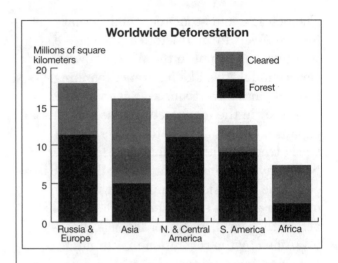

industrializing regions of India, China, and Mexico. Many forests in North America and northern Europe have been damaged by the acid rain that industry creates. Agricultural and industrial development is also damaging the earth's water supplies. Overuse, new irrigation plants, and a lack of sewage facilities have poisoned once pure rivers and lakes. Schemes to divert the direction in which river waters flow often backfire because the water that remains gets so salty that it kills off all marine life.

12A According to the graph, which three regions have cleared the largest <u>proportion</u> of forest?

_____

12B What are the motives behind deforestation?

_____

_____

_____

_____

_____

_____

196

Environmental Pollution: Who Will Stop It?

The damage inflicted on local environments by acid rain, overgrazing, and water depletion is severe but nothing compared with the *global* risk from the **greenhouse effect**.

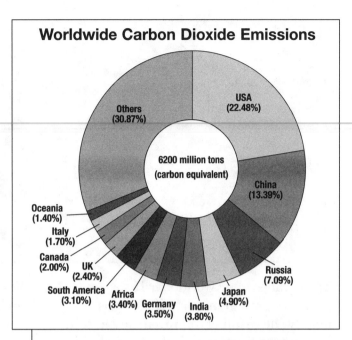

Worldwide Carbon Dioxide Emissions

6200 million tons (carbon equivalent)

Others (30.87%)
USA (22.48%)
China (13.39%)
Russia (7.09%)
Japan (4.90%)
India (3.80%)
Germany (3.50%)
Africa (3.40%)
South America (3.10%)
UK (2.40%)
Canada (2.00%)
Italy (1.70%)
Oceania (1.40%)

The sun's energy comes to us through radiation. Most of this radiant energy is reflected back into space. But when, as many scientists believe is happening today, that energy is trapped within the earth's atmosphere, the earth warms up. This energy gets trapped when gases like carbon dioxide (CO_2) and methane are released by the burning of fossil fuels like coal and oil. These gases then form an invisible curtain around the earth.

Industrialization and the growth in world population have led to an increase in the use of fossil fuels. The burning of logged trees poses a special problem. Trees and plants absorb carbon dioxide. But now there are fewer trees and plants to absorb it. There is no doubt that carbon dioxide levels have risen sharply over the past 30 years.

Some skeptics suggest that there is no such thing as global warming, or if there is, it is not the result of increasing levels of CO_2. But the scientific consensus is that temperatures have risen about 1° in the past 100 years. If the output of CO_2 continues to rise, the earth's average temperatures could rise by about 5.5° by 2050. This would cause ice caps to melt and sea levels to rise. Low-lying delta areas like Bangladesh, Egypt, and coastal China would be particularly affected. Rich nations might move people to higher ground or pay for protective measures; developing nations could not afford this.

A better way to address the problem is to prevent it. Many nations are limiting the amount of gases that industry and automobiles may emit. But these efforts are spotty and inadequate. Tree burning continues in Brazil and Indonesia; China and India continue to burn huge amounts of coal.

As the table shows, the worst culprit is the United States. It is responsible for releasing 17.6 per cent of all types of greenhouse gases. Developing nations are unlikely to reduce their CO_2 emissions unless industrial powers reduce theirs. Moreover, they have more immediate worries, such as declining water supplies and soil erosion. The U.S. industrial lobby is powerful, and Americans like to insist on their right to consume what they wish. These factors make it unlikely that the U.S. will provide leadership in the fight against global warming.

13 Explain in your own words how global warming occurs.

_____

_____

_____

_____

Science and Technology

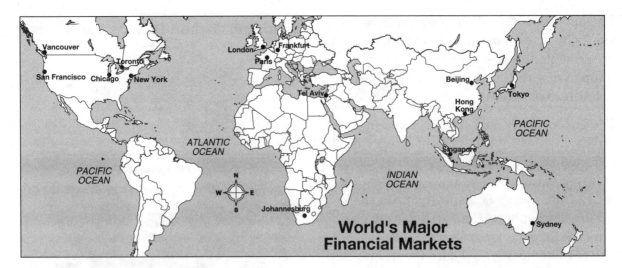

World's Major Financial Markets

The decades after World War II saw an explosive growth in world trade. This was mainly the result of improvements in technology, transportation, and communications. In the 1960's, computers began to change the way that banks, universities, and airlines operate. Factory automation allowed fewer workers to produce more goods. Scientific methods and mechanized equipment increased farm output. More recently, advances in telecommunications have created a worldwide information network. Sophisticated computer hardware and software, satellites, and fiber-optic cables have made it possible for financial traders across the globe to correspond with each other 24 hours a day. We can visualize this as hundreds of thousands of computer screens hooked into a single global communications system.

The communications revolution has taken place mainly in industrial nations. But the boom in hi-tech gadgetry—cell phones, beepers, and e-mail—has also reached parts of the developing world such as the busy cities of West Africa. Internet service is available, but web-surfing has not become a way of life for the people of this region. The new technologies are hobbled by the cost of computer equipment or the shortage of phone lines. Over the next 3 years an American aid program expects to provide 20 or so African countries with their own high-speed Internet access lines.

The globalization of communications has impacted politics, too. Authoritarian governments find it increasingly hard to hide bad news from their people. The nuclear disaster at **Chernobyl** was photographed by a French satellite that transmitted the information to the Chernobyl region and to the rest of the world. The Chinese government's suppression of student demonstrators in Tiananmen Square was reported back to China by radio, TV, and fax. As the Communist regimes of Eastern Europe fell, pictures and reports reached neighboring nations encouraging them to follow suit.

14 List the kinds of information to which large parts of the world have immediate access.

_____

_____

_____

_____

_____

Launching of
Space Shuttle Columbia

The same technology that launched communications satellites has also sent people into space. Russia launched *Sputnik,* the world's first satellite, in 1957. The United States sent three men to the moon in 1969. Most satellites are used to bounce radio signals around the world, but they can also be used to gather scientific information about outer space.

The technological revolution has been matched by a biological revolution. The Green Revolution was made possible by the development of new high-yield seeds. These seeds have helped developing nations feed their rapidly expanding populations. After scientists worked out the structure of **DNA**, the building blocks of life, it became possible to use genetic engineering to create other new strains of plants and animals. Genetic engineering can also help in the fight against disease. In cases like the one described on the right, scientists can use gene therapy to control inherited diseases.

Laser equipment allows surgeons to perform surgery in their offices that previously would have required a hospital stay. A vast array of new drugs can help victims of arthritis, heart disease, ulcers, depression, AIDS, and many more diseases. Organ transplants can prolong the lives of those who would surely have died. These advances have increased life expectancy in the countries where they are available.

On September 14, 1990, researchers at the U.S. National Institutes of Health (NIH) performed the first approved gene therapy procedure on a four-year-old girl named Ashanti DeSilva. Born with a rare genetic disease, Ashanti lacked a healthy immune system and was extremely vulnerable to infection. Children with SCID usually develop overwhelming infections and rarely survive to adulthood; even a common childhood illness like chicken pox is life-threatening. Ashanti led a cloistered existence, avoiding contact with people outside her family, remaining in the sterile environment of her home, and battling frequent illnesses with massive amounts of antibiotics.

In Ashanti's gene therapy procedure, her own white blood cells were genetically modified and then infused back into her bloodstream. Laboratory tests show that the therapy has strengthened Ashanti's immune system. She no longer has recurrent colds, has been allowed to attend school, and has been immunized against whooping cough. This gene therapy procedure is not a cure, however. The genetically-treated white blood cells only survive for a few months and must then be replaced, but Ashanti's future is much brighter because of the new therapy.

15 **Which consequence of the Scientific Revolution would have surprised Thomas Malthus (see page 129)? What arguments might Malthus use in defense of his theory?**

_____

_____

_____

_____

_____

_____

_____

_____

_____

_____

The Nuclear Menace

The nuclear age began in 1945 when the United States dropped atomic bombs on two Japanese cities to hasten the end of World War II. The Cold War saw a nuclear arms race between the two superpowers.

In 1968, 175 nations signed the Nuclear Nonproliferation Treaty (NNT) pledging to stop the spread of nuclear weapons. After the dissolution of the Soviet Union in 1991, five nations admitted that they owned nuclear weapons: the United States, China, Russia, Britain, and France. The Ukraine, Belarus, and Kazakhstan had been left with nuclear stockpiles when the U.S.S.R. collapsed. Ukraine and Kazakhstan agreed to return their nuclear warheads to Russia and to destroy the remaining missiles. Belarus will soon follow suit. Even so, there is deep concern that some Soviet nuclear weapons are being stolen or sold.

In addition, there is evidence that several other countries have developed or are in the process of developing nuclear weapons. India and Pakistan have both tested nuclear weapons. The tensions between the two countries remain high, as does the threat of nuclear war between them. Israel is said to have stockpiled hundreds of nuclear weapons which it could use against Arab nations in the most desperate emergency. Libya, North Korea, Iran, Argentina, and Iraq are also alleged to be developing nuclear weapons.

More is known about the situation in Iraq than anywhere else. The U.N. began sending inspectors to Iraq after its troops defeated Iraq in the Gulf War. These observers found that Iraq had obtained hi-tech equipment from suppliers in Britain, Germany, and the U.S. which would allow it to build nuclear weapons. Iraq had signed the NNT but had continued to try to build nuclear weapons. In 1998, the U.S. began

bombing military and other installations when Iraqi leaders stopped UN inspections. It is unclear whether the bombings have affected Iraq's nuclear capability.

Despite these concerns, there are reasons for optimism. The NNT was extended permanently in 1995. Then in a UN vote in 1996, all nations except Pakistan and India signed a Comprehensive Test Ban Treaty prohibiting nuclear explosions whether for peaceful or military purposes. It will come into force when 44 nations have ratified it.

16A What does this cartoon mean?

_____

_____

_____

_____

_____

16B What caption would you give it?

_____

_____

The Role of the United Nations

The **United Nations** is the foremost international organization today. By 1997, 179 nations had signed its charter and become members. The branch of the UN that attracts the most attention is the Security Council. The United States is one of its permanent members along with China, Russia, Britain, and France. The Security Council is the peace-keeping arm of the UN. During the Cold War, the Council was often deadlocked since a permanent member can veto any decision.

It is not always possible to settle international disputes diplomatically, so the Council may recommend the use of UN peace-keeping forces. However, UN troops may act only as watchdogs; they can only use their weapons in self-defense. This limits their usefulness. One limitation on the success of UN peace-keeping efforts has been that the nations that provide their troops (and this includes the U.S.) often want to pull them out if casualties are heavy. The UN's ability to support peace-keeping operations is also limited by financial difficulties. Each member nation is expected to provide it with funds. But many nations have fallen behind in their payments. In 1998, the United States was the largest debtor and owed the United Nations over two billion dollars.

By 1995, the UN had participated in 35 peace-keeping missions. Sometimes it was able to keep the peace, sometimes it failed. Some of its most successful actions have involved trade embargoes. The economic sanctions levied against South Africa were observed by nearly all UN members and helped to bring apartheid to an end.

UN agencies have helped people throughout the world. The World Health Organization has wiped out deadly infectious diseases such as smallpox. Today it is fighting a global war

THE UNITED NATIONS

| Security Council | International Court of Justice |

| General Assembly | Special Agencies | Secretariat |

| World Health Organization (WHO) | UN Children's Fund (UNICEF) |

| International Monetary Fund ((IMF) | World Bank |

against AIDS. The UN International Children's Fund (UNICEF) sends aid to poor mothers and their children. The World Bank provides loans and technical advice to developing countries. The International Monetary Fund (IMF) promotes world trade.

17 Select two UN peace-keeping actions and discuss their success or failure.

_____

_____

_____

_____

18 Which UN agency do you think is most effective in resolving international problems and why?

_____

_____

_____

_____

Looking to the Future

The World Bank believes there will be less poverty in every part of the world except Sub-Saharan Africa by the year 2000. In Africa, too, there are some hopeful signs. Apartheid has disappeared from South Africa under the leadership of Nelson Mandela. The World Bank has provided loans to African nations committed to economic reform. Some African nations like Kenya have seen major improvements in living standards.

Population growth remains a major obstacle to growth. Traditional African belief systems measure a woman's usefulness and virtue by the number of children she can bear. The social attitudes that encourage women in industrial nations to delay childbearing—education, career-building, and a desire for independence—hardly exist in African societies. Environmental catastrophes prevent population growth from being matched by an increase in output. Africa's indebtedness is also becoming a serious burden. Originally, foreign capital was used to build infrastructure; now it is used to pay for imported oil or to feed the hungry. The region's problems are made worse by civil wars and frequent government changes.

Latin America is also suffering the effects of a demographic explosion which is projected to double the population by 2025. There are wide differences in birth rates between nations like Chile and Argentina, on the one hand, and the other nations such as Brazil and Mexico. But overall, population growth is likely to cause a huge increase in child poverty and malnutrition, strain health-care services, and increase urban growth and environmental pollution.

Resource-rich nations—and this includes oil exporters like Saudi Arabia and the United Arab Emirates as well as the industrial West—are much better able to deal with economic and environmental problems than those without tools, money, and skilled workers. High educational levels are likely to increase environmental awareness. Poorer societies are too busy feeding their young populations to respond to floods and drought. Indeed, the industrial economies seem to have all the advantages. They are the ones with the capital, technology, communications, surplus food, and powerful multinational companies.

But some environmental issues—particularly the possibility of global warming—affect rich and poor nations alike. Only when the United States and other industrial nations sharply reduce the emissions of harmful gases can they expect developing nations to follow suit.

19 Some developed nations are using genetic engineering to produce food in laboratories. Why might this food NOT reduce the problems of nations with explosive population growth?

A Lab-produced food would sabotage the agricultural economies on which most developing nations are built.

B Nations have developed their own cooking styles and mass-produced food would be unpopular.

C The food does not contain enough vital nutrients.

D These nations lack the advanced technology required to create such food.

Section Review: Contemporary Issues

Part A

Below is a list of events or trends that have occurred since 1945. Select any THREE of them and explain why they have been crucial turning points in—

> EITHER: the reduction of world tension
> OR: the increase in world tension
> OR: the growing imbalance between developed and developing nations
> OR: the spread of knowledge

The creation of the United Nations
The formation of the EEC
The economic recovery of Japan
The Four Modernizations in China
Indian independence and partition
OPEC regulation of oil production
The spread of democracy in Latin America
The spread of nuclear weapons
The communications revolution
Space exploration

The collapse of the Soviet Union
The end of apartheid in South Africa
The Chinese Cultural Revolution
The end of European colonialism in Africa
The formation of the state of Israel
Improved health care in developing nations
The AIDS epidemic
The logging of tropical rain forests
The spread of Islamic fundamentalism

_____

_____

_____

_____

_____

_____

_____

_____

_____

_____

_____

_____

_____

_____

_____

_____

_____

_____

Part B

1 Which statement helps to explain the appeal of Communism in the Developing World?

1 According to Karl Marx, social and political revolution is most likely to occur in industrialized societies.

2 Communism preaches the withering away of the state.

3 Communists expressed their support for peoples oppressed by colonialism.

4 The Soviet Union was the world's most powerful nation after 1945.

2 China was to Deng Xiaoping as India was to

1 Ayatollah Khomeini

2 Jawaharlal Nehru

3 Nelson Mandela

4 Yasir Arafat

3 One similarity between postwar Europe and postwar Japan is that in both regions

1 new constitutions based on the American model have been introduced

2 the population is expanding rapidly

3 there has been a revival of militarism

4 U.S. aid helped their economies to recover

4 Which event occurred *first* in the collapse of Communism in postwar Europe?

1 Czechoslovakia was divided into two nations: the Czech Republic and Slovakia.

2 Lithuania declared its independence.

3 Gorbachev became the head of the Soviet government.

4 The Berlin Wall was torn down.

5 What conclusion can best be drawn from this postage stamp which celebrates the 70th birthday of Britain's queen?

1 Ex-colonial nations retain some ties with the power that colonized them.

2 Queen Elizabeth rules Uganda.

3 The civil war that devastated Uganda during the rule of Idi Amin has finally ended.

4 Uganda is a matriarchal society.

6 Fidel Castro differed from Juan Perón in that he

1 enjoyed the support of the working people

2 nationalized foreign-owned industries

3 supported revolutionary movements in other Latin American countries

4 was able to seize power because of the support of the army

7 The rulers of which nation are Islamic fundamentalists?

1 Algeria

2 Egypt

3 Iran

4 Iraq

Part C

	GDP in $ per person	% of GDP from agriculture	Life Expectancy Male	Female	% of Population Under 15	Over 65	Infant Deaths per 1000 live births
Afghanistan	175	59.7	41	42	46	4	172
Australia	17080	4.0	73	80	22	11	8
Austria	19240	3.2	73	79	17	15	74
Bangladesh	200	42.7	54	53	44	3	120
Bhutan	190	44.2	46	49	39	4	120
Canada	20450	3.2	73	80	22	11	8
Chad	190	41.4	45	47	43	4	127
Denmark	22090	4.6	72	78	17	16	7.5
Ethiopia	120	41.7	46	48	46	3	139
France	19480	3.6	73	81	20	14	7.3
Japan	25430	2.44	76	82	18	13	4.6
Malawi	200	37.9	48	50	48	3	137
Mali	270	39.6	43	46	47	4	113
Nepal	170	58.7	50	50	42	3	112
Netherlands	17330	4.7	74	80	18	13	6.8
Nigeria	270	26	48	49	45	2	114
Sierra Leone	240	39	41	44	44	3	147
Somali Republic	150	64.9	44	48	46	3	127
Tanzania	120	56.1	49	54	48	3	105
Uganda	220	6.9	50	52	49	2	96
United Arab Emirates	19860	1.7	69	73	35	1	25
United Kingdom	16070	1.4	73	79	19	16	8
United States	21700	1.9	72	79	22	13	9

Explain the difference in the GDP (Gross Domestic Product) statistics for Chad and the United Arab Emirates.

_____

_____

_____

_____

_____

How does the age structure of Japan differ from that of Nigeria. What causes this difference?

_____

_____

_____

_____

_____

Part IV: Practice Test

1 Which statement explains the title of this map?

1

THE "CAPITAL DISTRICT"

DUR-KURIGALZU

BAGHDAD

SIPPAR

SELEUCIA   CTESIPHON

AGADE

BABYLON

KISH

   It shows an area that used to be the headquarters of tribal leaders in southeast Africa.

2 It shows cities that were the capitals of Middle Eastern empires and civilizations.

3 It shows the district along the coast of China where the Tang, Ming, and Qin emperors built new cities for their courts.

4 It shows the district that contained the capital of the Ottoman Empire.

2 Which situation resulted from the Protestant Reformation?

1 Fewer people attended church services.

2 Rulers gained more control over their states.

3 The censorship of ideas became as widespread among Protestant nations as it was among Catholic nations.

4 The Protestant Churches became wealthier than the Catholic Church had ever been.

3 Over the last three decades, women in the West have worked mainly to achieve

1 legal equality

2 social and economic equality

3 the right to participate in combat on an equal basis with men

4 the right to vote

4 Hammurabi's Code is to Babylon as

1 Justinian's Code is to Byzantium

2 the Five-Year Plan is to the Soviet Union

3 the Napoleonic Code is to Great Britain

4 the Petition of Right is to Ireland

5 The technology of Ancient Egypt included

   1 a calendar that made it possible to predict when rivers would flood

   2 the ability to produce iron from ore and charcoal

   3 the invention and use of gunpowder

   4 the knowledge that the earth revolves around the sun

6 What was one consequence of the attitudes held by people like Lajos Kossuth?

   Kossuth and his friends genuinely believed that they were doing the non-Hungarians a kindness by giving them a chance of becoming absorbed in the superior Hungarian culture. To
   refuse this kindness was nationalist fanaticism; to impose it by force was to promote
   progress. The suggestion that Romanians, Slovaks, or Serbs were nations, with a national
   culture of their own, was simply ridiculous nonsense.

   Hugh Seton Watson, *Nations and States*, 1977

   1 a growing desire for self-rule among the Balkan peoples

   2 the assassination of Tsar Alexander II and the end of reform in Russia

   3 the outbreak of revolution in France in 1848

   4 the unification of Germany

7 Mansa Musa of Mali and Akbar the Great of India were both

   1 Moslems

   2 pacifists

   3 post-colonialists

   4 tyrants

8 Which Hindu belief or practice is described in this extract from the *Upanishads*?

   As a caterpillar, having reached the end of a blade of grass, takes hold of another blade, then
   draws its body from the first, so the Self, having reached the end of his body, takes hold of
   another body, then draws itself from the first.

   1 ahimsa or nonviolence to all living creatures

   2 dharma or duties

   3 reincarnation or rebirth

   4 the varnas also known as the caste system

British women trucking clay for brick making during World War I.

9 The activity of women like those above helps to explain why

1 female laborers permanently replaced men in most heavy industries

2 the Industrial Revolution began in Britain

3 so many men died in World War I

4 women in many nations won the right to vote after World War I ended

10 In both Latin America and the Balkan states, the coming of independence was quickly followed by

1 frequent wars among neighboring states

2 land reform

3 reconquest by the imperial powers

4 the spread of Marxist ideas

11 Which of the following made his epic journeys longest ago?

1 Christopher Columbus

2 Ibn Battuta

3 Marco Polo

4 Zheng He

Five Economic Goals	
Freedom	Workers can change jobs and join unions; consumers can decide how and where to spend and save; businesses can be established or closed or relocated.
Efficiency	Resources are allocated so as to maximize the benefits and minimize the costs of using them.
Equity	Wealth and incomes are distributed and taxes are levied in a way people think is fair.
Security	Protection of individuals against economic risks such as work injuries, unemployment, business failure, inflation, age and disability, and poverty
Growth	Increasing output of goods and services

12 Which of these five economic goals would you think command economies are **BEST** able to achieve?

1 efficiency

2 freedom

3 growth

4 security

13 Which of the following countries do you think has had the best results in promoting the five economic goals listed above?

1 Brazil

2 Communist Cuba

3 the present Germany

4 post-Soviet Russia

14 In what respect did the Meiji reforms in Japan resemble the Emancipation Decree of 1861 in Russia?

1 Both began the process of turning a feudal nation into a modern state.

2 Both transformed an absolute monarchy into a democracy based on universal suffrage.

3 Both transformed primarily agricultural nations into nations whose wealth was based on industry.

4 Both were followed by massive population growth.

15 Which of the following helps to explain the rapid spread of Islam?

1 Mohammed's skill as a military leader

2 the Arabs' reasonable treatment of the people they conquered

3 the Koran's teaching that each Moslem must create his own individual relationship with God

4 the weakness and decline of the Ottoman Empire

NOTICE: Photocopying any part of this book is prohibited by law.

209

16 The Mongol conquerors were contemporaries of

   1 the crusaders

   2 the Meiji Restoration

   3 the Renaissance popes

   4 the Tang emperors

17 Which of the following shows the influence of this clause from the Magna Carta?

   No free man shall be taken or imprisoned or dispossessed, or outlawed, or banished, or in any way destroyed, nor will we go upon him, nor send upon him, except by the legal judgment of his peers or by the law of the land.

   Magna Carta, 1215

   1 the Bill of Rights of 1689

   2 the Declaration of Independence

   3 the Edict of Nantes

   4 the United Nations Charter

18 Which development was a cause of the other three?

   1 the belief that natural laws can explain the workings of society

   2 the imposition of censorship by the Catholic Church

   3 the development of the theory of universal gravitation

   4 the publication of the knowledge that the earth revolves around the sun

19 How does Hinduism differ from Judaism, Christianity, Islam, and Buddhism?

   1 Its followers believe in heaven and hell.

   2 Its followers believe in monotheism.

   3 Its ideas did not originate with a major prophet or religious leader.

   4 It stresses the importance of spiritual rebirth.

20 Which of the following indicates how geography contributes to our understanding of history?

   1 It analyzes the artifacts that ancient cultures have left behind them.

   2 It investigates the structures and laws that people create to govern their societies.

   3 It shows how people have created settlements and structures on the Earth's surface.

   4 It shows how the forces of supply and demand shape human behavior.

21 [The Spaniards said] that there was only one God, that he governed heaven and earth, and that he was Lord of all…the Pope was lord of all the universe in lieu of God, and that he had conferred this land upon the King of Spain…The [Indians replied] that the Pope must have been drunk when he did so for he gave what was not his own, and that the King who asked for and accepted such a gift must be some idiot, since he asked for the property of others and came there to take it.

— Martin Fernandez de Encisco, *Suma de Geografia*, 1519,
describing his meeting with two Indian chiefs in South America

The statements contained in this quotation reveal

1 the different beliefs of the peoples of the Old and New Worlds

2 the reasons that Spain was able to build a colonial empire in the Americas

3 the way that Native American society was organized

4 why the Pope was able to control secular rulers during the sixteenth century

22 "The proletariat, economically enslaved by capital, cannot dominate politically unless it breaks [its] chains."

This statement reflects the ideas of

1 laissez faire capitalism

2 Marxism

3 totalitarianism

4 utopian socialism

23 The Sepoy Mutiny in 1857 took place in opposition to

1 British rule

2 German rule

3 Portuguese rule

4 Spanish rule

24 What is the author describing?

The one thing which was forced on one by the whole scene was that it was the revenge of France for 1871. It took place in a building which was really erected on the ruin and humiliation of Germany; it was also the room in which Germany, inflicted a great humiliation on France; France now once more having got the upper hand was having her revenge…It was merely an episode in the secular rivalry of two nations which has been the curse of Europe.

— Sir James Headlam-Morley, *Memoir of the Paris Peace Conference, 1919*

1 the arrangements made to resettle Europe at the Congress of Vienna

2 the occupation of Nazi Germany by French (and other) troops at the end of World War II

3 the end of World War I

4 the defeat of France in the Franco-Prussian War

First ships passing through the Suez Canal in 1869

25 This picture of the opening of the Suez Canal suggests that

    1 France was now able to control the Middle East

    2 merchants could now travel overland from North Africa to China

    3 steam power did not immediately replace wind power

    4 some ships still preferred to use the ocean route to India

26 Which twentieth-century leader nationalized the Suez Canal?

    1 Kemal Atatürk

    2 Menachem Begin

    3 Gamal Abdel Nasser

    4 Saddam Hussein

27 Which of these four twentieth-century dictators was aided by two of the others and opposed by the third?

    1 Adolf Hitler

    2 Benito Mussolini

    3 Francisco Franco

    4 Josef Stalin

28 Which nation benefitted from the Marshall Plan?

1 Japan

2 Mexico

3 the Soviet Union

4 West Germany

29 Forgiveness is to Christianity as

1 democracy is to despotism

2 supply and demand is to mercantilism

3 race hatred is to Nazism

4 violence is to Buddhism

30 The saviour of all mankind...whose provident care has not only fulfilled but even surpassed the hopes of all: for both land and sea are at peace, the cities are teeming with the blessings of concord, plenty, and respect for law, and the culmination and harvest of all good things bring fair hopes for the future and contentment with the present.

A decree from the province of Asia, issued at some date between 27 B.C.E. and 14 C.E.

This decree suggests some of the factors that

1 allowed Greek civilization to have such a powerful influence on future generations

2 enabled the Roman Empire to prosper for so many years

3 made it difficult for the Mongols to overthrow the Arab Empire

4 persuaded the Chinese emperors to expand their contact with the outside world

31 Which medieval practice do these Custumals describe?

And it is to be noted that none of the above-named villeins can give their daughters in marriage, nor cause their sons to be tonsured, nor can they cut down timber growing on the lands they hold, without license of the bailiff or sergeant of the lard, and then for building purposes and not otherwise. And after the death of any one of the aforesaid villeins, the lord shall have as a heriot his best animal, if he had any; if, however, he has no living beast, the lord shall have no heriot...The sons or daughters of the aforesaid villeins shall give, for entrance into the holding after the death of their predecessors, as much as they give of rent per year.

— From the *Custumals* [Customs] *of Battle Abbey,* 1305

1 the caste system

2 heresy

3 manorialism

4 universalism

32 Indira Gandhi is to Jawaharlal Nehru as

1 Catherine the Great is to Peter the Great

2 Elizabeth I is to Henry VIII

3 Margaret Thatcher is to William Gladstone

4 Theodora is to Justinian

33 What accounts for the rise in oil prices in the 1970's?

1 a shortage of oil created by the Iraq-Iran War

2 a reduction in the amount of oil produced and shipped to Israel's Western allies

3 the growing demand for fuel created by industrialization in East Asia

4 the growing power of Islamic fundamentalists

34 In what respect does Napoleon's statement (below) reflect the ideas of mercantilism?

All the raw silk from the Kingdom of Italy goes to England. I wish to divert it from this route to the advantage of my French manufacturers; otherwise my silk factories, one of the chief supports of French commerce, will suffer substantial losses. My principle is *France* first.

— Napoleon Bonaparte

1 He believed that the government should control and protect domestic industry.

2 He realized that competition between English and French silk makers would reduce prices and increase the sale of silk fabrics.

3 He thought that an aggressive foreign policy would create new markets for French industry.

4 He understood that the textile industries could be the spearhead of industrial growth.

35 Russia more than any other country needs a proper economic foundation for its national policy and culture...International competition does not wait. If we do not take energetic and decisive measures so that in the course of the next decade our industry will be able to satisfy the needs of Russia and other Asiatic countries which are—or should be—under our influence, then the rapidly growing foreign industries will...establish themselves in our fatherland...Our economic backwardness may lead to political and cultural backwardness as well.

— Sergei Witte, Minister of Finance, in a memo written to Tsar Nicholas II

Witte's memo above reveals that the government wished to extend

1 Bolshevism

2 democracy into Russia's Asian provinces

3 Russian imperialism

4 Russian trade with Europe

36 Who created China's Civil Service?

1 Emperor Hong Wu who founded the Ming dynasty

2 Mao Zedong

3 the Han emperor Wudi

4 the philosopher Confucius

37 I am also sending to the province of the Zapotecas, of which Your Majesty has already been informed, three captains to invade in three different directions, so as to conquer it as swiftly as possible. This will most certainly be very beneficial, not only because of the harm which the natives of that province do to others who have been pacified, but also because they occupy the richest mining lands to be found in New Spain, from which, once they have been conquered, Your Majesty will derive great profits.

Hernán Cortés, *The Fifth Letter*, ca 1525

What was one consequence of the actions that Cortés was planning?

1 severe inflation in the Spanish economy

2 the conquest of the Incas

3 the conquest of Peru

4 the extinction of the Taino people

38 Which factor helps to explain the different rates of population growth in developed and developing regions?

World Population Growth, 1750-2050

1 Industrial populations tend to have high birth rates.

2 Families in nations with a high standard of living generally have small families.

3 Famine and disease are severe problems in developing nations.

4 Ethnic strife has led to devastating wars with high casualty rates in Africa and Europe.

39 The Chinese conquest of Tibet and the Japanese occupation of Manchuria were both examples of

1 the search for raw materials

2 the survival of the fittest

3 the triumph of industrialization

4 twentieth-century imperialism

40 This Jacobin poster proclaims "Liberty, equality, fraternity, or death." What name do we give to the policy that grew out of this philosophy?

1 Imperialism

2 The Congress of Vienna

3 The Rights of Man

4 The Reign of Terror

41 How does Mandelstam's poem below differ from most Soviet literature of this period?

> His fingers are as fat as grubs,
> And the words, final as lead weights, fall from his lips,
>
> His cockroach whiskers leer,
> And his boot tops gleam.
>
> Around him a rabble of thick-necked leaders–
> Fawning half-men for him to play with.
>
> They whinny, purr or whine
> As he babbles and points a finger,
>
> One by one forging his laws, to be flung
> Like horseshoes at the ear, the eye or the groin.
>
> And every killing is a treat
> For the broad-chested Ossete [man from southern Russia].
>
> — Poem by Osip Mandelstam, written in about 1936

1 It celebrates the triumph of communism over evil, selfish leaders.

2 It deals with heroic working people.

3 It is abstract rather than realistic.

4 It is critical of the Russian dictator (Josef Stalin).

42 Absolute rulers like Peter the Great and Louis XIV increased their power by

1 avoiding war

2 policies of isolationism

3 reducing the independence of the nobles and subordinating them to the crown

4 distributing land to the peasants

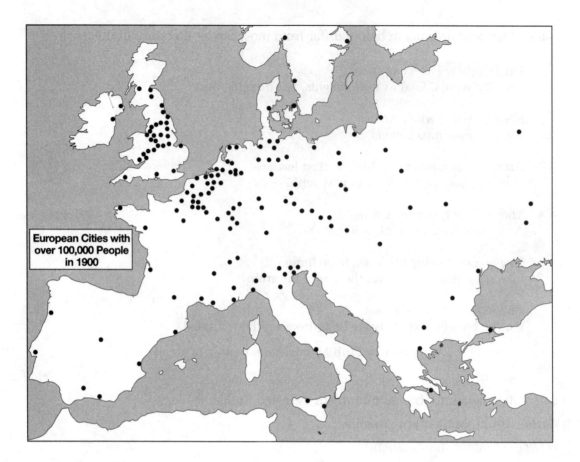

European Cities with over 100,000 People in 1900

43 This map suggests a relationship between

1 birth rate and environmental factors
2 climate and urbanization
3 industrialization and urbanization
4 medical technology and declining infant mortality rates

44 The race to send men into space was one aspect of

1 the Cold War

2 the Industrial Revolution

3 the rivalry between China and the Soviet Union

4 the Scientific Revolution

45 India's Gupta Empire is renowned for its scientific and cultural achievements which include

1 the development of the alphabet that forms the basis of Western languages

2 the development of the printing press

3 the invention of writing paper

4 the invention of the zero and of the number system we use today

46 What aspect of World War I does this letter confirm?

Everyone who is not wounded, everyone who can raise an arm, is up, and like a shower of hailstones our bombs pelt the attacking foe. The first wave lies prone in front of our holes, and already the second is upon us, and behind the English are coming on in a dense mass. Anyone who reaches our line is at once polished off in a hand-to-hand bayonet fight, and now our bombs fly with redoubled force into the enemy's ranks. They do their gruesome work there, and like ripe ears of corn before the reaper, the English attacking columns fall...Such is the battle of the Somme—Germany's bloody struggle for victory.

— Letter from Karl Gorzel, a German soldier, to his parents, October 1, 1916

1 the devastating effect of firepower that made it necessary to wage a defensive rather than an offensive war

2 that the war on the Eastern Front was much more mobile than the war in the West

3 that once the volunteer soldiers had been killed or wounded, governments introduced conscription to raise fresh troops

4 that German troops benefitted from a strong military tradition, whereas English soldiers were generally inexperienced and physically weaker

47 Japanese samurai like the one pictured below were to their daimyos as

  1 califs of Baghdad were to the Janissaries

  2 medieval knights were to their lords

  3 monks were to their abbots

  4 plebeians were to patricians

48 Why did nationalism play a role in the Mexican Revolution of 1910-1920?

  1 Mexicans wanted to rid themselves of a French emperor.

  2 Mexico's leaders wanted to use the army to expand their revolution into Central America.

  3 The Maya and other major Indian groups wanted to form independent nations.

  4 U.S. intervention in Mexican politics provoked a strong Anti-American, nationalist response.

49 The Chinese Cultural Revolution and Stalin's rule in the Soviet Union were similar in that both

  1 encouraged citizens to snoop into the lives of their fellow citizens

  2 had as their goals the celebration of a democratic way of life

  3 were designed to allow the introduction of private property

  4 were aimed at protecting individual liberties

50 The aspect of Greek culture below that influenced Renaissance art most deeply was

  1 Greek democracy

  2 the Greek focus on the individual

  3 the Greek mystery religions

  4 the Greek use of slaves

Document-Based Question

This task is based on the accompanying documents (1-8). Some of these documents have been edited for the purpose of this task. The essay is designed to test your ability to work with historical documents. As you analyze the documents, take into account both the source of the documents and each author's point of view.

Directions:

- Write a well-organized essay that includes an introduction with a thesis statement, several paragraphs explaining the thesis, and a conclusion.
- Analyze the documents.
- Use evidence from the documents to support your position.
- Do not simply repeat the content of the documents.
- Include specific related outside information.

Historical Context:

Since the beginning of human history, people, goods, and ideas have moved from one region to another. The documents describe some of these movements.

Task:

Travel can be dangerous, even today; in the past it could be a very hazardous undertaking. Even so, people journeyed thousands of miles over land and oceans. What has motivated men and women to risk their lives in this fashion?

Part A

Short Answer

The documents on the following pages relate to the movement of goods, people, and ideas. Examine each document carefully and then answer the question which follows it.

NOTICE: Photocopying any part of this book is prohibited by law.

221

Document 1

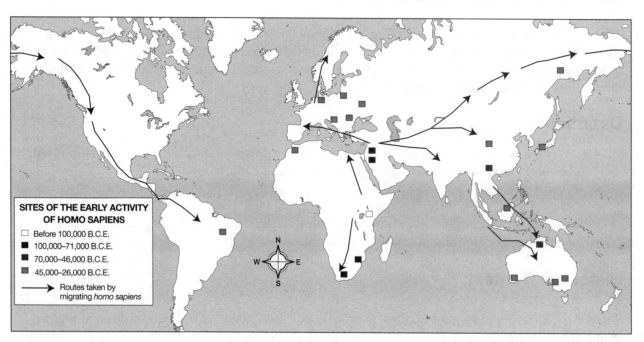

SITES OF THE EARLY ACTIVITY
OF HOMO SAPIENS
- ☐ Before 100,000 B.C.E.
- ■ 100,000–71,000 B.C.E.
- ■ 70,000–46,000 B.C.E.
- ■ 45,000–26,000 B.C.E.
- → Routes taken by migrating *homo sapiens*

1 Where did the first humans (homo sapiens) originate?

_____

Which were the first areas they migrated to?

_____

_____

Document 2

> Once, China had been cut off from the rest of the world by oceans, mountains, and deserts. The Tang emperors did not isolate themselves behind such barriers. Imperial armies guarded the Great Silk Road which linked China to the West. Merchandise and travelers moved safely along it in both directions.
>
> —Krieger et al. *World History: Perspectives on the Past*

2 What area did the Silk Road go through after it left China? What was the terrain like through much of its route?

_____

_____

What else besides merchants and merchandise moved along the Silk Road?

_____

_____

NOTICE: Photocopying any part of this book is prohibited by law.

Document 3

After this castle was built, certain traders began to flock to the place in front of the gate to the bridge of the castle; that is, merchants, tavernkeepers, then other outsiders drifted in for the sake of food and shelter of those who might have business transactions with the count, who often came there. Houses and inns were erected for their accommodation, since there was not room for them within the chateau. These habitations increased so rapidly that soon a large ville came into being.

—Medieval record describing the emergence of a town

3 How did the growth of towns change life in Medieval Europe?

_____

_____

_____

_____

Document 4

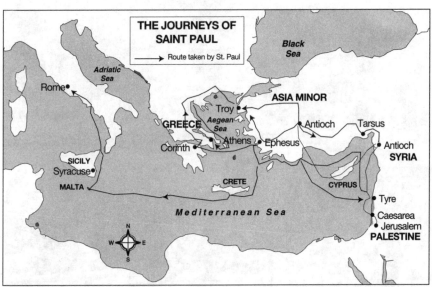

THE JOURNEYS OF SAINT PAUL

→ Route taken by St. Paul

4 What was St. Paul's message?

_____

_____

_____

How was this message received in Rome?

_____

_____

_____

Document 5

And in the year [1492], in the days of King Ferdinand, the Lord visited the remnant of his people [the Jews] a second time, and exiled them…The King gave them three months in which to leave…Many of the exiled Spaniards went to the Mohammedan countries to Fez, Tlemcen, and the Berber provinces under the King of Tunis…Many ships with Jews went to the city of Naples on the coast…Part of the exiled Spaniards went over the sea to Turkey. Some of them were thrown into the sea and drowned, but those who arrived there the King of Turkey received kindly as they were artisans.

—Account written by an Italian Jew in 1495

5 Why did the Ottoman Turks welcome Jewish refugees from Spain?

_____

_____

_____

_____

Document 6

1565 Engraving of one of the first encounters between Native Americans and Spaniards

6 How does the artist suggest that Native Americans and Spaniards treated each other?

_____

_____

_____

_____

Document 7

Moreover, while the majority of Africans inhabit rural settlements, the continent has been urbanizing at dizzying speed. Vast shanty cities have already emerged on the edges of national capitals (Accra, Monrovia, Lilongwe). By 2025, urban dwellers are forecast to make up 55 per cent of Africa's total population.

—Paul Kennedy, *Preparing for the Twenty-First Century*

7   Why are so many Africans moving to the cities?

_____

_____

_____

Document 8

NORTH AMERICA

Boston
New York
Charleston

Fish, furs, naval stores
Manufactured goods

Meat, fish, rum, lumber, grain

Tobacco, rice, furs, indigo

Manufactured goods

Slaves

Slaves & Molasses

Caribbean Islands

European goods

Rum

Slaves

Slaves

SOUTH AMERICA

PACIFIC OCEAN

ENGLAND

EUROPE

SPAIN

AFRICA

IVORY COAST

TRANSATLANTIC TRADE ROUTES IN 1760

8   How did early transatlantic trade affect the English economy?

_____

_____

_____

What "invisible items" were exported from Europe to the Americas and what impact did they have?

_____

_____

_____

Part B

Essay Response

Travel can be dangerous, even today; in the past it could be a very hazardous undertaking. Even so, people journeyed thousands of miles over land and oceans. What has motivated men and women to risk their lives in this fashion?

Your essay should be well organized with an introductory paragraph that states your position. Develop your position in the next paragraphs and then write a conclusion. In your essay, include specific historical details and refer to the specific documents you analyzed in Part A. You should add additional information from your knowledge of global history.

Thematic Essay

Themes: Change and Scarcity

Read the following statement:

> "Population growth is not the problem. The problem in the world today is
> that the industrial nations consume too much of the available resources,
> and the developing nations consume too little."

Task:

Write a five-paragraph essay to support or disagree with the above statement. You
must cite at least three examples in which population pressure or resource consumption are an issue.

Hints:

Among the situations you might want to consider are:

    Migrations of East African peoples

    Medical and scientific advances since World War II

    Deforestation in the Amazon rain forest

    Global warming

    Patterns of population growth among developing and industrial peoples

_____

_____

_____

_____

_____

_____

_____

_____

_____

_____

_____

_____

_____

_____

_____

_____

_____

GLOSSARY

BIOGRAPHY

&

INDEXES

GLOSSARY

Absolute   Having total power.

Acupuncture   Ancient Chinese practice of piercing body parts with needles to treat disease or relieve pain.

Agrarian   Relating to the land or to agriculture.

Ancien Regime   Social and governmental system that existed in France before the French Revolution.

Anschluss   Annexation of Austria by Nazi Germany in 1938.

Apartheid   Policy of racial segregation practiced by the South African government against black and other colored peoples.

Appeasement   The act of pacifying an aggressive power to avoid war.

Aqueduct   Channel for carrying water over a series of raised arched structures; widely used in the Roman Empire.

Archipelago   A group of islands.

Armada   Fleet of ships sent by Philip II of Spain against England in 1588.

Artifact   Item produced by humans (bowls, coins, etc.); used by archeologists to learn about past cultures.

Astrolabe   Instrument used to find the altitude of the sun or stars.

Authoritarian   Describing a system of rule that requires citizens to obey those in power (as opposed to one that favors individual freedom).

Axis Treaty   Coalition among Germany, Italy, and Japan during World War II.

Balance of Power   Distribution of economic or military strength among nations sufficient to keep any one of them from becoming too strong.

Barbarian   Term used by Ancient Greeks and Romans to describe a foreigner.

Barter   Exchange of goods.

Bazaar   Arab market place.

Bill of Rights of 1689   (See **English Bill of Rights**.)

Black Death   Bubonic plague which spread across Asia and Europe in the mid-fourteenth century and returned many times; killed millions of people.

Boat People   Vietnamese who, traveling in small boats over open seas, fled Vietnam after the Communist takeover.

Boer   Descendant of Dutch colonists in South Africa.

Bolshevik   Member of radical branch of Russian Social Democratic Party which seized power in Russian Revolution of 1917.

Bourgeoisie   Middle class; in Marxism, capitalists as opposed to the proletariat.

Boxer Rebellion   Unsuccessful anti-foreign rebellion led by members of a Chinese secret society in 1898–1900.

Buddhism   Religious and philosophical system that teaches individuals how to escape earthly suffering.

Bureaucracy The officials who administer government.

Bushido Samurai code of conduct that emphasizes loyalty, courage, simplicity, and honor.

Calligraphy Beautiful handwriting.

Capitalism An economic system in which people put their money into businesses in the hopes of making a profit.

Caravel Fifteenth-century sailing ship from Spain or Portugal.

Cardinal A high officer in the Roman Catholic Church who participates in the election of a new pope.

Cartographer Map maker.

Cash Crop Crop grown for sale rather than for consumption by the family or community.

Caste Hereditary Hindu social class. (See also **Varna**.)

Caudillo Latin American leader or commander.

Chernobyl Soviet nuclear power plant where an accident in 1986 caused large amounts of radiation to leak into the atmosphere.

Civil Disobedience Nonviolent opposition used to gain concessions from authority.

Civilization Country or people considered to have reached a high level of social and cultural development.

Code Napoleon System of civil law compiled in France in 1804 under the orders of Emperor Napoleon.

Cold War Period of distrust between the Western nations, led by the U.S., and the states of Eastern Europe, led by the U.S.S.R., that dominated world affairs between 1945 and 1991. They never fought each other directly, but both sides had nuclear weapons.

Collective Farm Large farm run by the state with hundreds or thousands of agricultural workers.

Columbian Exchange Transatlantic exchange of goods, people, and invisible items, particularly between 1492 and 1760.

Comintern International organization of Communist parties through which Soviets hoped to foster worldwide Communism.

Command Economy An economic system run by the government. The government decides what products will be made, by whom, where, and how much they will cost.

Commercial Revolution Expansion of trade, business, and finance that occurred in Europe between 1400 and 1700; often associated with the rise of capitalism.

Communist Someone who believes in a system in which the government owns all property and controls the economy.

Concentration Camp Camp for political prisoners or prisoners of war. Particularly used to describe Hitler's death camps.

Conquistador Spanish soldier who participated in the conquest of the Americas.

Consciousness Raising A sharing of experiences in order to become more aware of one's social, political, or psychological condition.

Constitutional Monarchy   Monarchy in which the power of the monarch is limited by custom or by a constitution.

Consul   Top-level official in the government of Ancient Rome.

Containment   Policy of preventing the spread of Communist rule.

Contras   Revolutionary group in Nicaragua that opposed the ruling left-wing government.

Cortes   Spanish representative assembly.

Cosmology   The study of the universe.

Council of Trent   Council of bishops summoned by the pope in 1545 to reform the Catholic Church and enable it to fight back against Protestantism.

Counter Reformation   Movement in the Catholic Church in the sixteenth century to oppose the advance of Protestantism.

Creole   Latin American of European ancestry or of mixed black and either French or Spanish descent.

Crop Rotation   System of growing different crops each year to preserve soil fertility.

Cultural Revolution   Social revolution in China in the 1960's sponsored by Mao Zedong and intended to stifle criticism of government and maintain revolutionary zeal.

Cuneiform   Ancient writing of Mesopotamia that used wedge-shaped symbols.

Daimyo   Japanese feudal lord who led an army of samurai.

Daoism (or Taoism)   Chinese religion and philosophy based on ideas of Lao-Tse that teaches simplicity and selflessness.

Declaration of Independence   1776 act by which colonists claimed they were free of British rule.

Declaration of the Rights of Man and of the Citizen   Statement of liberal and universal goals made by the leaders of the French Revolution in August, 1789.

Deforestation   Large-scale logging that often clears whole forests.

Democratic Socialism   Belief that socialism may be achieved by democratic (e.g., parliamentary) means.

Depression   Severe economic slow-down of the economy, in which people lose jobs and plants close.

Desertification   Spread of deserts into what was previously farmland, caused by human activity and climactic change.

Despot   Absolute ruler.

Diaspora   Term used to describe the scattering of Jews outside their original homeland in Palestine.

Dictatorship of the Proletariat   Absolute control of economic and political power by a government of the working class.

Diocese   Administrative unit within the Christian Church headed by a bishop.

Direct Democracy   Form of government in which citizens meet together to make political decisions and laws. (See also **Representative Democracy**.)

Directory   Government of five men that ruled France between 1795 and 1799 during the First Republic.

Divine Right   Supposedly God-given right to rule claimed by monarchs.

DNA (Deoxyribonucleic Acid)   Basic material in body cells that transmits hereditary patterns.

Dominion   Self-governing nation within the British Empire.

Domino Theory   Belief that if one nation in Southeastern Asia should come under Communist rule, the rest will soon follow.

Draft   Compulsory military service.

Duma   Russian Parliament created during Revolution of 1905.

Dynasty   Succession of rulers belonging to the same family.

Edict of Nantes   Declaration issued in 1598 by Henry IV granting French Protestants freedom of worship.

Elliptical   Oval-shaped.

Emancipation Decree of 1861   Measure by which Tsar Alexander II freed Russian serfs from bondage to their landlords.

Enclosure Movement   Widespread conversion of open fields to fenced-in lands by English landowners.

English Bill of Rights   Laws passed by English Parliament in 1689 designed to protect civil liberties.

Enlightenment   Philosophical movement of the eighteenth century that stressed reason and opposed blind faith.

Enlightened Despotism   Absolute rule exercised for the well-being of the people.

Entrepreneur   Person who owns or starts a business and takes the risks associated with running it.

Epidemic   Rapid spread of a disease.

Estates General   Chief legislative assembly in France before the Revolution.

Ethnic Cleansing   Term used to describe the elimination by one ethnic group of a different ethnic group by murder or expulsion.

Ethnocentrism   Belief in the superiority of one's own race, culture, or nation.

European Economic Community   Organization of European nations formed in 1957. Initially it was a six-nation customs union. Since then its membership has expanded to include most Western European nations and its goals to include economic and political unity. Also known as the **Common Market.**

Evangelical   Member of a Protestant church that stresses salvation by faith rather than power of sacraments (See **Sacraments**.)

Fascist   Member or supporter of the political dictatorship in Italy under Mussolini which stressed racist, nationalist, and warlike ideas. Or anyone who believes in racism and a totalitarian style of government.

Feminist   Someone (usually a woman) who supports a movement aimed at gaining rights for women that are fully equal to those enjoyed by men.

Feudalism   System in which land is held by vassals in return for military service.

Fief   Parcel of land held under feudal law in return for military service.

Four Modernizations Reforms based on free enterprise introduced into the Chinese economy by Deng Xiaoping.

Four Noble Truths Basic principles of Buddhist practice.

Fourteen Points Fourteen conditions set forth in 1918 by President Woodrow Wilson as a basis for post-war peace.

Frank Member of a Germanic tribe that created an empire which included present-day France, Italy, and Germany.

Fuller Cloth worker who brushes cloth fibres to thicken a fabric.

Gentile Non-Jew.

Gentry English land-owning class.

Ghetto Section of city where members of a particular ethnic group live; in European cities prior to 1945, area to which Jews were confined.

Glasnost Russian term meaning a policy of openness in the Soviet Union.

Great Wall 1,500-mile wall in northern China built between 300 B.C.E. and 1500 C.E. to keep out invaders from the north.

Global Interdependence and Globalization The way in which the economies of countries around the world are intermixed and dependent on each other.

Grand Vizir Chief minister to the sultan of a Moslem country.

Great Fear Panic that spread among French peasants in 1789 that aristocrats were planning to attack them. Prompted peasant attacks on their lords' property.

Greenhouse Effect Atmospheric warming caused when certain gases are released during the process of burning fuel.

Guild Trade alliance of medieval craftspeople or merchants.

Gulf War Three-day war fought between Iraq and a U.S.-led coalition in 1991 after Iraq invaded Kuwait.

Hajj Pilgrimage to Mecca.

Hanseatic League Medieval league of merchants of northern European cities.

Hapsburgs Dynasty with branches that ruled Spain and Austria.

Hellenistic Characteristic of Greek culture after the time of Alexander the Great.

Helot Slave; Helos was a Greek town whose inhabitants were enslaved by Sparta.

Heresy Doctrine or belief that a church holds to be false.

Hieroglyphic Ancient Egyptian written language that used pictures and symbols to represent words or syllables.

Hiroshima First Japanese city to be bombed by nuclear weapons in 1945 during World War II.

Holocaust The slaughter of about six million Jews by the Nazis during World War II.

Holy Roman Empire Empire in central Europe that was created in the medieval era and dissolved by Napoleon. In theory, the emperor was elected, but members of the Hapsburg family were regularly chosen after 1500.

Humanism Renaissance movement that stressed individual worth.

Icon Religious image or picture, particularly associated with the Eastern Orthodox Church.

Immunity Power to resist an infectious disease.

Imperialism Control by one nation of trade and government of another nation

Indian National Congress Group founded in 1885 with goal of increasing economic opportunities for native-born Indians. By 1900, self-government had become its aim.

Indulgence Pardon for sins that was sold by the Roman Catholic Church.

Industrial Revolution The shift from manufacturing things by hand to the use of machinery, along with the changes in social and economic life that this caused.

Inflation Sharp rise in prices.

Infrastructure Underlying foundations of a state or economy, especially its transport and communication systems.

Inquisition Court created by the Roman Catholic Church to investigate and suppress heresy.

Intelligentsia Educated class, particularly in pre-Revolutionary Russia.

Iron Curtain Imaginary divide separating Soviet-dominated Eastern Europe and U.S.-led Western Europe after World War II.

Islamic Fundamentalism Belief held by some Moslems that religious rules should govern political as well as private behavior; characterized by opposition to materialism and other aspects of Western culture.

Isolationism The policy of avoiding alliances with other nations.

Jacobin Member of radical club that met in Jacobin friars' convent during French Revolution; dominated French government between 1792 and 1794.

Janissary Turkish soldier.

Jihad A Moslem holy war against the enemies of Islam.

Joint Stock Company Association of individuals who own stock in an unincorporated company.

Justinian Code Code of laws compiled by the Byzantine Emperor Justinian.

Karma A person's lifetime actions that were thought in Hinduism and Buddhism to determine that person's fate in the next life.

Koran Sacred book of Islam that contains the revelations reportedly made by Allah to Mohammed.

Kulak Prosperous Russian farmer; as a class the kulaks opposed Soviet collectivization of agriculture.

Laissez Faire Economic theory that the state should avoid involvement in a nation's trade and financial affairs.

League of Nations International body formed after World War I to settle disputes peacefully.

Limited Government Principle that there are limits to a government's power and that individuals have rights that cannot be taken away.

Long March 6,000-mile retreat by the Chinese Communist army in 1934–35 from southeast to northern China to escape from Nationalist troops.

Magna Carta 1215 document in which King John promised to observe the rights of his barons and other freemen.

Mandarin A senior official of imperial China.

Mandate Territory temporarily administered on behalf of the League of Nations by another nation.

Manorialism System where peasants used parcels of their lord's land in return for services and rent (usually produce).

Market Economy (See **Capitalism**.)

Marshall Plan Plan conceived in 1947 by Gen. George Marshall, U.S. Secretary of State, that provided economic aid to European nations after World War II.

Martyr Person who chooses to die for his or her faith.

Mass Catholic service that celebrates the sacrament of the Last Supper.

Meiji Japanese term meaning "enlightened rule." Used to describe era which began in 1868 after overthrow of Tokugawa shogunate and in which Japan became a modern, industrial nation.

Mercantilism Regulation of national economy so as to maximize exports and increase nation's supply of gold and silver bullion.

Mercenary Professional soldier serving in a foreign army for pay.

Messiah In Judaism, the expected deliverer of the Jews; in Christianity, Jesus Christ.

Mestizo Person of mixed parentage (Hispanic, Native-American or black) in Latin America.

Mir Self-governing village community of peasant farmers in Russia.

Mission Church organized to spread Christianity among the American Indians.

Mixed Economy Economy in which some state regulation and perhaps ownership of industry is combined with private enterprise.

Monotheism Belief that there is only one God.

Monroe Doctrine President Monroe's 1823 warning to European nations to keep their hands off North and South America.

Monsoon Seasonal wind that brings heavy rains.

Mosaic Picture or design created by laying small stones in mortar; this art form was favored by the Byzantines.

Mummy Dead body preserved by the Ancient Egyptians through the process of embalming.

Munich Pact 1938 agreement between leaders of Britain, France, and Nazi Germany that approved Hitler's seizure of the Czech Sudetenland.

Muslim League Group founded in 1906 to press for Indian self-government and to protect Moslem interests; by 1935, the League was committed to the creation of a separate Moslem nation.

NATO (North Atlantic Treaty Organization) Military alliance formed by Western allies in 1949 to stop spread of communism.

Natural Law Rules of human conduct based on reason and an inborn sense of morality.

Nazi Member or supporter of the political dictatorship in Germany under Hitler which stressed racism, hatred, and nationalism.

Neolithic Revolution Process that took place about 10,000 years ago in which groups of humans settled in one place as farmers.

Ninety-Five Theses Arguments used by Martin Luther to attack the Roman Catholic Church and pinned by him to the door of Wittenberg Church in 1517.

Nonalignment Policy of refusing to take sides in the Cold War.

Oligarchy Form of government where power lies in the hands of a small group.

OPEC (Organization of Petroleum-Exporting Countries) Organization formed in 1960 by Middle Eastern oil-producing nations with the goal of maintaining oil prices by monitoring production.

Pacific Rim Industrial nations of East and Southeast Asia—Hong Kong, Japan, Singapore, Taiwan, and South Korea.

Parish A church district under the charge of a priest or minister.

Parliament (British) Legislative body made up of a House of Commons whose members are elected and a House of Lords where membership is by appointment or inheritance.

Patriarch Senior or chief bishop in the Eastern Orthodox Church.

Patrician A member of an old noble family in Ancient Rome.

Pax Romana The peace brought by Ancient Rome to the lands it ruled.

Pearl Harbor U.S. naval port in Hawaii bombed by Japanese planes; this event triggered U.S. entry into World War II.

Peninsulares European-born elite in Latin America.

Peon Member of working class in Latin America.

Perestroika Russian term used by Mikhail Gorbachev to describe reform of the Soviet economy.

Petition of Right Statement made by English Parliament of 1628 describing the liberties and rights of the people.

Pharaoh Ruler of Ancient Egypt.

Philosophe French Enlightenment thinker.

Plebeian A member of the lower class in Ancient Rome.

PLO (Palestine Liberation Organization) Originally a radical group led by Yasir Arafat whose goal was to eliminate Israel and create a Palestinian state by use of terror. It later renounced terrorism and became the official Palestinian organization for negotiations with Isreal over the formation of a Palestinian state.

Polytheism Worship of many gods.

Popular Sovereignty Belief that power originates with and belongs to the people.

Pogrom Organized massacre or attack on minority group; particularly attacks on Jews in Czarist Russia.

Predestination The belief that God has condemned some souls to damnation and some to salvation.

Primary Source Original documents such as diaries, government records, letters, and so on (See also **Secondary Source**).

Prime Minister Head of government in a parliamentary system.

Privatization Sale by the state to private enterprise of a state-owned industry or company.

Proletariat Working class.

Protectorate A state under the control of another, stronger state.

Purdah Hindu system of secluding women.

Purge Process of ridding a nation of "undesirable elements"; particularly used to describe policy of murder and exile carried out by Josef Stalin in the 1930's.

Puritan Revolution Anti-royalist rebellion in England; the Puritan victors subsequently imposed their own religious and social beliefs and practices on the nation.

Pyramid Huge triangular structure built by the Ancient Egyptians to serve as a tomb for a pharaoh.

Rabbi Teacher of Jewish law; spiritual head of a congregation.

Raj Term used to describe British rule in India or the parts of India that Britain ruled directly.

Reactionary Political conservative who wants to undo progress.

Recession Mild economic slowdown, where some people lose their jobs.

Reform Act of 1832 British legislation that enfranchised middle class male voters and provided representation to industrial towns and cities that had not previously elected members to Parliament.

Regionalism A focus on the politics and culture of a smaller region rather than a larger area.

Reincarnation The rebirth of the soul in another body.

Renaissance Great revival of art, learning, and literature in Europe in the fourteenth through the sixteenth centuries.

Reparations Compensation paid by a defeated nation to the victors.

Republic A nation where supreme power rests with the citizens; a state with an elected head rather than a monarch.

Representative Democracy The kind of government in which citizens elect their political leaders who then decide on policy and make laws. (See also **Direct Democracy**.)

Retainer Person of rank who owed service to a lord.

Sacrament Seven holy rites in the Roman Catholic Church.

Salvation In Christianity, the belief that Jesus gave his life to save the souls of mankind.

Samurai Member of a military class in feudal Japan who owed loyalty to a daimyo.

Sandinista Member or supporter of the leftist Nicaraguan government in 1980's.

Sans Culottes Paris citizen who supported the French Revolution.

Saturation Bombing Practice of dropping massive numbers of bombs to destroy everything within a target area.

Scientific Method Set of procedures that use observation and experimentation to prove or disprove a theory.

Schism Division within the Catholic Church. The schism of 1054 led to the final break between Catholicism and the Eastern Orthodox Church. The great schism of 1378 led to a temporary division within the Catholic Church to 1417.

Secondary Source Writings about events that are based on primary sources or on other secondary sources. (See also **Primary Source**.)

Serf Peasant tied to his lord's land.

Shiite One of two branches of Islam; its members reject the authority of the califs who succeeded Calif Ali. (And see **Sunni**.)

Shintoism Principal religion of Japan based on worship of ancestral spirits.

Shogun Military governor of Japan. (And see **Tokugawa Shogunate**.)

Show Trial Court trial staged by government in which the accused are coerced to confess to their crimes.

Slash-and-burn Agricultural technique of clearing land by burning and using the ash as fertilizer.

Smelt To melt an ore by heating so that the pure metal can be separated from impurities in the ore.

Socialist Realism Style of painting, sculpture, and literature that depicts heroic workers; used to glorify Soviet values during Stalin's rule.

Sphere of Influence Area of the world where a foreign power has powerful economic or political rights.

Stuart Scottish dynasty that also ruled England during most of the period between 1603 and 1714.

Suffrage Right to vote.

Sultan Moslem ruler, particularly ruler of Turkey.

Sunni Orthodox Moslem who accepts the Sunna teachings that supplement the Koran. (And see **Shiite**.)

Superpower Usually used to describe the U.S. and the U.S.S.R., the world's strongest post-World War II powers.

Supply and demand In a market economy, the theory that prices reflect the demand for a product and the quantity that is available.

Taiping Rebellion Rebellion of 1850-1864 in southern China that killed 20 million; finally suppressed with British help.

Talmud Collection of writings on Jewish civil and religious law.

Tariff Tax on imports, used to protect industry from foreign competition.

Third World Nations that were not part of Western or Communist blocs.

Three Principles of the People The basic principles which Sun Yat-sen and his colleagues wished to use in modernizing China.

Tokugawa Shogunate   Founded in 1603 by Tokugawa Ieyasu and surviving until 1868. Tokugawa shoguns wielded supreme political and military power. They re-imposed centralized rule over feudal Japan and brought stability, peace, cultural creativity, and political isolation.

Torah   In Judaism, the first five books of the Bible.

Totalitarian   Describing a government run by one person or group and controlling all aspects of life.

Triangular Trade   The trade in goods and slaves between Europe, West Africa, and Central and North America.

Tudor   Welsh dynasty that ruled England between 1485 and 1603.

Ulema   Moslem scholars learned in law and religion.

Ultimatum   Statement of conditions by one party or nation; their rejection by another party may lead to war.

United Nations   Post-World War II international organization intended to resolve issues peacefully.

Universal Gravitation   Scientific law dealing with the attraction exerted by dense matter on less dense matter.

Untouchable   Member of the lowest Indian caste.

Utopian   Describing a scheme for creating a perfect social order.

Varna   One of four principal social classes in ancient India.

Vassal   Feudal tenant who held land from a lord in return for military and other service.

Viet Cong   Communist guerrillas in South Vietnam.

Warsaw Pact   1955 defense pact among East European Communist nations.

Yeshiva   Jewish school.

Zen Buddhism   Most widespread form of Buddhism in Japan; its followers seek enlightenment through intuition.

Zhong Guo   Chinese for Middle Kingdom; based on Chinese belief that their empire lay at the center of the universe.

Ziggurat   Terraced pyramid of Ancient Mesopotamia that served as a temple.

Zionism   Desire among Jewish nationalists to build (or subsequently to support) a homeland in Israel.

BIOGRAPHY

Akbar the Great   (1542–1605)
Greatest Mogul emperor of India.
Fine administrator; followed poli-
cy of religious toleration.

Al-Razi   (865–925) Arab chemist and
physician. His written works
include a medical encyclopedia
and a handbook of diseases.

Alexander II   (1818–1881) Tsar of
Russia. Responsible for emancipation of the serfs. Assassinated.

Alexander the Great   (356–323
B.C.E.) King of Macedonia.
Conquered Persia and created
vast, short-lived empire that
reached to India.

Askia Mohammed   (ruled 1493–1528)
King of Songhai and excellent
administrator. Made Timbuktu a
center of Moslem scholarship.

Asoka   (?–232 B.C.E.) Emperor of
India's Maurya dynasty.
Converted to Buddhism; sent
Buddhist missionaries across Asia.

Atatürk, Kemal (Mustafa Kemal)
(1881–1938) Army officer and
statesman who founded modern
Turkey.

Augustus   (63 B.C.E.–14 C.E.) First
emperor of Rome. Attained sole
power after the defeat of Mark
Anthony. Reformed administration and promoted culture.

Bacon, Sir Francis   (1561–1626)
English philosopher and statesman. Recommended building theories that are based on observation.

Beauvoir, Simone de (1908–1986)
French Existentialist and author
of the ground-breaking feminist
work *The Second Sex*. Personally
and professionally associated with
philosopher Jean-Paul Sartre.

Benedict, Saint   (480?–547) Founder
of Western monasticism and of
Benedictine Order.

Bessemer, Henry   (1813–1898) British
inventor responsible for the
process named after him whereby
pig iron is made into steel.

Bismarck, Prince Otto von
(1815–1898) Prussian-born
landowner, statesman, and
Chancellor of Germany; largely
responsible for its unification.

Bolívar, Simón   (1783–1830) South
American soldier and statesman.
Liberated Venezuela, Colombia,
Ecuador, Peru, and Bolivia from
Spanish rule.

Bonaparte, Napoleon   (1769–1821)
General and Emperor of France.
Reformed French legal system
and administration. Conquered
and for a time ruled most of
Continental Europe.

Buddha (Enlightened One) (563?–483?
B.C.E.) Born **Siddhartha
Gautama**, son of an Indian rajah.
Philosopher, founder of Buddhism.

Buonarroti, Michelangelo   See
Michelangelo.

Cabral, Pedro   (1467–1520)
Portuguese navigator. Claimed
Brazil for Portugal.

Caesar, Augustus   See **Augustus.**

Caesar, Julius (100?–44 B.C.E.) Roman general, statesman, and writer. Conquered Gaul (France) and ruled as dictator of Roman Republic until his murder.

Calvin, John (1509–1564) French theologian and leader of Protestant Reformation. Created new branch of Protestantism that focused on predestination and church organization.

Cartier, Jacques (1491–1557) French explorer in Canada.

Castro, Fidel (1926–) Cuban revolutionary leader; premier since 1959.

Catherine the Great (1729–1796) Empress of Russia. Extended Russian territory; took part in partition of Poland.

Cavour, Count Camillo (1810–1861) Italian statesman and prime minister of Piedmont. Largely responsible for the unification of Italy.

Charlemagne (742?–814) King of the Franks; founder of the Holy Roman Empire.

Charles I (1600–1649) Stuart king of England and Scotland. Defeated by Parliamentary forces during English Civil War. Executed.

Charles V (1500–1558) Hapsburg Holy Roman Emperor and King of Spain as Charles I.

Churchill, Winston (1874–1965) English Prime Minister during World War II.

Clemenceau, Georges (1841–1929) French statesman known as "The Tiger." Founder of the Third French Republic and its premier. Headed French delegation at Versailles Peace Conference.

Colbert, Jean Baptiste (1619–1683) French minister of finance under Louis XIV. Fostered industry and commerce.

Columbus, Christopher (1451–1506) Italian explorer who in 1492 led first Spanish expedition to the New World.

Confucius (551–479 B.C.E.) Chinese philosopher. Founded Confucianism, a religion based on reason rather than spirituality.

Constantine (280?–337) Emperor of Rome; made Christianity the empire's official religion; moved capital from Rome to Byzantium which was renamed after him.

Copernicus, Nicolaus (1473–1543) Polish astronomer whose theory that planets orbited the sun (instead of vice versa) revolutionized cosmology.

Cortés, Hernan (1485–1547) Spanish conquistador. Conquered Aztec Empire in Mexico.

Cromwell, Oliver (1599–1658) English general and statesman. After the overthrow of the monarchy he became Lord Protector and ruled England as dictator.

Cyril (820?–875?) Greek scholar and missionary. Along with Methodius he developed Church Slavonic language and spread Christianity among Eastern Slavs.

Da Gama, Vasco (1469?–1524) Portuguese explorer who sailed around southern Africa to India. Established Portuguese trading power in the Indian Ocean.

Darius the Great (540?–486 B.C.E.) King of Persia; defeated by the Greeks at Marathon.

Da Vinci, Leonardo (1452–1519) Italian artist and scientist. Famous as painter of Mona Lisa.

Deng Xiaoping (1904–1997) Chinese political leader from 1976–1997. Modernized industry and privatized agriculture. Opened economy to foreign investors but refused to grant political freedoms.

Descartes, René (1596–1650) French scientist and philosopher. Stressed power of reason. Forced into exile by church opposition to his ideas.

Díaz, Porfirio (1830–1915) Mexican general and president. Policies brought foreign investment and economic stability to Mexico; also brought prosperity to the elite, and dire poverty to the masses.

Diocletian (245–313) Roman emperor; divided empire into four regions; persecuted Christians.

Disraeli, Benjamin (1804–1881) British conservative statesman and novelist. Responsible for 2nd Reform Act which created two million working-class voters. An ardent imperialist, he proclaimed Queen Victoria Empress of India.

Eisenhower, Dwight D. (1890–1969) American general and 34th U.S. President. Supreme commander of allied troops in Europe during World War II and later of NATO.

Elizabeth I (1533–1603) Queen of England. Brought peace and economic stability. Promoted culture.

Engels, Friedrich (1820–1895) German philosopher, socialist, and associate of **Karl Marx**. Wrote *The Communist Manifesto* in 1848.

Erasmus, Desiderius (1466?–1536) Dutch humanist and church reformer. Translated New Testament from Greek to Latin.

Ferdinand (1452–1516) **and Isabella** (1451–1504) Spanish monarchs who unified Aragon and Castile, financed Columbus's expedition to America, defeated the Moors, and expelled the Jews from Spain.

Franco, Francisco (1892–1975) Spanish general and dictator of Spain. Obtained power as the victorious leader of right-wing Nationalist troops during Spain's Civil War.

Franz Josef (1830–1916) Emperor of Austria-Hungary. Autocratic patron of the arts. His harsh policy towards Serbia helped bring about World War I.

Frederick the Great (1712–1786) King of Prussia. Doubled size of kingdom through foreign wars and Partition of Poland.

Gautama, Siddhartha See **Buddha**.

Galileo, Galilei (1564–1642) Italian physicist; discovered the laws of falling bodies; Vatican condemned him as a heretic and forced him to recant.

Gandhi, Indira (1917–1984) Prime Minister of India; daughter of **Jawaharlal Nehru**. Assassinated by Sikhs.

Gandhi, Mohandas (1869–1948) Nationalist leader of India known as the *Mahatma* (Great Soul). Used policy of nonviolent civil disobedience to win economic, social, and political change. Led Congress Party in fight for Indian independence. Assassinated.

Garibaldi, Giuseppe (1807–1882) Italian patriot and general. Led his "Red Shirts" in guerrilla campaigns through Naples and Sicily in fight for independence.

Genghis Khan (1167?–1227) Mongol warrior, founder of a huge Mongol empire in northern China and Central Asia.

Gladstone, William (1809–1898) British statesman and prime minister as leader of the Liberal Party. Social reformer.

Gorbachev, Mikhail (1931–) Soviet statesman and General Secretary of the Communist Party. Introduced policies of *glasnost* and *perestroika*. Awarded Nobel Peace Prize for permitting self-rule to return to Eastern Europe. Resigned when Soviet Union disintegrated.

Hammurabi (1815?–1750 B.C.E.) King of Babylon. Responsible for legal code named after him.

Hannibal (247–183? B.C.E.) Carthaginian general. Fought Second Punic War against Rome.

Haroun al-Rashid (766–809) Fifth and greatest Abbasid calif of Baghdad. Empire stretched from North Africa to India; ruled at highpoint of Arab culture. Appears in *Arabian Nights*.

Havel, Václav (1936–) Czech playwright and political leader. President of the Czech Republic.

Henry IV (1553–1610) King of France. Leader of Protestant Huguenots, he converted to Catholicism on becoming king. Issued Edict of Nantes. Brought unity and stability to France.

Henry VIII (1491–1547) King of England. Broke away from Rome and created Church of England with himself as head. Six wives.

Henry the Navigator (1394–1460) Portuguese prince who sponsored exploration and expansion.

Hidalgo, Miguel (1753–1811) Mexican revolutionary priest. Organized revolt against Spain in 1810; executed after its defeat.

Hitler, Adolf (1889–1945) German Chancellor 1933–1945, leader of Nazi Party, and brutal dictator who led Germany into World War II and was responsible for the Holocaust and other atrocities.

Ho Chi Minh (1890–1969) President of North Vietnam. Founded Vietnamese Communist Party. Resisted Japanese and French rule in Indochina. Tenacious leader during Vietnam War.

Homer (9th century B.C.E.) Greek epic poet; author of the *Iliad* and *Odyssey* which describe the siege of Troy and the wanderings of Odysseus.

Hussein, Saddam (1937–) Arab nationalist and president and dictator of Iraq. Launched Iraq-Iran war. His invasion of Kuwait led to Gulf War in which his forces were defeated.

Ibn Batuta (1304?–1406) Arab traveler who left an account of his journeys and the places he visited.

Ibn-Sina (980–1037) Also known as Avicenna. Persian physician and philosopher. Wrote work that was standard medical text until 1500.

James I (1566–1625) Stuart king of England and Scotland. Sponsored translation of Bible into English. His strict anti-Puritanism caused many Puritans to flee to America.

Jefferson, Thomas (1743–1826) American statesman, diplomat, and author. Drafted Declaration of Independence; 3rd U.S. President.

Jesus (4? B.C.E.–29? C.E.) Jewish religious teacher. Believed by Christians to be Son of God and Savior of Mankind. Crucified for treason against Rome.

Jinnah, Mohammed Ali (1876–1948) Indian Moslem political leader. Headed Muslim League and campaigned for independent Moslem state of which he became head in 1947 when Pakistan was created.

Johnson, Lyndon (1908–1976) 36th U.S. President. Responsible for "War on Poverty" and civil rights legislation. Declined re-election bid because of unpopularity that derived from the escalating Vietnam War.

Joseph II (1741–1790) Holy Roman Emperor and ruler of Austria. Reformer and despot.

Justinian (483–565) Byzantine emperor. Responsible for codification of laws named after him.

Kennedy, John Fitzgerald (1917–1963) 35th U.S. President. Led U.S. during Cuban Missile Crisis. Assassinated.

Kepler, Johannes (1571–1630) German astronomer; demonstrated that planets follow elliptical paths around the sun.

Kerensky, Alexander (1881–1970) Russian revolutionary. Head of provisional government; overthrown in Bolshevik Revolution.

Khomeini, Ayatollah (Ruhollah Moussavi) (1900?–1989) Spiritual and political leader of Iran. Returned to Iran from exile in 1979 and became leader of new Islamic republic.

Klerk, Fredrik Willem de (1936–) President of South Africa. Released Nelson Mandela from jail. His government repealed apartheid laws and supported political equality for all South Africans. Shared Nobel Peace Prize with **Mandela** in 1993.

Kublai Khan (1216–1294) Mongol emperor; grandson of **Genghis**. Founded Yuan dynasty in China which flourished under his rule.

Las Casas, Bartolomé de (1474–1566) Spanish missionary in Central America. Complained to Charles V about forced Indian labor. Wrote *History of the Indies*.

Lenin, Nikolai (Vladimir Ilyich Ulyanov) (1870–1924) Russian revolutionary and founder of Bolshevik (later Communist) Party. Returned to Russia from exile during 1917 revolution. Seized power as leader of Bolsheviks and ruled Soviet state until his death.

Lloyd George, David (1863–1945) Welsh statesman and British prime minister during World War I.

Locke, John (1632–1704) English Enlightenment philosopher.

Louis XIV (1638–1715) King of France known as the Sun King. Absolute ruler; built palace at Versailles. Hired able ministers to develop commerce and industry but squandered money on endless foreign wars.

Loyola, Saint Ignatius (1491–1556) Spanish soldier who converted to a religious life. Founded Jesuit Order.

Luther, Martin (1483–1546) German Protestant and leader of Reformation. Protested against papal abuses in 95 Theses.

MacArthur, Douglas (1880–1964) U.S. general. Commanded U.S. forces in the Far East during World War II. Led the reconstruction of Japan. Commanded UN troops in Korean War until his dismissal by President Truman.

Machiavelli, Niccoló (1469–1527) Italian political philosopher and diplomat. Author of *The Prince* which describes how an amoral prince can retain power.

Madero, Francisco (1873–1913) President of Mexico. Proclaimed the revolution in 1910. Deposed and murdered.

Magellan, Ferdinand (1480?–1521) Portuguese navigator who led Spanish-backed expedition that was first to sail around the world.

Maimonides, Moses (1135–1204) Jewish rabbi and physician. Born in Spain but lived and wrote in Egypt. Used reason to interpret Jewish scripture.

Mandela, Nelson (1918–) South African statesman. Led black protest movements and was sentenced to life imprisonment. Released in 1990 and elected President in 1994. Shared Nobel Peace Prize with **F.W. de Klerk** in 1993.

Mansa Musa (?–1337?) Ruler of Mali. Made hajj to Mecca and brought back Moslem scholars to Mali.

Mao Zedong (1893–1976) Chinese communist revolutionary and head of state.

Maria Theresa (1717–1780) Ruler of Austria and Hungary. Capable administrator.

Marx, Karl (1818–1883) German philosopher and founder of modern socialism. His analysis of economic and political aspects of capitalism in *Das Kapital* proved very influential.

Mazzini, Giuseppe (1805–1872) Italian patriot. Headed short-lived Republic of Rome in 1849.

Metternich, Clemens von (1773–1859) Austrian statesman. Helped to arrange peace terms at Congress of Vienna and to balance power among European nations.

Michelangelo (1475–1564) Italian sculptor, architect, and painter. Best known for painting the ceiling of Rome's Sistine Chapel.

Mohammed (570?–632) Arab prophet and religious leader; founded Islam; his teachings are recorded in the Koran; proclaimed himself the messenger of Allah.

Montesquieu, Charles (1689–1755) French political philosopher.

Moses (13th century B.C.E.) Hebrew law-giver and prophet. Led the Israelites out of Egypt into the Promised Land (the Exodus). By tradition, he received the Ten Commandments on Mount Sinai.

Mussolini, Benito (1883–1945) Founder of fascism and dictator of Italy. Ally of Nazi Germany in World War II. Shot.

Nasser, Gamal Abdul (1918–1970) Egyptian President; nationalized Suez Canal.

Nebuchadnezzar (605–562 B.C.E.) King of Babylon; destroyed kingdom of Judah and took Jews as captives to Babylon

Nehru, Jawaharlal (1889–1964) Indian statesman. First prime minister of India. Imprisoned for civil disobedience during 1930's. Leader of nonaligned nations.

Newton, Sir Isaac (1642–1727) English mathematician. Best know for theories of gravitation and optics and his development of calculus.

Nkrumah, Kwame (1909–1972) African political leader. First prime minister of Ghana which he led to independence. Deposed after becoming dictator.

Obregón, Álvaro (1880–1928) President of Mexico. Promoted political and economic reforms. Assassinated.

Owen, Robert (1771–1858) Industrialist and socialist. Set up Utopian community in Indiana.

Paul, Saint (?–64? C.E.) Christian apostle and missionary who spread the teachings of Jesus to the Gentiles. Wrote several epistles included in New Testament.

Perón, Juan (1895–1974) and Eva (1919–1952) Nationalistic and totalitarian president of Argentina and his hugely popular wife.

Perry, Matthew (1794–1858) U.S. naval officer. Obtained trading rights from Japan.

Peter, Saint (?– 64?C.E.) Leader of Jesus's 12 apostles. Regarded as first pope by Roman Catholics. Reportedly martyred at Rome.

Philip II (1527–1598) King of Spain; failed to crush Protestant rebellion in Netherlands; sent unsuccessful Armada against England.

Pizarro, Francisco (1474?–1541) Spanish conquistador; conquered Inca empire in Peru.

Plato (427?–347 B.C.E.) Greek philosopher; student of Socrates. Described ideal state ruled by philosophers.

Polo, Marco (1254?–1324?) Venetian explorer famous for his overland journey to China.

NOTICE: Photocopying any part of this book is prohibited by law.

247

Rabelais, François (1492?–1553) French monk and humanist. Author of *Gargantua* and *Pantagruel*, comic, bawdy books that explore serious themes.

Reagan, Ronald (1911–) Movie star and 40th U.S. President.

Reza Shah Pahlavi (1877–1944) Shah of Iran. As an army officer he lead a successful coup and later founded Pahlavi dynasty. Resigned under allied pressure in World War II.

Robespierre, Maximilien (1758–1794) Fanatical leader of French Revolution. Led radical Jacobins in National Convention; destroyed moderate opponents; began Reign of Terror; executed.

Roosevelt, Franklin Delano (1882–1945) 32nd President of the United States. Introduced the New Deal programs during the Depression. Led the nation to victory during World War II.

Rousseau, Jean Jacques (1712–1778) French philosopher. Major figure of the Enlightenment. Wrote *The Social Contract*.

Shakespeare, William (1564–1616) English playwright and poet. Widely held to be one of world's greatest writers in any language. Author of 36 plays, 152 sonnets, and several longer poems.

Smith, Adam (1723–1790) Scottish *laissez-faire* economist.

Stalin, Josef (Josef Vissarionovich Dzhugashvili) (1879–1953) Soviet dictator. Used position as General Secretary of the Communist Party to gain absolute power. Created totalitarian state. Allied with West during World War II. Subsequently imposed Soviet control over nations of Eastern Europe.

Suleiman the Magnificent (1494–1566) Ottoman sultan. Reign marked by successful wars that expanded his empire and by legal and cultural achievements.

Sun Yat-sen (1866–1925) Chinese political leader regarded as "father of modern China." Briefly served as President after overthrow of Manchu dynasty.

Timur Lenk, also known as Tamberlaine (1336?–1405) Mongol conqueror. Empire centered in Central Asia. Invaded India and massacred thousands.

Toussaint L'Ouverture (1774?–1803) Emancipated Haitian slave. Led slave rebellion. Ruler of Haiti.

Trotsky, Leon (Lev Davidovich Bronstein) (1879–1940) Russian revolutionary. With **Lenin** led Bolshevik seizure of power in 1917. Directed Red Army in civil war. Lost power struggle with **Stalin**. Exiled and assassinated.

Truman, Harry (1884–1972) 33rd U.S. President. Responsible for decision to use atomic bomb against Japan in World War II.

Tull, Jethro (1647–1741) English agriculturalist who invented a machine to sow seeds.

Villa, Pancho (1877–1923) Mexican revolutionary leader. Attacked and burned New Mexico town. Assassinated.

Voltaire (François-Marie Arouet) (1694–1778) French philosopher; major figure of the Enlightenment. Spent many years in exile. Wrote the satire *Candide*.

Walesa, Lech (1943–) President of Poland in post-Soviet era. Leader of Solidarity, a Polish labor-union movement that helped topple the Communist government.

Watt, James (1736–1819) Scottish inventor who developed an improved steam engine.

Wilson, Woodrow (1856–1924) 28th U.S. President. Asked Congress to declare war on Germany during World War I. Published Fourteen Points as prerequisites for peace; attended Versailles Peace Conference.

Wudi (ruled 141–87 B.C.E.) Emperor of Han dynasty in China during period of prosperity and stability. Expanded empire to north, west, and south. Encouraged commerce. Selected officials on basis of merit.

Xavier, Saint Francis (1506–1552) Spanish missionary and Jesuit; traveled to India and East Indies.

Yeltsin, Boris (1931–) President of Russia during period of economic turmoil.

Zapata, Emiliano (1879?–1919) Mexican revolutionary whose chief ambition was to return land to native people. Assassinated.

Zheng He (1371–1435) Moslem Chinese admiral under Ming dynasty. Sailed to Southeast and South Asia, and to Arabia and East Africa creating trade relations between China and these areas. Also demanded submission to authority of Ming.

Zhou Enlai (1898–1976) Chinese Communist leader and prime minister.

INDEX OF MAJOR THEMES
AND CONCEPTS

GENERAL INDEX